THE ENGLISH LINE

Also by John Powell Ward:

Poetry and the Sociological Idea (1981)
Wordsworth's Language of Men (1984)
Raymond Williams (1981)
The Poetry of R. S. Thomas (1987)
To Get Clear (poems) (1981)
The Clearing (poems) 1984)

THE ENGLISH LINE

Poetry of the Unpoetic from Wordsworth to Larkin

John Powell Ward

MACMILLAN

First published 1991

Published by
MACMILLAN EDUCATION LTD
Houndmills, Basingstoke, Hampshire RG21 2XS
and London
Companies and representatives
throughout the world

Phototypeset by Input Typesetting Ltd, London
Printed in Hong Kong

British Library Cataloguing in Publication Data
Ward, J. P. (John Powell) 1937–
    The English line : poetry of the unpoetic from Wordsworth to Larkin.
    1. Poetry in English – Critical studies
    I. Title
    821.009

ISBN 0–333–47168–7
ISBN 0–333–47169–5 pbk

Contents

Preface

Writing on several poets at once, one draws on man
resources. For intellectual stimulus and their patience and sup
port in various ways, times and places, I am indebted t
Dannie and Joan Abse, Peter Forbes, Jeremy Hooker, Sue Roe
Gordon Stuart and John Turner; to Beverley Tarquini, Carolin
Egar, Alison Kelly and Sue Cope of Macmillan; to my wil
and sons, as always; to University of London extramural stud
ents at Ongar, Essex; and most of all (because the idea for th
book came from their stimulus) to the students who took m
course on twentieth-century poetry at University Colleg
Swansea, in 1985–8.

JOHN POWELL WAR

Acknowledgements

The author and publishers would like to thank the following for permission to quote copyright material: the Estate of Robert Frost, Jonathan Cape Ltd and Henry Holt & Co. Inc. (USA) for excerpts from 'Home Burial', 'The Mountain', 'Mending Wall', 'The Ax-Helve', 'Stopping by Woods on a Snowy Evening', 'After Apple-Picking', 'The Oft-Repeated Dream' and 'Tree at my Window' from *The Poetry of Robert Frost* edited by Edward Connery Lathem; and the Trustees for the copyright of the late Dylan Thomas, J. M. Dent & Sons Ltd and New Directions Publishing Corporation (USA) for excerpts from 'Fern Hill', 'Poem in October' and 'The Force that through the Green Fuse'. Extracts from *High Windows*, *The Whitsun Weddings* and *Collected Poems* by Philip Larkin; from 'Autumn Journal' from *The Collected Poems of Louis MacNeice*; and from 'In Memory of Sigmund Freud' from *Collected Poems* by W. H. Auden are reprinted by permission of Faber and Faber Ltd. The excerpt from 'This Be The Verse' from *High Windows* by Philip Larkin (copyright © 1974 by Philip Larkin) is reprinted by permission of Farrar, Straus and Giroux, Inc. (USA). The excerpt from 'An Interview with *The Observer*' from *Required Writing* by Philip Larkin (copyright © 1983 by Philip Larkin) is reprinted by permission of Farrar, Straus and Giroux, Inc. (USA). The excerpt from 'In Memory of Sigmund Freud' by W. H. Auden is reprinted by permission of Random House, Inc. (USA).

Hardy's poems belong to an English tradition that goes bac
to Romantic poets like Wordsworth and John Clare, an
beyond them to the anonymous beginnings of the Englis
lyric in the Middle Ages. It is a poetry, essentially, of norma
tive experience: plain, low-pitched, physical and abiding. :
says that life goes on, and that human beings think and fee
in much the same way from one generation to another, an
from one century to another, and that because they thin
and feel, they are capable of tragedy, and of poetry. It i
the principal tradition in English verse.

Samuel Hynes

La mélancholie n'est pas française

Julia Kristeva

He is the poet of unpoetical natures

John Stuart Mill (on Wordsworth)

O woe, woe, etcetera

Ezra Pound (on Housman)

Some time ago I agreed to judge a poetry competition – yo
know, the kind where they get about 35,000 entries, an
you look at the best few thousand. After a bit I said, wher
are all the love poems? And nature poems? And they said
Oh, we threw all those away. I expect they were the one
I should have liked.

Philip Larkin

Does the land wait the sleeping lord
        or is the wasted land
that very lord who sleeps?

David Jones

1
Introduction

Here are two poems. The first is the sonnet 'Leda and the Swan' by W. B. Yeats:

A sudden blow: the great wings beating still
Above the staggering girl, her thighs caressed
By the dark webs, her nape caught in his bill,
He holds her helpless breast upon his breast.

How can those terrified vague fingers push
The feathered glory from her loosening thighs?
And how can body, laid in that white rush,
But feel the strange heart beating where it lies?

A shudder in the loins engenders there
The broken wall, the burning roof and tower
And Agamemnon dead.
                              Being so caught up,
So mastered by the brute blood of the air,
Did she put on his knowledge with his power
Before the indifferent beak could let her drop?

The second poem is 'A Thought in two Moods' by Thomas Hardy:

I saw it – pink and white – revealed
    Upon the white and green.
The white and green was a daisied field,
    The pink and white Ethleen.

And as I looked it seemed in kind
    That difference they had none;
The two fair bodiments combined
    As varied miens of one.

A sense that, in some mouldering year,
  As one they both would lie,
Made me move quickly on to her
  To pass the pale thought by.

She laughed and said: 'Out there, to me,
  You looked so weather-browned,
And brown in clothes, you seemed to be
  Made of the dusty ground!'

The differences between the two poems are very clear. Yeats is drawn to something outside himself rather than a personal experience within. It is the legend of the rape of Leda by the god Zeus who took on the form of a swan as a disguise for his action. As a result of the rape Leda gave birth to Helen of Troy, about whom was fought the ten-year siege of Troy, one of the most far-reaching events of the ancient world. The story seems to be told mainly by its rich embodying vocabulary. And the story itself is so palpable and solid, that it, rather than any poet, seems to ask the question in the poem's second half about the relation between knowledge and power. The poet stands outside the question, and asks it publicly. He lets, or makes, the words do the work, as though trusting that the poem's strong rich vocabulary is itself what contains the story's historical, mythical and psychological material.

    This verbal power works from the start. The first two stanzas are a cluster of nouns, each with its carefully placed adjective. 'Sudden blow', 'great wings', 'staggering girl', 'dark webs'; these and the rest follow in close succession, as though by attending to such details the poet could find the answers to his questions. As a result the individual nouns and adjectives gain weight, as though we could feel them like stones in our hands. The poem's words exhibit a choiceness in the poem, and take on extra rarity through the charge the poet gives them. In the second half of the poem the evocation is even more marked. The effect of the single act of love-making is put not as brooding thought or logical proposition, but as vivid detail. One 'shudder' as the love-making ends moves direct, by juxtaposition and without intervening explanation or process, across to the actual details of the battle; 'broken wall', burning roofs and dead war-general. Similarly the question of how knowledge and power are engendered is made urgent through what actually happened; mastery by brute blood, and the slack body of the rapist letting the woman go.

'Leda and the Swan' was written in 1923. Hardy's poem 'A Thought in two Moods' appeared in his collection *Moments Of Vision* published in 1917, one unusual for Hardy in mainly containing poems quite recently written. So, as broad periods of literature go, these two poems are nearly contemporary. Yet Hardy's tone, feeling and mode of working are very different from that of Yeats. As the title suggests, it is the thought itself rather than its reference that draws the reader's attention. The words by contrast are thin and transparent, as though to gain their effect by getting out of the way of what is felt and thought, rather than themselves being the physical means of lifting it forward into view. If Yeats's words are gold or stone models of what they evoke, Hardy's are a liquid cellophane parting silently before us, like air or water, so that we go through them into the unknown of our own dark minds. And it is less what the poet saw and more what it then felt like to see it, that mattered.

As part of this effect, the details are very few. We don't know if the poet is walking, standing at the field's corner or staring from a window. We can only guess who the woman is or what she looks like. The poet is struck by one thing; the contrast between her pink dress and the green of the field. Even those few details offer no simple story. We enter the poem and glimpse its images; yet they are uncannily taken away again. They are not joined to the objects they supposedly colour by any squads of clear words as in Yeats's poem. There is just woman, field, pink and green. They can thus become quickly mingled with the poet's mind and emotion and he turns at once to his own feelings about them.

As a result, the poem turns out to be made of mind and emotion themselves. It is only to that end that its words are chosen. With no material component, established myth, or traditional symbol or contemporary technological substance to retain us, we are drawn down to something more intangible. The poem is apparently about death, yet that word does not occur. We are drawn in to supply the word and idea ourselves.

The woman furthermore views the matter differently from the
man. She sees the poet himself as already the colour of the
earth where we shall all end. Even the poem's title is left
ambiguous. Perhaps the two moods are both the poet's, or his
and his friend's, or perhaps the physical presence in the first
and last stanzas sandwich the more drifting, internal rumi-
nations of the second and third.

Hardy is a central representative of a kind of poetry which
is the subject of this book. Broadly speaking, it is characterized
by a melancholy moodiness, a certain elusiveness of its
material as we have seen, and a sense of the presence of the
familiar and everyday as the only things – if even those –
that can be relied on at least to be present. A greyness and
colourlessness fills the present, making for a yearning for the
past, childhood and what is lost more generally; there is a
certain boundlessness too, as though the sharp edges of reality
are not distinct. It is commonly lyrical, which is its attraction;
but equally inward and subjective, as though that elusive subject we mentioned is forever the poet's own feelings, thoughts,
fears and disturbances. The poetry is commonly spoken in the
first person. This first-person quality, which to some readers
is excessively self-regarding[1], claims however to be exemplary;
it suggests that humanity is broadly the same everywhere; and
as a result, insofar as this poetry is political, it may provisionally be called social democrat – hard on the rich, compassionate
towards the poor, and saying that despite great material difference all are capable of feeling and suffering the same things.

But finally, and from a poetic point of view most importantly, the language is what is often called 'simple' or 'ordinary'. The poets seem to write as they might speak, and indeed
often state their positive suspicion of any sumptuous language
or poetic adornment. This apparently wilful denial of the very
thing a poet might most be expected to want to exploit – the
riches, linguistic variety and width of reference of language
itself – as though painters always worked with only one colour,
or musicians always wrote for only one instrument, raises
questions about the nature and status of this line, and of
poetry generally. As the critic Walter Pater put it of Wordsworth, 'His words are themselves thought and feeling'[2]. This
is to say that the words' sole aim is to express mind and

emotion themselves. This feature, perhaps originating in a puritanical feeling about art altogether, is the starting-point from which to enquire what is behind the wider poetry's characteristics.

Over the last two hundred years there have been a number of poets whose work shows these characteristics. William Wordsworth, John Clare, Thomas Hardy and Robert Frost all produced large bodies of work of this kind. Poets with the same consistency of type but who wrote much less include A. E. Housman and Edward Thomas, and there are other groups of poets with, to some extent, a similar tone and mood, most notably the Georgian poets of the second decade of this century. As far as one can identify such a thing, these are the 'pure cases', though this of course is not to say that they are superior to poets of other kinds.

Then there are other poets, some of considerable significance, whose work embodies the same tendencies but in bursts or periods, or who practise it most of the time but with some features modified or muted. Their poetry draws on more explicitly verbal, mythological or narrative traditions. Such cases include the Victorian poets Alfred, Lord Tennyson and Matthew Arnold, profoundly influenced by the Wordsworthian mode but suspicious of aspects of it. With them much of the poetry is as we have described, while elsewhere they treat of classical and mythological subjects. In his 'conversation poems' Samuel Taylor Coleridge also wrote briefly in the Wordsworthian way, while Wilfred Owen was drawn by the suffering, bleak landscape and mud of the First World War away from a more robustly verbal poetry to this greyer mode. Louis MacNeice varies from the very personal and melancholic to his own curious mixture of classical and surrealistic. The group known as 'The Movement', flourishing in the 1950s, has some affinities with Philip Larkin, the chief though rather exceptional exponent among them of this kind.

There are also a number of poets, of whom two are included here and one omitted, who illustrate from an interesting angle just where this kind of poetry starts and ends. This is less a matter of their being 'halfway cases' than of their either nearly approximating to the type, or very nearly avoiding it, without in either case finally doing so. Thus W. H. Auden, certainly

in the 1930s, has many of this poetry's marks. Yet he took the
crucial different step of treating his own inner feelings as no
longer reliable if spontaneously rendered, and in effect checked
them, as they came, against the texts of Marx and Freud.
Auden re-enters the *gravitas* of a different poetry: again and
again his own feelings are seen from the outside, as it were
by a majestic silent professional watching himself, even while
he is still feeling them as a man. Auden may well have marked
the beginning of the end for this kind of poetry.

Conversely Gerard Manley Hopkins and Dylan Thomas
might seem fully and delightedly verbal. Yet I include them,
for they show that the verbal interest can at times come from
a more brooding subjectivity. They, at the other end of the
continuum from Auden, never wholly renounce the inward
pull of mind and emotion as starting-points. Their vocabulary,
rich as it is in both substance and treatment, is always chosen
within the wider parameter of melancholy's grey familiar
world. But in all three cases there is no claim that they 'belong'
where they don't. The aim, in omitting Auden and including
Hopkins and Dylan Thomas, is simply to show by wider example how the features of this kind of poetry pull with or against
each other, and some of the varieties of effect that result. No
doubt other people would choose other poets. But Wordsworth, Hardy, Housman, Frost and Edward Thomas are fully
of this kind all the time; the central impulses remain the same
across all their work.

Taken as a group, these and comparable poets have been
called 'the English Line'. Samuel Hynes, Andrew Motion and
others use the term explicitly, and the idea of 'Englishness'
has figured in much discussion of these poets[3]. There is a
danger in using this title. 'English' now, in literary studies,
has often come to refer to the widespread attempt, over a
hundred years ago, to establish the idea of a unified English
national culture, and the allied attempt to set up English as a
subject of study (perhaps supplanting classics) in schools and
universities. This is already an oversimplified view of what
happened. But, in any event, it occurred before most of the
poets discussed in this book had written. It centred on Spen-

ser, Chaucer, Shakespeare and Milton, with Wordsworth the most recent major name. Furthermore the later critics who are usually credited or discredited with the attempt to establish an English canon – T. S. Eliot and F. R. Leavis – by and large ignored this particular 'English Line' as their exemplars. Eliot, as is well known, looked to the seventeenth-century metaphysical poets and Elizabethan dramatists and clearly thought little of Wordsworth and Hardy (though more of Tennyson), while Leavis's three major twentieth-century poets in his influential book *New Bearings In English Poetry* were two Americans and an English Catholic, Gerard Manley Hopkins, included in the present book as the most marginal case.

'English' in the present context refers to something narrower and more typological than adulatory – not that the present writer does not greatly admire these poets. But presumably nobody could envisage a 'national' and supportive culture relying for its poetic expression on something so melancholic and introverted, and it can go dangerously close to the exiguous on many occasions. Its strength is as an elegiac accompaniment to our lives; it voices, without rich verbal mediation, the elusive places of our most intense emotions. And its 'Englishness' lies in the characteristics typical of how the English are often seen, or were seen, by others. It lies in the verbal reserve and the pragmatic and laconic suspicion of the visionary or the extravagant, for which the English were commonly renowned. These features in their turn probably stem from the position of the middle class in a gradually secularizing world in which the landscape and terrain were increasingly altered, many would say marred, by the encroachment of industry. This poetry spans the period from about 200 years ago until the present, when the industrial and technological revolutions have seemed to threaten the presence of 'nature' and a common knowable landscape more than ever before, and at least some of the newly powerful middle classes felt the first tremors of guilt at their more fortunate position in the world. The poets were compromised in a contradictory position not of their own making: seeing the natural world ravaged by a commercial enterprise they themselves deeply suspected and perhaps hated but of which they were also undeniably beneficiaries. But like most other poetry, this too is not merely

social or political. It is sad in the presence of love and the
inevitable expectation of death. The value of the poetry lies,
not in the extent to which its immediate detail reflects these
historical movements, but in taking them further; using them
to embody a sadness applicable more widely, to any sadness,
any loneliness, bereavement or despair or indeed more exult-
ant feeling, anywhere and at any time.

By contrast the poetry of Blake, Shelley, Keats, Browning,
Eliot, Yeats, Auden and a few more enriches English poetry
(now in a wider sense) by conscious dissatisfaction with these
characteristics. They contain the contrary outgoing thrust without which English poetry of the last 200 years would be sparse
indeed, and its introversion and melancholy debilitating. This
other poetry may either extol the works of civilization or,
conversely, tirade against them and their political systems.
This again makes it unprofitable to try and tie it, as a type, to
any one political position, as the opposing positions of Eliot
and Yeats on one side and Blake and Shelley on the other
testify. Yet in all four of these cases the poetic attention, and
therefore the verbal material, draws on previous human
attempts to structure the physical world, in art, myth, military
conquest, human groups, technology, tools, decorations and
language seen as an artefact itself. The central longing is not
for the natural world. Nor is it for any past Eden; rather,
classical achievements are treated as present resources. This
other poetry then becomes richer and more exhilarating verbally, and aspires immediately to cultural inclusion; indeed in
modernist and post-modernist poetry the poet's own voice is
not valued as a personal matter even though, as Maud Ellmann
has recently suggested, how far such poets succeed in minimiz-
ing the presence of their personalities may be limited[4].

As to 'the English line' poets, a notable fact is that the
nineteenth and twentieth centuries differ from each other as
to how far these poets are indeed English in birth and background. Apart from Christina Rossetti, all the poets from the
nineteenth century discussed here were English pure and
simple, so far as any such condition is possible. In the twentieth century many of the most typical and central poets are not
English. Edward Thomas, MacNeice and others, most obviously Robert Frost, originate and/or have parentage elsewhere

in the English-speaking world, whether in these islands or outside. It is then a matter of the reader's political opinions as to how far we see this as a colonizing process from England itself or, by contrast, a gradual intrusion into a line previously clearly associated with one country, and now modifying it. The lesser melancholy of Frost – cognate in all other respects – and the larger, though compromised, verbal compulsions of Wilfred Owen and Dylan Thomas (possibly originating in the Welsh language in both cases) are signs of the silent change already under way early in the twentieth century itself. For comparable reasons, indeed, this line would now appear to be ending, and I share to some extent, if less strongly, the view expressed by Anthony Easthope on that matter in various places[5].

We should also stress at this point that these poets did not necessarily learn from each other, nor had they always even heard of each other. It is as much a set of characteristics, a type, as a line. And whether a 'canon' of poetry was consciously or otherwise constructed, whether historical determinants brought about recognizably similar poetry for a particular period, or whether a language, separately reached, made possible a new aesthetic which could alleviate sadness – these are questions of critical theory. To answer such questions one must first identify the features these poets share, and judge just what they are and what is expressed by them. It is this matter that the book attempts to explore.

As the Hardy poem suggests, this poetry is written in what appears to be simple and unadventurous language. It is remarkable how often these poets have insisted, outside their poetry, that they are to some degree suspicious of language. From Wordsworth to Larkin they have stressed not just the simplicity but the ordinariness of their language. They are suspicious of richer or more elaborate vocabularies. In emphasizing his determination to employ only 'real language of men' and 'a man speaking to men' in his renowned *Preface* of 1800, Wordsworth wrote also that 'there will be found in these pieces little of what is usually called poetic diction'; the 'gaudiness and inane phraseology' as he preferred to call it. For Wordsworth the matter was fundamental existentially. Language was 'like the power of gravitation or the air we breathe'; not palpable objects but the invisible element we inhabit. Arnold's praise of Wordsworth's poetry lay in that it 'has no style'. Hardy tried for a slight sense of carelessness in his work, while Edward Thomas spoke strongly against the unreal verbal elaborations of his former mentor, Walter Pater. Robert Frost saw not words but sentences as a poem's essential medium. Larkin said a poem is merely a verbal device by which an emotion in one person is made available to another. So long as that is done, there is no need to attend directly to words for their own sakes[6].

The characteristic comes from the secularization of the world in the last two centuries, and the connected feeling that language need not be sacramental. There is no one-to-one connection between individual words and real things, whether physical or spiritual, in a reality conceived of as neither divinely created nor static and knowable. Rather, language has life in communication to another person, colleague, lover, friend or enemy across a gap. Meaning is constantly negotiated and renegotiated, rather than attained by reference to and permutation of assured entities. Language exists far more now merely to keep us in touch with each other, to get our feelings or beliefs out of ourselves into the open. Individual words carry power to that end.

Again the strongly Protestant and perhaps Puritan inheritance behind this poetry is evident; the suspicion of the luxurious or guiltless, or even the confident. From such a stance words might not seem a worthwhile medium for poetry at all. And it is as though the poets we are attending to here, in one sense stuck with words, seem almost to have been actively seeking another art altogether. This view can be supported by taking literally the idea that poets work with a medium as do painters and composers. Artists work with raw material: colours, sounds, stone. They seek to shape such materials into something hitherto not articulated or solidified. But it is as though these 'English line' poets are left, in a world of thinned and untrusted words, with only their minds and emotions themselves as what is to be shaped. It is as though not paint, not sound, not stone, not words, or even sentences, but mind itself, emotion itself, was all that remained to be shaped in a world of such doubt and uncertainty. And, since 'mind and emotion' are still nonetheless *not* media that could be worked like stone or paint, words themselves have to be brought in as a kind of second-order medium, to stand in for the actual experiences of mind and emotion themselves, if not fully, at least as nearly as possible.

This is why in the subtitle I follow J. S. Mill in calling this the 'poetry of the unpoetic'. The writing is then retrieved as poetry because a different, salving pleasure appears. The words are enjoyed, not for their own sakes as palpable and richly semantic media, but as embodying the rhythm and shape that seem to manage and ease the very pain they try to express. It is as though the drift, pain and swirl of such feelings, internally, has itself to be shaped to allay their pressure or to eject them cathartically. Put this way, much of what the English line poets seem to have been groping for becomes clearer as to its intention. The words themselves are not succulent or savoured for their own sakes, for they aim mainly to embody the darker interior of mind and feeling themselves.

It may still seem a melancholy approach to what is, one might say ought to be, one of the human race's most rewarding activities; making, creativity, self-expression, art. Yet this simplicity is deceptive, and one soon finds that something elusive is being sought or expressed. There are complexities of syntax and rhythm, deliberate hesitations and downplayings, and much weight put on the seemingly innocent parts of grammar; the verb 'to be', the conjunctions and qualifications, if, perhaps, I might, and yet, because, oh, and so on. And this too is a central feature: a melancholy pervades these poets. At times it is morbid, a graveyard preoccupation with the bodies of the dead, as in Housman, of death occurring by accident, as with Wordsworth, or excessive fear of one's own extinction, as with Larkin. At other times it is a more formal sense of the elegiac. It is present as loss, a real or imagined childhood or garden of Eden or loved person never to be retrieved from alienation or death; a perpetual longing for something whether knowledge or terrain, always out of reach. But the question then arises as to which way round these melancholic poetic events occurred. Either these poets historically felt themselves cut off from a previously reliable tradition of words for their art, and so became victims of a sort of vocational pessimism; or conversely melancholy itself, through depression and perhaps neurosis in new circumstances (Puritanism, guilt at privilege, fear of change, and other things) led some poets into habitual recourse to the appropriate, colourless vocabulary, the confess- edly dismal lexicon which was all that was realistically left to them. Much that we consider in the following pages will be an implicit attempt to answer this very question. Either way the outcome is the same, that a certain minimalism of lan- guage, and a melancholy associated with that in one who is after all poet himself, are found in close association. The poets often despair of themselves and their work, as with Words- worth, or swear coarsely at books or the world, as with Larkin, or feel deep hesitation, a fluttering of 'if' and 'perhaps', as with Edward Thomas, or deliberately spin out page upon page of full-bodied cliché itself, as with MacNeice, or simply let life's irony display itself without seeming to bother much about words themselves, as with Hardy.

The poetry of simple language, or its shape and drift without substance, is thus inward, troubled, grey, boundless and uncertain. Its saving grace is that it sings, and when it does it is beautiful. To more robust spirits such poetry will not much appeal. To put it bluntly and extremely, such poets have been attributed with anything from excessive mother-bond to auto-eroticism. Yet a more charitable view would point else- where; to a certain stoical sturdiness, including physical sturd- iness, and a discontent, dissatisfaction and restlessness which pushed human enquiry to the point where the self itself seems to be endangered and even dissolved in the uncompromising attempt to know truth by being it. The song is the poetry's heart. However sad, lonely or even reprehensible is one's mood, the poem of this kind, by attending to phrase or passage rather than word, can make it bearable, meaningful and lovely, by making the mood itself sing, be parts of music, or come from music itself. How can my mood be bad, if reading this poem makes me say, yes, that's just how I so often feel, and this poem gives it a shape that makes it compare with all one thinks most worthwhile? Perhaps I too am not so bad, if the sweetest music of the race does not scorn to express such a sadness of mine, or alchemically so transmute it.

There are a couple of other qualities in the poetry to be mentioned here. One is the general phenomenon of desire, whether sexual or epistemological. The other is the matter of the familiar landscape, the unexotic out-of-the-window or on-a-walk terrain that often accompanies them. This matter has led to some controversy, again concerned with 'Englishness', although the prevalence of the relevant feature in the poems is not denied. A somewhat insular society and readership, recognizing such landscape, will then simply regard the resulting poetry as 'English', much as cricket, pubs and driving on the left are English – not to mention not speaking before being introduced, preferring understatement to enthusiasm and making religion a matter of refinement and compromise.

Two sides of this second aspect of the matter can be identified. These are: why the poets should so need to rely on a familiar, often rural landscape as psychological sustenance, and what happens when it seems to be threatened. The need for familiarity has causes and results. If the poets are sad or afraid, and if a sense of divine providence guarding you wherever in the world you are has declined, then the familiar is reassuring. But equally, the familiar is by definition neither surprising nor exciting. This is of course a highly relative view. The power of the natural world to delight and satisfy is not denied. The question is of the degree of familiarity and newness in any one case. The ecstasy and awe at the unknown apparently felt by Wordsworth in many of his 'natural' settings does not obviate a wider sense that the lakes and mountains were familiar too. Or, where that newness is present, then indeed Wordsworth's larger aspiration to put melancholy behind him, if temporarily, does mark him out from many of the rest of these poets. Trees, rivers and grass are brought in, by and large, not so much as objective correlatives for an inner feeling, but more as its very source. And because those things are not themselves restless they suggested solace for such poets. It is notable that these poets seldom refer to animals. If they do, the animals are static, perhaps grazing. There is little interest in what they do, how they breed or migrate or how they are predatory. The poet of mind is more compulsive

about wind, air and water, and earth itself, the very elements
of which nature seems to be made, and which give direct rise
to the flowers, trees and grass which come from it but remain
physically joined to it, rooted in it. Nature is conceived of as
permanent, the very medium of our existence.

However, when nature is threatened, the picture becomes
different. The expression of longing for the past, and for a lost
paradise, becomes prominent in the poets as the decades pass.
At first it is an inner matter, as Wordsworth moves from the
legitimately 'natural' world of the Lake District mountains,
confronts his own education and the French Revolution, and
senses that the world, though not gone, suddenly looks and
feels different. Later the pressure of new industry and the new
world-picture of pure science affects the poets more and more.
The scarring of the natural world by endless hurrying change
throbs in Arnold's 'The Scholar-Gipsy' in every stanza. There
is also geology. The strata beneath the landscape we see, their
fossils and skeletons, worried Tennyson as he brooded over
his religious doubts brought on by the early death of his friend
Arthur Hallam. By the time of Hardy nature itself has a dead-
ness, a blank neutrality, while much of MacNeice's *Autumn
Journal* responds to the suburban as now half the environment.
By Larkin's time the threat is overwhelming. Larkin evokes a
changing landscape of roadworks, railways, supermarkets and
suburban housing. His fellow-poet Charles Tomlinson coined
the word 'manscapes' for Larkin's scenes. Nature becomes a
lost paradise; yet that too declines, when nature becomes the
planet's spinning ball, and the suns and stars of the galaxy
itself.

The other consideration is the theme which sways in and
out of the poems, seldom named as a subject but always
present; the cluster of factors associated with desire. This
desire may be sexual or epistemological or, as Foucault has
suggested, in combination from a common root[7]. The compulsion to fill a lack or absence, to enter a void simply because
it is there and its unknown extensiveness is part of reality
itself, pervades these poets. It could be argued, generally, that
the constant preoccupation with the self *by* the self makes any
search impossible, for the seeker and the sought become the
same thing. As a result any imaginably objective entity in

which to seek simply dissolves. The poet is left only with his language; the palpable physical world in which, perhaps, satisfaction is available if invisible; and the possibility of another human with whom to make a physical and personal relationship and so fend off the emptiness if only temporarily. Wordsworth's poetry is full of mysterious people, usually women, just drifting into and then back out of sight. Hardy is said to have fallen in love with every woman he met, a fact which decreases, rather than otherwise, any sense that he would thereby have found an answer to his desperation and sense of inadequacy. For Larkin loneliness is both sad and necessary at once.

This endless desire for what is by its nature missing, is also associated with these poets' kind of language. The poet's incessant need is to catch up with an inner identity and outer reality, both receding. Yet, on the other hand, the suspicion of substantive language comes out as doubt that such knowledge can ever be attained. For language, to these poets, is such that no full-bodied reasoned account of reality, either of nature, death or the fullest human love, can ever be given. The language can only ever mourn its lack. Wordsworth wrote in *The Prelude* that what passes within even the philosophic mind, 'lies far hidden from the reach of words'. W. D. Shaw has written that in *In Memoriam* Tennyson is always reaching for what cannot be said. He cannot translate the unattainable into ordinary language, and therefore words (the words in the poem) can only cease when a vision beyond words is reached[8]. With Hardy, the result is often that poems end by declaring that he does not know this or that, about a person or a place. With Larkin, satisfaction is achieved by ending with an image, a palpable embodiment, of endlessness itself. This occurs in 'Dockery And Son', and also 'Here', where the poem ends not 'here' at all but with the poet staring out over shingle and breaking waves at 'unfenced existence:/Facing the sun, untalkative, out of reach'. With Housman it is not sea but those 'blue remembered hills' where, of course, he 'cannot come again'. The area not known, so to speak, is left very large; it is what humans have not yet attained to or understood, whether in galactic exploration, philosophy or human sexual love.

Other poets are quite different. They elaborate words richly, or point them outwards to what they seem solidly to name. They feel, but about things outside themselves. They are concerned less with nature than with how humans civilize nature with buildings, works of art, clothes, ships and ideas and forms of law and institution. They go away from the familiar. Shelley and Byron went to live in the ancient world of Greece and Rome, and Eliot and Pound exploited European and Far Eastern culture for materials for their work. Indeed such poets go to worlds beyond ours; as Blake put it, 'the real and eternal World of which this Vegetable Universe is but a faint shadow' (*Jerusalem*, 77). They have pain and sometimes neurosis, but also happiness and exaltation, and like Keats exhilaration in front of the beautiful. Like Shelley and Browning they are firm and raspingly confident as much as mournful. They trust the objective world for exciting and already informed experience. They accept clearer demarcations between aspects of reality, a tendency suggested in T. S. Eliot's recurring image of stairs and staircases, rather than in Arnold's pervading image of water. The past is a bank of earlier cultural and historical possession, not a wistfully longed-for dream. Their own death would be that of hero not suicide.

The English poets seem to isolate, in the realm of knowledge, one feature of it; namely, that it can never be complete. The incompleteness is what is voiced, and it feels often like an emptiness of self and of language. That it can seem to have captured the subliminal senses of countless educated and uneducated people for 200 years suggests that it has touched a vein in English consciousness that might otherwise have remained unlocated, unarticulated. It is perhaps a consciousness that English middle-class males endured, or brought on themselves, in the high peaks of the industrial revolution. Yet the implications are further-reaching than that still. A political and social explanation is necessary but would not be enough. These poets arrive, perhaps through the route of their social and economic circumstances, at existential positions which occur to most people confronting birth, sexual reproduction, death, and the physical world in the parts where it has not been altered by human intervention, laudable or otherwise. At best, they sing our deepest fall-back experience.

As to contemporary critical theory, the approach of this book will be that of direct response to actual texts, but seeing this on a continuum from theory rather than across a divide from it. The elements of personal response and theoretical application are not easily separable. Even when, as it were, simply reading the poems, we have for some time now been unable to avoid asking whether poems come largely from historical and ideological positions; whether they have hidden unconscious origins, perhaps sexual; whether a disposition to enjoy is not a privilege; whether poetry, and literature generally, are continuous with all other writing or different in kind; whether a poem can ever usefully be valued over another poem, and if so from what standpoint; and whether language itself is not the final predisposing factor, changing with the ages yet always recognizable, even over millenia, as not so very different from what linguistically went before. Rather than trying to answer these questions overtly here it seems best to let my own predispositions emerge in the main body of the book. However, certain things can be said as preliminary.

Certain features of critical theory have informed this book's approach. First, the view that everything is political, if taken exclusively of other considerations, is itself patently inadequate. For one could as easily say everything is sexual, biological, divine, meteorological or all manner of things; or indeed that language itself, that millenia-old phenomenon, is what shapes how our minds 'think' about anything at all. Nevertheless, having made this reservation, it is clear that this group of 'English line' poets did obviously respond to a varying degree to the social, political and economic situation with its power, privileges and human relationships. It is not coincidence that such homogenous work appeared in this two-century period, one in which Britain became a world industrial power and then, to a degree at least, has declined.

The historical research of Marilyn Butler, Jerome McGann and the many current biographers such as Lawrance Thompson, Peter Ackroyd, R. B. Martin, Stephen Gill and the rest has gone a long way towards demystifying the notion of timelessness often attached to the poets themselves. Yet that does not disperse the idea that 'poetry' itself proceeds independently in part. As Harold Bloom put it, 'The Marxists say, do not make the mistake of trying to destroy the precursor by taking his place. . . . My sad reply must be: No newly strong poet can reduce the significance of the precursor's mastery. . . . The dialectics of poetry are never those of nature or of society or of history.'[9] Poets do in practice draw linguistic resource from outside their own era: they may be if not (unacknowledged) legislators, certainly primal shapers of the very means by which a society speaks, and so thinks, at all; and the very possibility of 'ideology' itself may thus depend on the availability of certain kinds of language at any time. The individualist ideology of liberalism need not have been either accepted or rejected, as such, by the poets. Rather, they took it aboard as material to be worked, by putting language to work. The ideology, social class and material circumstance they began with was not itself the poetry; it was the materials for the poetry. This view does not dispose of the political one. While some people write poetry and others read it, others remain oppressed, with no shelter and nothing to eat. The dilemma suggests that the 'aesthetic' itself needs reconsideration. We must ask if we can, need to or should enjoy the valued cultural product when many in the world are deprived not only of that opportunity but of almost everything else.

On the question of language, the most fertile insight of the last few years has been Derrida's suggestion that a (Western) metaphysics of presence is suspect in its unitary blandness, and that in fact 'difference' – primal metaphysical distinction – is necessary for any meaning whatsoever to be possible[10]. Mere bland unity would mean nothing, an observation incidentally also made by Aristotle. However, Derrida's famous 'mark, trace, rupture' on reality leads on to his view that writing precedes speech rather than the reverse. The precedence is not only chronological. Rather, writing is the larger entity that contains speech as only one of its forms, rather than the other way round. All meaningful act(s) of signifying can be seen as a kind of writing: whether gesturing; the fossil record and the trees blowing in the wind; colour and tone; sexual activity; all are an impression or mark on the face of reality, or within reality itself. The result for poetry is a suggestion that such signification is already inherent to a considerable degree in words themselves. The play of *écriture* across reality leads to further play, further combinations and significations, and these can be 'read' without reference to some 'intention' on the part of the author, or even an author at all. The writing-speech reversal throws light on the present poets, as well as tying up with comparable distinctions in linguistics (particularly Saussure's signifier/signified) and some distinctions in contemporary psychoanalysis.

The English line poets we are discussing seen different. They seem to speak rather than write. The voice, real or illusory, emanates from an equally real or illusory self. The ever-present first person, the 'I', seems to deny the equally deconstructive suggestion (this time from Foucault and Barthes[11]) that the author is discountable. And possibly the attempt to make poetry as though words were transparent only, is itself melancholic. The attempt of the poet to take the 'mark' of language back down into a psyche by its nature dispersed and provisional (where is one's 'psyche'?) is failure or refusal to see language's universal presence as language. It is an attempt to make a unitary self dominate over writing's differentiated nature. Yet this does not invalidate the poetry. Rather, it makes clear that it too is one more signification, one more *écriture*, but on a wider scale; one in which the very fact of this poetry's existence is a mark on the whole of language. Such poetry may, in historical terms, be short-lived, or at most move in alternation with the different poetry (as of Eliot and Pound and post-Modernism) which seems closer to the individual word-mark; the pun, the alliteration, the citation from another language, the literary reference. The 'mark' of the English line poets is a larger-scale signification at the level of paragraph or period, or at least (as Frost thought) sentence. It is a sort of occasional reminder, in literary history, of one aspect of language's basis. So, when Edward Thomas makes a gently arcing curve from the apparently unpoetic 'And I am nearly as happy as possible', he has simply recast or resituated an unremarkable sentence in a way that makes poignant tension *between* that very generally unexceptionable saying and the particular occasion which he has set up emotionally. And when Robert Frost looks out of his window and thinks, 'Tree at my window, window tree', he makes richness and a singing tone not by enriching the vocabulary but by sending it round

again, re-arranged, as though a different feeling about the tree
is captured, and nothing new about the tree itself.

From psychoanalysis provisionally (i.e. without commitment
to a belief that all expression comes from a desire ultimately
sexual) we can again take insights which elucidate these poets
further from a different angle. Psychoanalytic criticism stems
from Freud's investigation of the unconscious, and particularly
the views of Freud's re-interpreter, Jacques Lacan, that 'the
unconscious is structured like a language'[12]. Lacan differs from
historicist critics in believing that poetry is 'the supreme pin-
nacle of language'. Since Lacan gives language such a central
role in the very definition of humanity itself, he sees poetry
as larger than merely a fortunate gift of tongues granted to
some people. The unconscious mind has a content, shape and
grammar which in effect generates the language we then
speak. This view is especially useful in approaching English-
line poets, for they already work with mind and emotion
(rather than words) as their medium, as we have said. Lacan's
idea that a psychiatric cure is not a re-enacted trauma as Freud
thought, but a re-attachment of the psyche to active language,
to *verbe*, emphasizes the role of language in active relations in
everyday, that is 'ordinary', life.

The French psychoanalytic critic Julia Kristeva has developed
Lacan's view in a special area. She sees a distinction between
the largely physical language of infancy and the later more
meaningful language of society achieved, in traditional societ-
ies, by the influence of the father in drawing the son away
from the mother. This approach too is applicable to English-
line poets. The division between the stages occurs because any
infant will learn rhythm, hear noises and sounds, before it
internalizes language's meanings – an event which incidentally
underlines language's material nature and makes poetry possible at all. Poets like Browning, Eliot and Yeats do not have
to go right into the stream of communal discourse of 'ordinary
language' (though later Yeats modified his view on this),
because they remain in touch with the language resources of
infancy and wander with it to any new departure. 'Wander'
is Kristeva's word, and she cites Joyce's *Ulysses*, the wanderer
of the ancient world, as prototype[13]. These poets use foreign
traditions, esoteric stories and language and ungrammatical

structures. The English-line poets by contrast stay home with the familiar, with what they experience as the home society's natural community. It is arguable that this English-line type of poetry derives from certain developmental phases in childhood and adolescence.

Finally there is the theory of canon-construction, which seeks the nature of 'literature' by asking how works and authors get chosen as belonging to it. The silent suggestion is commonly that certain bodies of work – the 'canon' – become regarded, not always justifiably, as the society's 'literature' while other work is neglected. Again the attempt in this book is not to consider the question theoretically, but to bear in mind watchfully the risks it points to in this sort of enterprise. A useful view is that of Altieri and Felperin[14] that *some* sort of selection is necessary, indeed inevitable, if there is to be any discussion of literature in practice. The community of literary criticism is the arena of an always provisional debate as to what kinds of writing have appeared, where they have come from, what they amount to, and when and whether they will finally fade away. The present book is such an attempt. I have to declare finally my own belief that the poets discussed here – like numerous others, not discussed, of quite different aim and character and of equal value – are in some sense worthwhile. However, such value may be brought out less by explicit praise than by asking how the poets are as they are, and so by implication where they stand up or fall down in contrast with other, equally rich, equally valuable and significant, equally English poets.

Part I

Part I

2
Wordsworth's Precursors

As will be seen, Wordsworth is the first poet fully to enter the cluster of attitudes to self, poetry and feeling which were described in the last chapter. But no one poet starts a tradition from nothing. For centuries poems have been written that move toward some of these features. The Old English poem 'The Seafarer' is a searing poem of toughness and fear in face of rock, sea, wind and winter. William Langland's *Piers Plowman* (late fourteenth century) precurses *The Prelude* just enough to be intriguing, with its 'field full of folk' and its poet wandering on the Malvern hills. Robert Burton's prose text *The Anatomy of Melancholy* appeared in 1621, and the melancholic refugees in the forest pervade Shakespeare's *As You Like It*. John Donne occasionally touched a combination of dejection and natural setting typical of the nineteenth century:

> And that this place may thoroughly be thought
> True paradise, I have the serpent brought.
> ('Twicknam Garden')

It was these scattered tendencies which, to put it shortly, William Wordsworth internalized as something of a cogent group, in a way which was to influence at least the first two-thirds of the nineteenth century. However, the more immediate thrust on Wordsworth himself and then through him the later poets, can be seen stemming from two sources: Milton, and the later eighteenth century poets of 'sensibility'. The earlier major influence was unquestionably Milton, particularly in *Paradise Lost*, which sets up a myth which the nineteenth century of this line never really escapes. God places Adam and Eve in an unspoilt paradise, the garden of Eden, at the beginning of the earth's existence. They are innocent and obedient. But Eve falls prey to the temptation of Satan (in the guise of a serpent) to eat of the fruit of the Tree of Knowledge, and she persuades Adam to do the same. God therefore expels them from their garden, and they now have their eyes open to knowledge, but also to labour and suffering, and their paradise is gone. It scarcely needs underlining why the poets of the first industrial and liberal age, with its growing technology and belief in education, should have so responded to this narrative. The implications of the story for poetry however are deeper. Adam's first conscious action when he was made by God was to name every plant and creature. But he is expelled; and the poetry that follows, in this particular English line, does its naming by expressing; by voicing and mourning this lost paradise, rather than by attaching labels to all that glorify it and inhabit it. Meanwhile the woman gets the blame, but in Wordsworth's own poetry a new and puzzled attitude to this facet of the matter enters.

Furthermore it is Satan, scourge of the world God made, who turns out to be the compelling figure in the poem, as is so often emphasized. This was not intended by Milton, the blind poet who does not know how true are his own words, but who does know that what he says is way beyond the daily world all others see but he cannot himself. (Milton, of course, went totally blind in middle age, probably his early forties.) Satan justifies his rebellion against God to his diabolical followers by saying he was never created by God in the first place. He was 'self-begot, self-raised' (*Paradise Lost* V 860). This optimistic claim contains the key to the whole matter. A hundred and fifty years later Wordsworth began his life poem *The Prelude* with words which almost exactly echo *Paradise Lost*'s end, 'The earth is all before me' (*Paradise Lost* XII 646; *The Prelude* 1805 I 15). English line poets also write as though they are of their own selves begot, and are melancholic from the experience. Wordsworth majestically and morally replaces God by nature, but the idea diminishes as technology and new human and psychological disciplines approach. The poets are left, as Adam and Eve were, with bourgeois marriage, poetic blindness and some confusion. They are very male, very serious and very vulnerable. Larkin's resistance to marriage is from this standpoint an end phase.

The good-evil duality in Milton which affects the later poets is not found in *Paradise Lost* alone. It is strong in the ode 'On the Morning of Christ's Nativity', to some extent in Lycidas (the poem that so moved Housman) and in the pleasure-pain pair of poems, 'L'Allegro' and 'Il Penseroso'. The divide inaugurates what we see as the Puritan streak in the English-line poets. Here more than anywhere the English line departs from the verbally richer tradition of Shakespeare[1]. The battle in Wordsworth and his successors becomes inward, and indeed may cease to be a battle. Rather, in the eighteenth century, what had been thought a battle turns into a precondition of human psychology, a set of uncertainties which simply present difficulty. It is the century of Hegel (born like Wordsworth in 1770) with his monumental conception of the universe itself as Absolute-Thought-discovering-itself, which it duly does in that in this period, in Arnold's phrase, 'the dialogue of the mind with itself has commenced'[2]. It is this process that sets going the whole tendency toward a poetry in which mind and emotions are themselves what the poet writes with.

Equally, and as the historical deconstruction of early nineteenth-century 'Romanticism' as a supposed entity proceeds in current criticism, the eighteenth-century 'poets of sensibility' become increasingly relevant to our present topic. They are regarded as preceding Wordsworth and the later trend with more obvious continuity than has normally been admitted. They led up to it, and indeed reached that edge themselves, without ever taking the final step into subjectivity itself.

There has long been a belief that the eighteenth century was a period of neo-classical reason and decorum, with romanticism a vigorous reaction to it. This view is now called into question. A valuable summary of the real change is provided by Marilyn Butler[3]. Well before the French Revolution new weekly journals, the new science of the Royal Society and the economic pessimism of Adam Smith led to a disenchantment with material luxury. Attention to the lowly and down-and-out also begin to have a rural setting. The country parson, gentleman or at least well-provided individual sympathizing with the deserving poor begins to figure, as with Crabbe, Cowper and Gray. The scientific objectivity, as far as it was that, of James Thomson's poem *The Seasons* (1730; final version 1746) stands back from romantic ego-involvement with nature, but equally it is miles from the literature of ownership of land

and country house estate. Gothic sentimentality too and the idea of the 'noble savage', epitomized in Crusoe's Man Friday, are hardly decorous, nor are the fear and unease which accompany this. Dr Johnson underwent sadness and neurotic terror of death even though we now think of him as the common sense critic *par excellence*. His poem 'The Vanity Of Human Wishes' (1749) and Edward Young's *Night Thoughts* (1742–5) both embody a disturbed rather than even-paced sensibility. Not that the classical ideal is always so far from such emphases. The Roman sad severity of Cicero and Vergil is a silent presence in Gray and Crabbe even if Catullus and Ovid are not.

The relevant poets of this time include Burns, Crabbe, Cowper, Dyer, Thomson, Collins and Gray. To oversimplify somewhat, they elaborated a tendency in poetry which Samuel Johnson traced back to the mid-seventeenth-century poet John Denham. In such poetry some poetic identification between morality and nature was attempted; what Samuel Johnson, writing of Denham, referred to as 'a new scheme of poetry' which he called '*local poetry*, of which the fundamental subject is some particular landscape, to be poetically described' (his emphasis)[4], with or without the meditative element. Our interest is in how far this is what finally went toward the subjective internalizing, the mind and emotion medium, that later became the English-line hallmark. The topic is discussed and Johnson's passage cited in another influential book two decades before Butler's, by Robert Langbaum. Langbaum argued that the key change came when the early nineteenth-century romantic poets underwent a disturbing *experience* in the face of some natural scene, which they had to come to terms with[5]. The eighteenth-century poets of sensibility did not quite do that. Many of them were moved to an internal *reflection* on what they saw, not shifting their own preconceptions, less still their sense of self, even though it is often quiet and sobering enough, as with Gray. What happens is that these poets write within a landscape, with the simple language befitting attention to the poor and deprived, but with their own personalities integrated and not in question. In James Thomson, for example, there is certainly a compulsion to make the move into nature:

> Wherefore should we choose?
> All is the same with thee. Say, shall we wind
> Along the streams? or walk the smiling mead?
> Or court the forest glades? or wander wild
> Among the waving harvests? or ascend,
> While radiant Summer opens all its pride,
> Thy hill, delightful Shene?
>
> (*The Seasons*, 'Summer' 1402–8)

That surely prefigures the opening lines of *The Prelude*, where Wordsworth too has the glorious freedom to wander wherever he likes. But with Thomson it isn't yet a question on which much will depend. There is something hypothetical about the alternatives in the lines. Wordsworth greatly admired the poem in his early years but went beyond it.

Wordsworth also admired Burns, especially 'The Cotter's Saturday Night' for its restoration of peasant life into poetry; and equally Young's *Night Thoughts*, where the silent meditation inside the oddly jerky and shrill exterior is real enough. Yet Young meditates, inwardly and without landscape, on sets of thoughts he has as propositions not experience. He does not discover the psychological disturbance within his own classical decorum. William Collins, who also verged on insanity, wrote poems on what were to become the early nineteenth-century themes of Simplicity, Liberty, Pity, Fear and Evening, but in the classical ode forms which he did not escape. Decades later the 'Ode to Evening' was praised by Gerard Manley Hopkins, who tried to set its 'heavenly beauty' to music (he was a competent amateur composer). Hopkins said that 'what came out was strange and wild and (I thought) very good'[6]. But from even so verbal a poet as Hopkins that wildness contrasts Collins, who is seeing the scene from indoors:

> Or if chill blustring Winds, or driving Rain,
> Prevent my willing Feet, be mine the Hut,
>   That from the Mountain's Side
>   Views Wilds, and swelling Floods . . .
>
> ('Ode to Evening' 33–36)

George Crabbe's poetry was admired by Jane Austen, Byron

and Ezra Pound, and disliked by Wordsworth. Hardy, however, said it first taught him realism in poetry. There are currently signs of revived interest in Crabbe's poetry[7]. It too
touches the edge of the later involvements, and Crabbe had
enough experience of calamity in his own life, being poor for
years and addicted to opium. Crabbe gradually attempted a
new kind of poetry, he wrote about poverty and the poor and,
like Larkin so much later, believed that happiness is not
poetry's subject: 'Amusements, Pleasures, Comforts, Days of
Joy/ May a Man's Mind, but not his Muse, employ'. In *The
Village* (1783) and *The Borough* (1810) Crabbe wrote long descriptions of the life and lot of poor people. There is no denying
the angry feeling of this work, nor his continuous attempts to
relate these topics to the question of poetic truth. But here too
Crabbe does not reach the point of merging poverty, countryside or truth with inner feeling. Those things come out as
strong external statements:

> By such examples taught, I paint the Cot,
> As truth will paint it and as bards will not.
> Nor you, ye Poor, of letter'd scorn complain,
> To you the smoothest song is smooth in vain;
> O'ercome by labour and bow'd down by time,
> Feel you the barren flattery of a rhyme?

Crabbe's feeling is sincere and real, but he has no inner difficulty in the poem itself, for his ethical position is already
unexceptionable. He therefore can't go into the implications
within the poem, of being a man himself, and of sharing the
same human situation.

The nearest any of these comes to self-consciousness, still
without quite getting to it, is Gray in his 'Elegy Written in a
Country Churchyard'. Gray was a quiet Cambridge recluse
who produced little poetry. His elegy was written in the years
1742–50. Right at the start of it the poet puts himself into a
spot from which he cannot, perhaps would not, withdraw:

> The Curfew tolls the knell of parting day,
> The lowing herd winds slowly o'er the lea,
> The plowman homeward plods his weary way,
> And leaves the world to darkness and to me.

The first-person 'me' comes after three balanced and objective observations, and it never returns. There is no first person pronoun in the poem again. Instead there is a succession of what appear to be deeply felt but carefully ordered observations. The judicious selection of words in slow procession seems to come from real respect for the dead poor he is thinking of. The second stanza continues:

> Now fades the glimmering landscape on the sight,
> And all the air a solemn stillness holds,
> Save where the beetle wheels his droning flight,
> And drowsy tinklings lull the distant folds.

Something is in the air, it throbs with expectation. Once the visual image has faded the remaining sounds, beetle's hum and distant cowbells, are clear-cut and tiny. They suggest a growing concentration as the subject's importance dawned on the poet, gathering and intensifying his feeling. The poet's eyes seem to lower from the further horizon and feel drawn down and near to the bare, plain mounds of earth at his feet. This is perhaps why Johnson famously decided that unlike much of Gray which he disliked, this poem 'abounds with images which find a mirror in every mind, and with sentiments to which every bosom returns an echo,' and why F. R. Leavis having just cursorily dismissed this line of eighteenth-century 'Romantic precursors' (his phrase), could add that 'from the general censure of this account Gray's *Elegy* claims exception[8]'. Throughout what follows Gray, decorously and quietly yet tenaciously and insistently, urges more and more examples and implications upon us, of the poverty he has so strangely focused on. Often the piling-up of instances and rhetorical insistence goes on from stanza to stanza, but the fifth and sixth conveniently show it in miniature:

> The breezy call of incense-breathing Morn,
> The swallow twitt'ring from the straw-built shed,
> The cock's shrill clarion, or the echoing horn,
> No more shall rouse them from their lowly bed.

For them no more the blazing hearth shall burn,
Or busy housewife ply her evening care:
No children run to lisp their sire's return,
Or climb his knees the envied kiss to share.

Gray doesn't mind resorting to the simplest words – the 'ordinary language' – when something just has to be said and by implication faced in his twilight solitude. In stanza five the unexpectedly simple fourth line clearly contrasts the decorously planted nominals of the first three, so that an undeniable truth is faced, and more and more inferences about these poor people, now dead and buried, can then be drawn further down the poem. The inferences widen and widen: that none of these people was famous, or famously cruel, or artists, or can be blamed, or can ever return; nor can the renowned who have more glorious burial. The poem is full of this slowly proceeding language which Gray ponders as he goes, and equally full of melting lines in which psychic condition and present emotion seem inseparable: 'And waste its sweetness on the desert air'; 'Implores the passing tribute of a sigh'; 'Nor cast one longing ling'ring look behind'.

Yet Gray does not know how to wind it up; he cannot take the logical-emotional step by which his very self is exposed and vulnerable as the poem's originator. That is why he never gets back to the 'me' of the first stanza. Stephen Bygrave has put it that the poem 'evokes a twilight which it cannot then move beyond', for it is read as 'a poem whose time has not quite come'[9]. This apparently is why Gray finished with the curious and not quite explicable epigraph in the poem's last four stanzas; the awkward ending in place of the real ending he could not yet arrive at. One wonders about this twilight, like Collins' 'Ode to Evening' and Cowper's more cheerful lines on evening in 'The Task' Book iv, and which no doubt led on to Wordsworth's 'An Evening Walk' in his earliest years. Wordsworth thought much of Collins and highly of Gray's elegy. He used two stanzas of the latter for the epigraph to his own second *Essay on Epitaphs*. Twilight precedes darkness. Milton the general precursor was blind, and the traditional blindness of the great poet begins to take on new significance as attention to the inner self replaces colourful perception of a world humans were intended to inhabit and from which they would derive meaning. The eighteenth-century parallel interest in the picturesque as a generous and happy landscape (the labouring poor invisible) gives way. Insight, one might say, begins to control outsight[10].

Many later poets of this English line – MacNeice, Hardy, Larkin – are meticulous observers in the sense of always looking, staring at a landscape, which they do record in sharp detail. But despite the apparently authoritative voice of the watching speaker, they have no guarantees for what they see. There is the bewildered secular community, and then a boundlessness further out and not yet known at all. That is in effect their way of being 'blind seers'. Only the confident Augustans or the mediaevalists could be so sure that what their eyes saw was what the creation contained, what God had made. One devotee of Gray's *Elegy* was Thomas Hardy. He quoted it frequently, titled a novel (*Far From The Madding Crowd*) from one of its lines and once said that for him Stinsford churchyard, where he was finally buried, was always the Stoke Poges churchyard where Gray wrote[11]. In his poems Hardy calls Stinsford 'Mellstock'. Possibly 'stock' is 'Stoke', and hearing has displaced seeing once more, not on the surface but in the mind's echo.

3
William Wordsworth

It is very hard to describe Wordsworth's poetry. The extraordinary haunting voice, so moralistic and yet so eerie, so stern yet so guiltily vulnerable, so ghostly and so dull at once, at times so firm while elsewhere, or even in the same passage, so liquid and elusive. It has been called 'echo humanised', 'pedestrian hauntedness' and a number of other things, not all complimentary. The remarkable thing is that what ought to be dreary turns out so deep and lasting. And it is the weird mixture of the two voices which stays throbbing in the minds of those who take to him, for many for the rest of their lives. At best it becomes what was called 'that thrilling utterance' by the poet A. E. Housman, whose illicit visits to the male flesh-pots of France and North Africa would have made one more expect he might have despised it.

The idea of the dreary trembles irresistibly in one of Wordsworth's most memorable passages. Once as quite a small child he had been in the hills with his horse and an adult companion. Inadvertently wandering away by himself, he came to a spot where many years earlier a murderer had been hanged. Further back up the hillside, overlooking a lake, he passed a girl carrying a pitcher. He remembered it all:

> It was, in truth,
> An ordinary sight, but I should need
> Colours and words that are unknown to man
> To paint the visionary dreariness
> Which, while I looked all round for my lost guide,
> Did at that time invest the naked pool,
> The beacon on the lonely eminence,
> The woman, and her garments vexed and tossed
> By the strong wind.

(*The Prelude* 1805 XI 307–15

The passage rings of Wordsworth and what is unique to him. An ordinary sight, yet somehow otherworldly at the same moment, uncanny and strange, no doubt because of the characteristic morbid touch in the unnatural death by hanging and the survivor beside it, one of Wordsworth's commonest scenarios. The oxymoron 'visionary dreariness' is one of many cases in the poetry where the weird mix of pleasure and pain are seen in a new way. The hollowed-out emptiness of the scene (made resonant by the monosyllables in line 311) is also restoratively touched in, in the last few lines, by the quick one-by-one list of nouns: pool, beacon, woman, garments and wind, all strangely irritated emotionally, 'vexed and tossed'. And of course the compelling sense that, in the act of sorrowfully saying that he cannot find the words, he has found them, and that the scene is therefore beyond formal dictionaries and words, and must be referred to, even by a poet, with some awe and at a distance. The simple language of these poets finds here one of its most eloquent liturgical pronouncements.

Wordsworth was born in 1770. He was thus already a young man a decade before the nineteenth century started. He grew up in the Lake District and then went to the University of Cambridge. At least twice in his early twenties he visited Europe, including extended stays in France immediately after the French Revolution. He became totally identified with that movement and was not far from enlisting with the revolutionaries with whom he made friends. But events were to prevent that. Britain's declaration of war against France in 1793, the revolution's idealism turning to horror and terror and Wordsworth's own earlier liaison with the young French woman Annette Vallon, by whom he had an illegitimate daughter Caroline, led him to a desperate trauma in London, probably in the summer of 1795. It took him months if not some years of harrowing self-doubt and self-examination to deliver himself from it. To achieve this recuperation he first went down to the west country, in that year of 1795, where later he met and began a lasting friendship with Samuel Taylor Coleridge; and then, after a trip to Germany with Coleridge and his own sister Dorothy, finally at the end of that year 1799 went with her to settle at Dove Cottage, Grasmere in the Lake District and his own 'native hills'. They moved twice more in later

years, but always in the same small area round Grasmere
which they never left again for any length of time, although
there were tours in Europe again or to Scotland, and shorter
trips to London. Wordsworth became Poet Laureate in 1843
and died aged 80 in 1850[1].

Many of these and earlier events in Wordsworth's life appear
in the long poem *The Prelude*, published after his death and
subtitled 'Growth of a Poet's Mind'. By virtue of its topic it
has been a main source of understanding of the work of these
'English line' poets. Wordsworth always acknowledged the
sustaining support of his sister Dorothy through his crisis years
and of her and his wife Mary Hutchinson for the rest of his
life, from Dorothy at least until her later permanent mental
illness. Feminists today argue that the poet did a bit too well
out of her loyalty, for she was always an embryonic poet
herself, a view for which there is certainly evidence.

In the decade from about 1797 to 1807 Wordsworth wrote
most of the poetry by which he is remembered. After some
distinguished long early poems which already bear his hallmark, the first real step toward major influence was the
defiantly challenging project, with Coleridge, to write poetry
in 'language really used by men', resulting in both the *Lyrical
Ballads* of 1798 and their famous Preface of 1800. The book
contained many ballads about country peasants living hard
lives and was written in unadorned language of disturbing
nature. Yet none bar the last poem, 'Tintern Abbey', discovers
what sooner or later must happen if you really want to write
in simple language while probing the material very deep. It
turns you inward as well as outward, and it is likely that this
discovery and its powerful and rewarding effects are what led
Wordsworth to feel that poetry, as much as political action,
could be his justification for his activities in the world. Certainly he 'withdrew' to the Lake District, but those who still
castigate him for this need to account too for his having already
written 'Tintern Abbey', the mysterious Lucy poems and a
draft of the first two books of the poem of his life.

From then on in this decade Wordsworth pursued his ever-
receding poetry of inner language, mind and heart through a
number of scenes and subjects. He gradually found what
seemed unaccountable; namely, that exploring his own past

in the mountainous region, remembered as both happy and haunted, itself brought on a sense of profound loss at its passing, and a loss of the childhood first-vision of that world. This led to the famous 'Ode: Intimations Of Immortality', other poems like 'Peele Castle' (the elegy written the year after his brother John was drowned at sea) and the continual rewriting of and adding to *The Prelude*. He wrote of the same matters in that poem more externally too, as well as in narratives of the lives of lakelanders who had suffered privation and loss. Such poems included 'Michael', 'The Brothers' and 'The Ruined Cottage', the last-named later to become the first book of *The Excursion*. In those poems the inner sense of self he had painfully come to incorporate is transferred across into those poems' characters. He also wrote the political sonnets of 1802 and, finally, those mysterious poems and passages of boundlessness, where reality is present but recedes before you, or comes from behind seeming to catch you up. The egg-stealing and bird-killing incidents in the first book of *The Prelude* have this and there are also, for example, the two poems written as a result of and two years after the 1803 tour of Scotland, 'The Solitary Reaper' and 'Stepping Westward'.

We need to begin, however, by returning to the French Revolution. That cataclysmic event set Wordsworth on the road from which he discovered his poetry-politics distinction. But it also predisposed the whole modern world of the last two centuries in which the poets we are considering flourished, perhaps now to die out. Thanks to the new pre-eminence of historical criticism, and no doubt also the bicentenary (1989) of the major event this year in which I am writing, there has been recent and heated debate about just what did happen to Wordsworth after the French Revolution and in subsequent years. Some critics, notably new historicists, argue that his departure to the lakes was a U-turn leading to a withdrawal which can only be called escapist. Others say that the process was essential because it deepened permanently his root in a single familiar, domestic and natural region, an essential for his kind of poetry. The English line poets without fail, even if to varying degree, require this sense of a familiar region. The debate is fundamental, not only to Wordsworth but as to how far poetry, and art, may claim to be autonomous forms of understanding like any other (such as philosophy or science), a positive formulation that historicist critics by nature of their ideologies can't allow. This discussion is central to any discussion about the language and tendencies of Wordsworth and the line that followed.

Marilyn Butler believes Wordsworth's actions imply a withdrawal to an attitude which was 'domestic, withdrawn, quietist, meditative and very consciously English'. From then on, she says, he became even more conservative, and this set in as early as the writing of the 'political' sonnets of 1802. Butler says that, however unconsciously this was made, it was a very political decision. This view is not peculiar to the late twentieth century. It was, for example, the subject of Robert Browning's poem 'The Lost Leader' and there were other cases. Butler's list is most interesting for our argument, for while her tone is hardly that of approval, her list of adjectives includes many we have already strongly associated with this kind ,of poetry. Recent disagreements have also occurred between George Watson and John Beer over the degree of Wordsworth's participation in such events and what extent of violence he would have been willing to commit; and between E. P. Thompson and Nicholas Roe about how radical the poet really was and how long it lasted[2].

In another trenchant article, Gayatri Chakravorty Spivak considers the writing of the French Revolution episodes in *The Prelude* (1805 IX-XI). This writing she argues was, for Wordsworth, an act of exorcism of his illegitimate fatherhood; a way of coping with the revolution experience by turning it into a text; and a justification of poetry as a better response to the oppression of mankind than politics was[3]. Her psychoanalytical reading of many passages in this part of the poem is interesting and persuasive; for example of Book XI lines 76-8 and 344-67 especially so. It seems an attribute of this whole line of poetry that the absence of sharp-edged language to block off the subconscious lets in deep resonances many of which are inevitably sexual. It is also obvious that Wordsworth's response to the revolution was of enough importance to him that he made these books the climax, even if not the most memorable poetry, of the poem. They are the structural counterpart of Milton's battle in heaven in *Paradise Lost*; the 'great argument' from which the wider intellectual energies are drawn and where the deepest conflicts are found.

To say as much however is to risk begging the question. When Wordsworth went to France he had already undergone the childhood experiences which vibrate through the poem's first two books. He had also already taken on the vocation of poet, as the poem makes clear. In any poetry at all the unconscious, the social and political scene, the gender situation and the actual language, constrained by its rhythms and its twenty-six letters, are all there as material the poet works with. So, since some poets lean to any one of these aspects more than others, it is neither surprising nor questionable if one tradition, in this case the English-line poets, find that language and rhythm constantly draw out their unconscious and, indeed, troubled thoughts and emotions more than do other poets. This is their vocation, it is what they find they have to do. Yet these critics tend to beg these questions, or seem to, by praising the poems' 'poetry' as a separate skill which is simply applied. Marilyn Butler puts it aside as being 'gifted with tongues' (p.10) while Spivak doesn't 'underestimate "the verbal grandeur" ' (p.221). But Wordsworth's massive achievement was to give conscious experience the stamp of the real itself, rather than to take that inner experience as merely the centre of a network of political, social and economic conditions. He wrote of all together, demonstrating their inseparability and with self-consciousness, feeling and knowledge of that feeling, entailing duties as great as those of external political action. The theme and its accompanying feelings haunt the English line for 200 years. The increasingly melancholic accompaniment occurs when the feelings overwhelm the individual, or are thwarted only with great resulting tension.

Another line of criticism argues that the very tentativeness of Wordsworth's poetry, the way it probes itself, uncovers its own puzzlement as it goes, and feels profound guilt about what emerges, is what contains its true character, and is itself what gets written. This has been argued by, among others, Paul Hamilton[4]. The point about the remembered childhood incidents and experiences, Wordsworth's famous 'spots of time', is that their nature was obscure to Wordsworth himself. The hesitancy of their expression, the knowing and not-know-

ing that marks English line poets all over, is epitomized by
the very act of writing a poem of the growth of a mind. For
it is the mind itself which is carrying out that task. In the
same way, as George Watson points out, *The Prelude* is not an
epic but an apology for not writing one. It was unfinished,
and the 'great philosophical poem' which Coleridge wanted to
see was never written. Meanwhile the hesitancy about what
his mind and emotions are really doing is explored through a
recollection of the experiences of hesitancy, emotion and
motion themselves.

This sense of hesitancy and guilt is often underlined in
apparently objective, scenic contexts which yet are themselves
a matter of things in motion. 'Emotion' is of the mind, 'motion'
is out in the physical world; yet they always seem to be connected in the life Wordsworth lives and feels. The early scenes in
The Prelude both throb with this motion and disturb the poet
as they do so. The poet steals and probably kills a bird found
in someone else's trap:

> and when the deed was done
> I heard among the solitary hills
> Low breathings coming after me, and sounds
> Of undistinguishable motion, steps
> Almost as silent as the turf they trod.
> (*The Prelude* 1805 I 328–32)

And when he stole eggs from a bird's nest high on a precipi-
tous hill rock:

> Suspended by the blast which blew amain,
> Shouldering the naked crag, oh, at that time
> While on the perilous ridge I hung alone,
> With what strange utterance did the loud dry wind
> Blow through my ears; the sky seemed not a sky
> Of earth, and with what motion moved the clouds!
> (1805 I 345–50)

The mixture of motion and emotion become entwined here
with another pairing and contrast; that of sight and sound.
We see both scenes, yet a look at their vocabulary shows that

in each of them something heard is the deepest experience. Harold Bloom believes that in the progressive movement of the poem 'Tintern Abbey' Wordsworth gradually recognizes this. The 'five long summers' of the poem that have passed since his previous visit to the spot, during which he has learnt to hear 'the still, sad music of humanity', encapsulate the eighteenth-century's gradual change from valuing the straight 'picturesque' to a new mixture of feeling, seeing and hearing. As Bloom says, this is again a move back to the Miltonic blindness. It means simply that nature's details are no longer servant to any objective appraisal but themselves move within the mind and its emotions[5]. In 'Tintern Abbey' the poet realizes that visual dominance has gone, that 'I cannot paint what then I was'. But to paint you have to be still, and here as elsewhere neither mind nor body can be still:

> And so I dare to hope,
> Though changed, no doubt, from what I was when first
> I came among these hills; when like a roe
> I bounded o'er the mountains, by the sides
> Of the deep rivers, and the lonely streams,
> Wherever nature led: more like a man
> Flying from something that he dreads, than one
> Who sought the thing he loved.
>
> (lines 65–72)

But in all this hesitant movement inward and outward, walking, seeing, hearing, and puzzlement about those things, there is one crucial change from the eighteenth-century poets. That is Wordsworth's own continuous self-consciousness of it: his sense, all along, that he is himself stumbling on how he feels, how he senses himself to be growing and feeling and thinking, and, indeed, *being* at all. It is this feeling that becomes the dark interior of this English-line poetry for almost the next 200 years. That is in effect the step Wordsworth took. It is epitomized by the first book of the poem about his own development, in which he only stumbles on this new subject in the process of writing it. One can open *The Prelude* at more or less any page and find him always watching what he is doing, and feeling it. 'I was left alone/ Seeking the visible world, nor knowing why'; 'I seem/ Two consciousnesses – conscious of myself/ And of some other being'; 'Not seldom I had melancholy thoughts'; 'whate'er/ I saw, or heard, or felt, was but a stream/ That flowed into a kindred stream'. These are random and brief examples, taken from hundreds. Often whole paragraphs are turned to this swelling rhythmic capture of 'the life within', and it is never absent from the story. While writing the poem Wordsworth more than once revealed anxiety that so long a poem should have such a subject. 'It seems a frightful deal to say about one's self, and of course will never be published (during my lifetime, I mean), till another work [*The Recluse*] has been written and published . . .' '. . . a thing unprecedented in Literary history that a man should talk so much about himself'[6].

The new self-searching is found in other contexts. In the 'Elegiac Stanzas Suggested by a Picture of Peele Castle' Wordsworth again seems to feel his own reactions more than anything else:

> So once it would have been, – 'tis so no more;
> I have submitted to a new control:
> A power is gone, which nothing can restore;
> A deep distress hath humanized my Soul.

But the 'deep distress' was the drowning at sea of his brother, John, the year before, and Wordsworth never tells us this. He is reminded, because the painting in question (by his friend Sir George Beaumont) is of the castle battered by storm and waves. It gives the poem's inwardness a tremendous power, for the pressure to understand one's own feelings is suddenly very moving and understandable.

The constant slight motion, which can never settle except by provisional moral decisions along the way, results in another major entry into this English-line poetry. This is the sense of the boundless. There is seldom a known horizon or further edge; there is always 'something evermore about to be' (*The Prelude* 1805 VI 542). In the very first lines of *The Prelude* Wordsworth sets out walking without knowing where to. He takes the whole of the first book to decide what the poem will be about; then recounts ceaseless journeyings both literal and metaphorical; is even disappointed when he finds he has crossed the Alps in Book VI; and ends the poem with it still only, supposedly, the first of three works in a major overall poem *The Recluse*, never finished. Nature itself recedes, like the 'huge cliff' in *The Prelude* (1850 I 357–424) which both towers over and pursues the young boy yet in fact, though always seeming higher and higher, is really slipping further away. In the book already cited Paul Hamilton shows interestingly how even the poor vagrants Wordsworth meets, in this poem and elsewhere, are somehow always just beyond his assistance. The power of imagining them and their lot is always necessarily greater than the practical means to help. This boundlessness is thus a mental and poetic attitude, perhaps uncontrollable, and again would be countered in a different kind of poetry by the stopping-points of the strong language of the finished artefact: jewel, coin, reason, cooked food, theatre, philosophical system, weapon and the rest.

Wordsworth is on the edge of the unknown in most contexts. For example, the three quite different settings of a political sonnet on looking out at France, the search for the homely cuckoo, and a chance meeting with women while walking in the Scottish highlands, all express this. In the sonnet 'It is a beauteous evening' he is walking on the beach in France with his daughter Caroline. A clear context both political and familial, yet he must always see the infinite dimension in the sea itself:

> Listen! the mighty Being is awake,
> And doth with his eternal motion make
> A sound like thunder – everlastingly.

The cuckoo is the bird which one always hears at the start of spring, yet one can never find it however hard one looks:

> To seek thee did I often rove
> Through woods and on the green;
> And thou wert still a hope, a love;
> Still longed for, never seen.
>
> ('To A Cuckoo')

More mysterious is the meeting with strangers in a wild place:

> '*What, you are stepping westward?*' – '*Yea.*'
> – 'Twould be a *wildish* destiny,
> If we, who thus together roam
> In a strange Land, and far from home
> Were in this place the guests of Chance:
> Yet who would stop, or fear to advance,
> Though home or shelter he had none,
> With such a sky to lead him on? . . .
>
> The voice was soft, and she who spake
> Was walking by her native lake:
> The salutation had to me
> The very sound of courtesy:
> Its power was felt; and while my eye
> Was fixed upon the glowing Sky,
> The echo of the voice enwrought
> A human sweetness with the thought
> Of travelling through the world that lay
> Before me in my endless way.
>
> ('Stepping Westward')

This unsharp vocabulary of the infinite and eternal lies right across Wordsworth's poetry, in the end to the imprecise edges of what we know and where we find ourselves. The poem that goes to the outermost was written several years before, probably late in 1798:

> A slumber did my spirit seal;
>   I had no human fears:
> She seemed a thing that could not feel
>   The touch of earthly years.
>
> No motion has she now, no force;
>   She neither hears nor sees;
> Rolled round in earth's diurnal course,
>   With rocks, and stones, and trees.

This is one of the 'Lucy' poems, in which, however, the girl or spirit Lucy is as far removed from our apprehension as could be imagined. It highlights in present context the question of how far this boundlessness stands in for an unattainable sexual desire, and it is relevant that not only 'Stepping Westward' but also its pair poem of the Scottish tour 'The Solitary Reaper' figures a woman in some sense out of reach. In the Lucy poems the girl is a very elusive figure. She is usually named, or only appears at all, at the end; she arrives, in fact, just in time to leave. She is glimpsed and then is gone, still just unattainable. Monumental research attempts to establish who she might have been have got nowhere, and many critics believe positive identification would enhance the poetry little. As Jonathan Wordsworth has phrased it, 'What put it into Wordsworth's head to write these beautiful, elegiac love-poems we shall never know'. Many critics in recent years, of varying critical persuasions and not only Wordsworth specialists, have seemed compelled to write about this poem, and Seamus Heaney, Jerome McGann and Janet Montefiore are only some who have written about it, just as, for example, E. D. Hirsch and others had done so in general works a generation earlier[7].

Again the boundlessness, as well as the hesitant motion, is marked by constant self-consciousness. Wordsworth sees mind, and his own mind, as boundless in scope. 'Oh mystery of man, from what a depth/Proceed thy honours' is how he put it, to describe what he elsewhere called the 'mind's abyss'. And when this boundless terrain is inhabited by down-and-outs of all kinds, male and female, his sense of guilt preoccupies him. He feels 'admonished' by the plight of the emaciated 'ghastly soldier' in *The Prelude* Book IV, and moved to new moral determination after depression by the stout-heartedness of the poverty-stricken leech-gatherer in 'Resolution And Independence'. These figures too seem to come up out of the mist and drift back into it. Yet along with both Wordsworth's sense of the limitless and his self-preoccupation that arises when witnessing it, there arises also the matter of sheer deprivation and neglect as something to be dealt with extrovertly and with social awareness. This is dealt with in the fuller pictures in the group of narrative poems, 'Michael' and others. They are firmly based in the natural community, on familiar ground inhabiting the landscape, also living lives of hard and exiguous labour, and in some aspects must be taken as mimetic. That is to say, these poems tell stories which could happen in the real world, or have done so.

In these poems the poet's mental activity comes again from his own deepest stirrings, this time seen as originating in kinship and the sexual and biological bond. As a result these three poems, 'Michael', 'The Brothers' and 'The Ruined Cottage' are premised on the three foundations of (male) traditional sociology of kinship; the father-son bond, the brother-brother bond, the husband-wife bond. *Poetic* awareness of a mind not one's own becomes possible only if one believes all language is from the same source, for Wordsworth a communal and kinship source. But as well in Wordsworth's case, all three poems are marked by anxieties drawn from his own life, which he then uses as a way of seeing into the lives of others. In 'Michael' the not unkind but strongly puritan father trains his son up to take over their small peasant holding. But the poem repeatedly reminds the reader that, though he is Luke's father, Michael is easily old enough to be his grandfather. A generation is missing. It would have been enough to have Michael say 'I have been toiling more than seventy years' (line 228). But Wordsworth puts it several more times. For example, 'So lived he till his eightieth year was past' (line 61) and 'At eighty-four/ I still am strong and hale' (lines 389–90). It is as though Wordsworth's own father, who he resented and disliked, is being expunged.

In 'The Brothers' a sailor returns to his Lake District home village unrecognized to enquire whether his family is still there. The poet surely has in mind his own mariner brother John who was also away from home years at a time. In the poem the well-meaning but imperceptive rector does the talking while Leonard the brother asks the occasional brief question. But John Wordsworth was equally well known for his taciturnity. Leonard's sad departure without finding his family is no doubt not premonitory (the poem was written before John's death), but it does show a sad sense of what mattered most to Wordsworth and his longing for reunion. In 'The Ruined Cottage' (also *The Excursion* Book I) Wordsworth's own happy marriage means that the tragic event has to come from outward circumstance; namely, the husband Robert's need to join an army regiment because two crops have failed and war threatens the surviving economy. The real-life Wordsworth enters the poem by the back door as the poet who hears the story told him by the Pedlar, who heard it from the wife Margaret herself.

The poems thus show Wordsworth writing about external matters of economic and social significance to demonstrate his democratic belief in what he called 'the one human heart', but using for the purpose the inward thrust of his own strongest experiences. He needs to locate them in that same heart and its restless, activated motion which he apparently believed gave life to the only language his poetry could use. Yet this time his purpose is outward, and he actually went to the length of sending his poems to the Member of Parliament, Charles James Fox, with a long explanatory letter drawing particular attention to 'Michael' and 'The Brothers'. He said that 'the two poems which I have mentioned were written with a view to shew that men who do not wear fine cloaths can feel deeply'[8]. By showing their deep feeling in his own inward poetic language he silently shows that language's communal nature.

The simple and often monosyllabic language of these poems can be puritan at times, at others very moving. When Wordsworth describes Michael and his family working, the language seems to breathe distrust of the luxurious and excessive.

> I may truly say,
> That they were as a proverb in the vale
> For endless industry. When day was gone,
> And from their occupations out of doors
> The Son and Father were come home, even then,
> Their labour did not cease; unless when all
> Turned to the cleanly supper-board, and there,
> Each with a mess of pottage and skimmed milk,
> Sat round the basket piled with oaten cakes,
> And their plain home-made cheese. Yet when the meal
> Was ended, Luke (for so the Son was named)
> And his old Father both betook themselves
> To such convenient work as might employ
> Their hands by the fire-side; perhaps to card
> Wool for the Housewife's spindle, or repair

Some injury done to sickle, flail, or scythe,
Or other implement of house or field.

(lines 93–109)

With its consciously biblical echoes, that is English-line plain
puritanism in its extreme form. But the texture is different
again, even though still monosyllabic, when a character
speaks. Margaret in 'The Ruined Cottage', having lived with
only a baby for several months in a damp cottage near the
breadline, approaches breakdown. She tells the Pedlar of this
on his next visit:

> 'I perceive
> You look at me, and you have cause; today
> I have been travelling far; and many days
> About the fields I wander, knowing this
> Only, that what I seek I cannot find;
> And so I waste my time: for I am changed;
> And to myself,' said she, 'have done much wrong
> And to this helpless infant. I have slept
> Weeping, and weeping have I waked; my tears
> Have flowed as if my body were not such
> As others are; and I could never die.'
>
> *(The Excursion* I 762–72)

In context this is moving in the extreme, yet one is left wondering whether the tears flow as, for such poets, words too are
believed to flow. When there is emptiness, the reader is necessarily drawn as into a vacuum into the emotions that yearn,
both of inner hope and outward sustenance. In 'The Brothers'
too, since the rector talks and Leonard is silent, the reader has
space in which to become rather thoughtful about the events
in the poem which *don't* happen; the hoped-for reunion with
his brother, his planned return to the village to live there, and
even the priest's recognition of him from boyhood. The gap
is what always brings on the unbearable, and one wonders
what results when it is evoked.

It brings us to the question of melancholy in this English-line
poetry, and how that seems curiously, if not always wisely,
connected with pleasure. Is it self-indulgent? Wordsworth's

contemporary and friend Thomas De Quincey thought so of
'The Ruined Cottage', and there are many suggestions of a
dangerous morbidity in Wordsworth's poetry as we have seen.
Wordsworth himself was aware of the danger:

> But, O dear friend,
> The poet, gentle creature as he is,
> Hath like the lover his unruly times –
> His fits when he is neither sick nor well,
> Though no distress be near him but his own
> Unmanageable thoughts . . .
>
> *(The Prelude* 1805 I 144–9)

In 'The Ruined Cottage' the Pedlar considers the matter during
interludes in the story and is frank about the temptation. He
says that to 'hold vain dalliance with the misery/ Even of the
dead; contented thence to draw/ A momentary pleasure' would
be a 'wantonness, and would demand/ Severe reproof' (*The
Excursion* I 626–30). But why then should it ever be permitted
at all? Why even go close?

The phenomenon is doubtless associated with the one
Wordsworth tries to face and overcome in his 'Ode: Intimations of Immortality'. It is probably the longer poem of
Wordsworth's that most people know best. Dejection and fear
get intertwined because the loss of childhood happiness and
security, seen in nature's failure to bring inspiration even on
a glorious May morning, don't just mean that he happens to
lose a bit of pleasure. They bode ill more widely for all his
future, and he realizes that childhood and the past is simply
going to slip further and further away. But there is pleasure
in expressing this; a briefly sardonic enjoyment at the very
recognition of what has gone blank:

> The Rainbow comes and goes,
> And lovely is the Rose;
> The Moon doth with delight
> Look round her when the heavens are bare;
> Waters on a starry night
> Are beautiful and fair;
> The sunshine is a glorious birth . . .
>
> (lines 10–16)

For Wordsworth, the way out of this desperate situation is via
an opposite, the huge sublimating idea of the child's descent
to this earth from a pre-existence. The poet comes to feel that
what he is grateful for – what gives pleasure – is precisely that
he can ask about what recedes, what is boundless:

> . . . those obstinate questionings
> Of sense and outward things,
> Fallings from us, vanishings;
> Blank misgivings of a Creature
> Moving about in worlds not realized,
> High instincts before which our mortal Nature
> Did tremble like a guilty Thing surprised
>   (lines 142–8)

The gain results from a new determination which, however,
still has a sad origin:

> We will grieve not, rather find
> Strength in what remains behind;
> In the primal sympathy
> Which having been must ever be;
> In the soothing thoughts that spring
> Out of human suffering . . .
>   (lines 180–5)

This sense of a necessary mix between melancholy and pleasure is one of the central risks the English line poet takes.
Housman, Edward Thomas and Larkin were prone to it, as
often were Tennyson and Arnold too. It would appear to arise
because if one really is going right down to the depths of one's
own feelings, 'the mind's abyss' as Wordsworth called it, then
to do so without at least some compensating pleasure could
make the enterprise unbearable. Yet the task has to be under-
taken if self-knowing is to be attained, or even attempted. For
Keats, the pain-pleasure tie-up happens simply because joy is
always already slipping away as you enter it. The sexual
climax, like the glass of wine, goes as it comes, 'Joy, whose
hand is ever at his lips/ Bidding adieu'. But for the equally
sexual but more philosophical poets, the matter has more sig-

nificance psychologically than aesthetically. Edward Thomas, as we shall see, puts pleasure and pain in an exact fifty-fifty balance almost as though wilfully to say that how they relate cannot be resolved.

In the English line later, down to Larkin and R. S. Thomas, as often as not there is wry sardony at lost love or loneliness, or wintry witticism at society's or one's own inadequacy. The basis is no doubt a bourgeois affluence which still can't avoid the fundamental sufferings of existence, and the dry comedy of living in a godless world with plenty to do and enjoy but with no reason why we should have this good fortune when others do not, nor indeed any apparent ultimate reason for being on this earth at all. To that extent this melancholy is democratic in feeling. Wordsworth was the first to experience it as self-conscious feeling as well as social anger, as the eighteenth-century poets of sensibility had, and to express it in the disembodied language it demanded. In his poetry the extremes of philosophical brooding and spontaneous impulse are as wide as in any subsequent poet. Later in his life they fossilized, all still centring on the one familiar place, the Lake District, to which he always returned, however much he went away to other places.

4

Samuel Taylor Coleridge and John Clare

Coleridge was Wordsworth's greatest friend. The serious personal quarrel of 1810–11 perhaps never quite healed over, but they still saw much of each other and there is sufficient evidence of their continued attachment and regard. Yet Coleridge's very different personality, his powerful, disorganized, fluttering mind meant that the poetry he wrote is for the most part rooted differently from Wordsworth's. Much as he thought Wordsworth's the greatest poetic talent since Milton, he thought it was misused. Coleridge's own poetry was subordinated to his shapeless aesthetic and philosophical investigations, snatches of insight, and always articulate perplexity. His contribution to the English line is thus smaller, for instead of reflection and poetry being one thing in his consciousness, reflection was always a pursuit of its own, as to truth's inclusive nature.

Indeed the poetry he is remembered for by most people is probably the three surrealist poems 'Kubla Khan', 'Christabel' and most of all that extraordinary visionary and surrealistic poem, emanating from a far more suppressed unconscious than the English-line poets display, 'The Rime of the Ancient Mariner'. And Coleridge did not long remain a poet. In 1801 he wrote to William Godwin that 'the Poet is dead in me; my imagination . . . lies, like a Cold Snuff on the circular Rim of a Brass Candlestick'[1] – a notion that Wordsworth would never have entertained, no matter what he was producing in his later years. Nonetheless Coleridge can be seen to contribute centrally if briefly to the continuity as here defined. As Bloom said, Coleridge had no precursor, and as Thomas McFarland has argued, his very strength is his irresoluteness, his leaving of thought open[2]. McFarland shows in great detail how Coleridge's very search for fulness, his 'response to the full range of our common need for connections' brings on or is dragged down by his 'neurotic inability to get down to business'. The brilliant chaos of, for example, Coleridge's *Lectures on Literature* (1809–19) bear the point out. So he was all the more dependent on Wordsworth when that more integrated poet was his close companion. We cannot go into the evidence on both sides here, as to which of the two influenced the other most, but there is little doubt about Coleridge's views of it. He revered Wordsworth.

By whatever path, the result is the group of 'conversation poems', most of them written in the years 1795 to 1798, that is up to the time of the joint publication with Wordsworth of *Lyrical Ballads*. Coleridge called them 'conversation poems' not because of their tone but because he was uncertain how far to call them poetry. The interesting ones for this argument are 'The Eolian Harp', 'This Lime-Tree Bower my Prison', 'Frost at Midnight' and the later and longer 'Dejection: an Ode'. This last was written in anxious answer to Wordsworth's 'Ode: Intimations Of Immortality', but also in the distress of Coleridge's unrequited love, despite his being married already, for Sara Hutchinson, sister to Wordsworth's wife Mary and who was part of the family *entourage* in the Lake District for decades. Even if it sounds rather cursory to say so, the last two poems would probably be allowed to be among the major poems in this English tradition.

These poems share important features. One is that their subjective mental activity flickers and darts about, rather than evincing the more brooding rumination of most comparable poetry. A second is that they are all set in a room looking out at nature instead of being out there from the start. Third, another person, one held in affection, is silently present in the poem, somewhat as the silent listener later appears in Browning's dramatic monologues. These characteristics mean a small departure from the English line, but mentally their evident concern to express a cheerfulness based on turbulence keeps them still under its larger umbrella. They show and come from a self-conscious man wrestling with his place in the world that Wordsworth and those after him think of as home always.

In 'The Eolian Harp' the poet sits with his wife near an open

window through which, as at the start of *The Prelude*, comes
a gentle breeze. The breeze plays across the strings of the
harp, or lute, the ancient instrument designed for just that
purpose. Thinking of the customary metaphor in this for
poetry's origin, Coleridge attempts, but fails, to get a sustained
meditation, and is all too aware of the fact. He remonstrates
with himself, and calls his jumpy thoughts:

Bubbles that glitter as they rise and break
On vain Philosophy's aye-babbling spring

and concludes by seeing himself as gently reproved by his
wife (also called Sara) and as 'A sinful and most miserable
man'. Coleridge elsewhere calls himself a 'whirl-brain'; his self-
knowing is not inaccurate. But in so speaking he was not
searching for self-knowledge. With him, enquiry into truth
was always a separate issue.

In 'This Lime-Tree Bower my Prison' Coleridge and some
friends have been sitting in a summerhouse when these friends
decide to go for a walk. Coleridge does not, having sustained
an accident to his foot earlier in the day. The poem has the
same jerky movement as 'The Eolian Harp', this time parallel-
ing the moments when the friends disappear and reappear in
the dips and rises of land as they get further away. The landscape swims and trembles (Coleridge's words) before the
poet's eyes as he sees his 'gentle-hearted Charles' – incidentally the essayist Charles Lamb – move further off. Yet the
meditation is still not a deep one, and Coleridge's conclusion,
'Henceforth I shall know/ That Nature ne'er deserts the wise
and pure', feels too unrooted, Wordsworth's 'Nature never
did betray/ The heart that loved her', the comparable line in
'Tintern Abbey' did not feel.

In 'Frost at Midnight' nature's presence is not only in the
icicles in the moonlight outside but also in the coldness perme-
ating the world. It affects not just the eyesight but the whole
body. Equally while, as in the other two poems, there is
another person present who is object of deep affection, this
time it is Coleridge's baby son, asleep in his cot. Coleridge's
intellectual ambitions are vested there to some degree; and
these two features, the frost and the babe, stir the poet to

thoughts of greater implication. The calm itself 'disturbs and vexes meditation', and the 'film, which fluttered on the grate' (the phenomenon of the invisible nimbus shimmering round the flame), is, like the poem itself, 'the sole unquiet thing'. (This 'sole unquiet thing' will be picked up more than a hundred years later as 'the only other sound' in a poem we shall come to, 'Stopping by Woods on a Snowy Evening'. The poet was aptly named in the circumstances: Robert Frost.)

But it is here perhaps that one sees what is behind all these poems. Despite his deeply unhappy marriage Coleridge had the temperament to adore his family and friends. Yet it seems he unconsciously deflects on to all of them what he secretly does not want for himself but feels strongly he must try to be – a deep, ruminative nature poet; that is to say, a Wordsworthian poet. This seems to be why there is always another loved person present or to hand in the conversation poems. And ironically that very dilemma makes him such a poet, if only for a while, through the manifestation of his own inadequacy. For like Wordsworth in the 'visionary dreariness' passage cited earlier, Coleridge's expression of failure becomes his success. It is subjective and familiar and retreats from unattainable poetic ambition into simple terms.

As Kathleen Wheeler has put it of 'Frost at Midnight', these three poems have a curious instant happiness and 'nowness', from moment to moment, rather than the reaching for the hard-won exaltation of Wordsworth's 'Ode: Intimations Of Immortality'[3]. But 'Dejection: an Ode' reverses this. It was written in April 1802 and, according to Dorothy Wordsworth's journal, only about three weeks after the first version of Wordsworth's 'Ode' and in clear response to it. Its very sad self-castigating quality is no doubt what led Wordsworth to answer back, as he did with 'Resolution and Independence', a poem written out of despondency but which ends commending its title's qualities. Coleridge's final version however was then first published in the *Morning Post* on 4 October 1802, the day of Wordsworth's marriage to Mary Hutchinson, sister of Sara to whom Coleridge's poem was addressed[4]. It would probably be a mistake to see this exchange as a sort of showdown between the poets (Coleridge later wrote a generous poetic tribute, itself a fine poem, to Wordsworth after the first family reading of *The Prelude*). But Coleridge's 'Ode' does come out of very complex emotions compounded by his black sense of failure as poet, lover and, perhaps, friend.

Again the poet is inside looking out, and again a loved person is the object of affection. This is Sara Hutchinson, though Coleridge concealed this in earlier versions. There is also an Eolian lute. But this time it is night, windy and rainy, and the lute 'screams' as the wind blows across it. In black mood the poet reflects that he no longer responds to nature. For no one can do so without the spirit in us to cherish it ('O Lady! we receive but what we give'), and this spirit is named as joy. Here follow two revealing pronouncements. For the inner power, which for Coleridge has failed, was 'my shaping spirit of imagination', a phrase which was to influence and perhaps direct literary criticism down to quite recent times. And what has caused this main loss of imagination, which he says 'nature' had given him at birth (line 85), was the 'abstruse research' (line 89) which came to 'steal/ From my own nature all the natural man' (line 90). This abstruse research, which Coleridge increasingly turned to for much of the rest of his life, came to 'infect the whole' (line 92), accompanied by opium addiction, ill-health and an inability ever to deliver a work in good shape, on time and to meet the needs of lecture audiences or publishers. If 'natural' in line 90 means 'unregenerate', the result of its loss was degenerate poetically, though not entirely in other ways. Certainly in our present terms here, it ends Coleridge's phase as an English-line poet. Yet all these sad feelings in the poem stem from that most melancholic thing, 'A grief without a pang' at the start of the second stanza, the black mood which is depressive, not frenzied or hysterical.

Especially with the *Biographia Literaria* of 1817 Coleridge became and remained a major force in English poetry and critical theory. He will probably not be neglected so long as there is interest, as now, in the history of attention to the points where art and reality coincide. Yet he also briefly entered this kind of English poetry by his awareness of poetry's many possible modes, his selfless and accurate understanding of Wordsworth's importance and his own poetic pain at the personality which had that awareness.

John Clare (1793–1864) was born a farm labourer, though not a destitute one, in rural Northamptonshire. He became a poet, in fact the prototype 'peasant poet' briefly taken up as such by London literary circles. He got into endless wrangles with his publishers and had some reputation, possibly exaggerated, for drunkenness and womanizing. Beneath all this however lay a strong if melancholic sense of purpose and an attitude to life and nature which resulted in a poetry of quality, consistency and detail. This continued furthermore after his confinement in 1837 in Dr Matthew Allen's asylum at High Beech, Epping Forest. He was there for four years, and then in the St Andrew's Asylum in Northampton for a further twenty-three years, worrying about his wife and children and seeing them only occasionally. In the High Beech period he must also incidentally, mutually unaware of the fact, have seen and been seen by Tennyson on their walks in Epping Forest. Equally ironically perhaps, Tennyson's friendship with Allen was what gave him (Tennyson) the knowledge of madness and madhouses he was to employ in the poem *Maud*. Since Tennyson had a strain of madness in his own background and feared for his wife's sanity, the basis of his and Clare's different success might seem to be that of education and class.

However, maybe that is too routine an answer. More positively one might ask how much conscious real education, self-acquired or not, the melancholic-meditative poets needed if they were to be more than just descriptive poets of country life. Coleridge said in the *Biographia Literaria* that the poetic imagination is 'a repetition in the finite mind of the eternal act of creation in the infinite I AM'. This borrowing of the biblical 'I AM' could be the subjectivity in bourgeois liberalism, but here is John Clare on the same subject, after very likely seven or eight years already in confinement:

> I am – yet what I am none cares or knows,
>   My friends forsake me like a memory lost;
> I am the self-consumer of my woes,
>   They rise and vanish in oblivions host,
> Like shadows in love – frenzied stifled throes
>   And yet I am, and live like vapours tost . . .
>   ('I Am')

There is perhaps more here than meets the eye. Melancholy, subjectivity, ordinary speech, imprecision, memory of loss, all the features we were looking for; yet one wonders if Clare cares or knows what a curious back-to-front touch he has put on them. Here it is the poet himself who is a 'memory lost' to others, not the poet's own past lost to himself. And, if we hear a pun on 'wares' in 'woes' in the third line, then Clare becomes not a privileged consumer of the labour of others but one who eats up his own toil. He may not have thought of it like that, and I for one hear in the first line the extra words 'not even myself', for he really *was* interested in nature in its fullest detail rather than how the human mind responds to that.

For in a Northamptonshire terrain where as he himself said hills are molehills, what he has uniquely is a meticulous observation of tiny detail which sings exactly with the metre of the line. It is seemingly unstoppable in the way it carries us along:

> From nights dull prison comes the duck
> Waddling eager thro the muck
> Squeezing thro the orchard pales
> Where mornings bounty rarely fails
> Eager gobbling as they pass
> Dew worms thro the padded grass
> Where blushing apples round and red
> Load down the boughs and pat the head
> Of longing maid that hither goes
> To hang on lines the drying cloaths
> Who views them oft with tempted eye
> And steals one as she passes bye
>
> ('September')

This short passage can hardly convey the full effect of the rather astonishing poem it comes from, *The Shepherd's Calendar*. The poem is over 3000 lines long and repeats no detail in its month-by-month record. An ominous threat of monotony one might suspect, and Clare's own editor James Hessey wrote back to him with evident exasperation when he first read the manuscript:

The great fault of the whole of them is that they abound too much in mere description & are deficient in Sentiment and Feeling and human Interest. You have already described [in earlier poems] in admirable colouring the Morning & the Noon & the Evening, & the Summer & the Winter, & the Sheep & Cattle & Poultry & Pigs & Milking Maids & Foddering Boys – but the world will now expect something more than these - [5]

The homogeneity across the work does become a strain. There are no sweeps and depths, no exaltations and darkness, no pressure of reason, no society and experience. Yet John Clare's knowledge of the natural and animal world make individual details by the hundred ring with authenticity; we are being taught. But one must point to the language's unambitious nature as well, for if the poet's absorption with it persists, then his own urgency is likely to draw him back down into the mind's actual movement whether looking to do so or not, as though into a vacated territory. Clare's words don't enrich the farmyard, only capture it. Solitude is encountered if it wasn't there already, and this produces something both melancholy and meditative, as Clare's life demonstrates. For when he first discovered his poetic leaning, he did not merely turn to descriptive writing. He investigated poetry's nature as far as he could in poems like 'An Effusion to Poesy' and 'To the Rural Muse'. Against Yeats's 'Words alone are certain good' Clare takes something much nearer the English line's view:

> True poesy is not in words,
>   But images that thoughts express.
>   ('Pastoral Poesy')

And he is quite clear just as early, that one's feelings about rural life bring up feelings about one's own situation:

> O winter, what a deadly foe
> Art thou unto the mean and low!
> What thousands now half pin'd and bare
> Are forced to stand thy piercing air
> All day, near numbed to death wi' cold

Some petty gentry to uphold,
Paltry proudlings hard as thee,
Dead to all humanity.
　　　　　　　　　('Impromptu on Winter')

He goes on with dry wit:

But why need I the winter blame?
To me all seasons come the same:
Now winter bares each field and tree
She finds that trouble sav'd in me
Stript already, penniless,
Nothing boasting but distress.

Clare's purposefulness meant he expanded his reactions to
nature and to his situation in a writing career of much larger
output, one imagines, than many people who have only heard
of him might credit. He doesn't look into it with the depth
that educated thinking enables – that is to say, when education
or cultural background are the only available means. This lack
prevented him from explaining this distress, or fully exploring
it even for himself, and his frayed reactions and tense
depression were a predictable outcome. He, therefore, cannot
take a larger place in the tradition because he has not the
consoling power of therapy to the depression of others, nor
can he place it in proportion in the larger world. As his editors
J. W. and Anne Tibble put it, 'Wordsworth's incessant effort
to comprehend experience would itself have been incomprehensible to Clare'[6]. But true as that is, Clare did have such
experience and the reader feels it. His painful but clear sense
of all that he did not know or understand is what commands
poetic respect and makes poetic dignity. This itself gives Clare
a position at the further end of the line, a pure case of sadness
in the 'ordinary language' and the familiar which the more
sophisticated and self-knowing English poet equally adheres
to. In the different context of peasant toil and no formal education, it is the same powerful feeling Wordsworth began with.

Part II

Part II

5

Alfred Lord Tennyson and Matthew Arnold

In 1850, exactly halfway through the century, Wordsworth died. In the autumn of that year Tennyson succeeded as Poet Laureate, and when in the following February he went to the queen to receive this honour formally, he wore the court dress overcoat which had been Wordsworth's[1]. This is often seen as a ritual handing-on to the successor Wordsworth himself had more than once implied he would himself have chosen. We can also see Tennyson putting on the outer garment of Wordsworth's copious and seamless language, without letting on how far he had the body inside to wear it.

In many of Tennyson's longer poems especially, the language and voice are Wordsworthian, but lie flat and distended. The fatigued tone and unspecific ('boundless') reference, the lines ending in 'die' and so on, are not forced upward from a dark turbulence below:

> the wreath of flowers fell
> At Dora's feet. She bow'd upon her hands,
> And the boy's cry came to her from the field,
> More and more distant. She bow'd down her head,
> Remembering the day when first she came,
> And all the things that had been. She bow'd down
> And wept in secret; and the reapers reap'd,
> And the sun fell, and all the land was dark.

This goes on for a couple of hundred lines and is from 'Dora' (lines 100–107), one of the *English Idylls* published in the early part of Tennyson's career. The poem was greatly admired by Wordsworth, who said that, despite many attempts, he had never written a better pastoral himself[2]; and like much of this writing of Tennyson's, it is highly readable and seems to embody what, once somewhere, was sincerely enough felt. But the repetitions, the sideways 'ands', the wreaths and the dark feel reached for as routine scenery without too much desire. The inner pressure of the self is not in the poem.

The Victorian poets were faced with a new difficulty. A reaction to the Wordsworthian ego-voice, the 'I', set in, the problem being that of how far one could presume one knew or expressed the objective world if one took that wholly subjective standpoint. This, after all, was the new age of biological science and heavy industry; new aspects of old things were appearing as plain fact, in industry, the fossil-record, medical advance and elsewhere, quite aside from what the subjective mind felt about them. That is to say, the 'objective world' was pressing itself on to the consciousness; in quite new ways, it was drawing attention to its objectivity. The problem has been discussed at length by Langbaum and more recently Carol T. Christ[3]. Her summary, simplified, is that the way out lay in the dramatic monologue. In that form the voice could be of the first person but not the poet's. By this means the inner feelings of the self might be kept present, but a certain detachment of commitment exist also. The form thus rose to prominence in the Victorian period, and was used frequently by Tennyson himself in his early period and notably in *Maud* later. Tennyson himself remained ambivalent, for he shared Victorian doubt about the precariousness of all-out subjectivity, yet he profoundly admired Wordsworth and inherited the Wordsworth voice. This makes Tennyson and Arnold intriguing exponents of this kind of English poetry for they employ much outward material, narrative, mythological and classical, but it is so often drawn downward and inward by the undertow of the same grey, inner and troubled intonation.

Both Tennyson and Arnold move back and forward between plain, wearied, often deeply poignant writing of the English line, and mythological narrative, often borrowed from classical legend, which commonly brings in the exotic and even sumptuous. In Tennyson's 'The Lotos-Eaters' the surviving fatigue is luxurious not exiguous. Arnold in fact is more humdrum than Tennyson, more tied up with English educational and newly-industrial life. But in one case Tennyson reverts to the fully inward and first-person poem, namely *In Memoriam*

A. H. H. It is this poem that appeared in the course of the events referred to earlier, those occurring between the death of Wordsworth and the acceptance of the laureateship. Assembled out of sight over seventeen years, *In Memoriam A. H. H.* is a kind of extraordinary silent centre of Tennyson's work; his own poem above all others. *In Memoriam* is thought of by many as the central Victorian poem; indeed, *the* Victorian poem, and if there is to be one major poem thought of as the link between Wordsworth and Hardy, this would have to be it. What we think of it ourselves will depend on how we see the path of the English line in Victorian poetry.

It is compelling too in the circumstances of its writing. Tennyson met Arthur Henry Hallam when they were undergraduates at Trinity College, Cambridge, and however their friendship was consummated there is little doubt that it can be called love in a full sense. They shared both personal intimacy and high ideals and aspirations, cultural and political. Hallam was engaged to be married to Tennyson's sister Emily. It seemed unthinkable that their lives should not contain each other for the foreseeable future. But in 1833, only three years after they both left Cambridge, Hallam died very suddenly in Vienna.

Just exactly what Tennyson felt at the time of Hallam's death is hard to know. Genuine grief, certainly, but there was probably a mixture of emotions, including a sense of opportunity not long delayed. The first result was not the elegy but the curiously grey poems – dramatic monologues – about the old men of classical legend, 'Ulysses' and 'Tithonus', and other poems on loneliness and unrequited love. *In Memoriam* itself was a collection of well over a hundred quite short poems, published as a single sequence in 1850, seventeen years after Hallam's death, and at first anonymously. The poems were written over most of that period, one by one or in groups. The first were written in the first few weeks after Hallam's death. Others have been dated fairly accurately by editors and Tennyson scholars, while still more remain uncertain as to date, although the writing did certainly continue on from 1833 well toward the middle 1840s[4]. It was a long time before Tennyson told even close friends much about them, and they were not written in the order in which they are printed. *In Memoriam* is a deeply subdued series of responses to and broodings about not only the loss of a close friend, but mortality itself, science, one's own doubts and inadequacies, and many other things.

In *The Princeton Encyclopedia of Poetry and Poetics* an elegy is defined as a lyric 'suggested either by the death of an actual person or by the poet's contemplation of the tragic aspects of life'[5]. This double definition is paralleled in the context of this poem by a remark by W. David Shaw in his study of the relation between poetry and philosophy in confronting truth-questions in the Victorian age. Shaw says, 'Like most autobiographical poems, *In Memoriam* frames experience twice. Hallam's life, death and afterlife are first framed by the immediate reactions of the mourner whose sorrow is recorded, and then by the retrospective experience and aesthetic commentary of the recording itself'[6]. A unique quality of *In Memoriam* is that, of these two things, the mourning of immediate death and the mournful reflection on something wider, the second gradually leaves the first behind, and guilt and philosophical doubt attend that very fact. Tennyson believed that Gray, in a limited sphere, was 'a great poet, with a wonderful ear'[7], but Gray connected the actual dead with the tragic aspects of life by taking the former as exemplary. Tennyson finds that the wider elegiac experience begins to move in on and dilute the particular example.

Here is poem 78, which illustrates well this and a number of the features of *In Memoriam* generally:

Again at Christmas did we weave
　The holly round the Christmas hearth;
　The silent snow possess'd the earth,
And calmly fell our Christmas-eve:

The yule-log sparkled keen with frost,
　No wing of wind the region swept,
　But over all things brooding slept
The quiet sense of something lost.

As in the winters left behind,
　Again our ancient games had place,
　The mimic picture's breathing grace,
And dance and song and hoodman-blind.

Who show'd a token of distress?
  No single tear, no mark of pain:
  O sorrow, then can sorrow wane?
O grief, can grief be changed to less?

O last regret, regret can die!
  No – mixt with all this mystic frame,
  Her deep relations are the same,
But with long use her tears are dry.

The sense that grief is passing can itself feel like a guilty loss. It may take its place, as in *In Memoriam*, in an understanding of how existence itself fades away, no matter what happy or sad experiences went to form it. In *In Memoriam* the pacing of the years and seasons since Hallam's death (three Christmases, for example), and the introduction of different themes, now this now that, as the poet casts about for both consolation and relief to puzzlement, are tied to the poet's reflection on immortality and after-life. If the loved friend is finally dead in this world, then the survivor must either believe in an after-life or bear the grief that the relationship is gone for ever. But it is also threatened by the survivor's new friendships and activities in social and political life, none of which the deceased friend will ever see, so that the memory of him itself becomes obsolete. Tennyson's sense of widowhood (sic) from Hallam suggests too that ageing takes one away from the parallel process the friend would have had if he had survived, remaining a contemporary. In the later part of the whole poem Tennyson has the odd glimpse of Hallam, for example when the poet visits their old college at Cambridge in poem 87, or in the reminiscence of poem 100. Tennyson's mood cycles and recycles; by poem 90 regret has seemingly returned, even if there is a touch of defensiveness: 'Whatever change the years have wrought/ I find not yet one lonely thought/ That cries against my wish for thee'; and by poem 116 he is able to suggest that a transfer forward of any remaining sorrow into time ahead is a next step which is happening to him:

Yet less of sorrow lives in me
  For days of happy commune dead;

> Less yearning for the friendship fled,
> Than some strong bond which is to be.

Tennyson doubtless saw that this could turn into an endless deferral until his own death. In fact both the poem and its continued growth toward Tennyson's middle years were such a deferral. Every new year or friendship would shift the emotion and the memory, both loosening the tie and yet reconfirming it by longevity. Tennyson wondered seriously whether not to publish the poem in his lifetime, and declined to add to it when this was suggested by a friend[8]. All this is reminiscent of *The Prelude*, which was published after Wordsworth's death by his wish, yet the conclusion of *In Memoriam* with the 'Epilogue' celebrating the poet's sister's wedding to the new friend Edmund Lushington feels more like the deliberate ending of Gray's 'Elegy' with its formal epitaph. Elegy may do the work of grief, but is then tragically only successful in that aim if the grief is itself allayed, leading to Milton's 'fresh woods, and pastures new' where the mourned person can never accompany. Tennyson articulates the relation between grief, meditation and the necessarily more practical emotions without which ordinary life could not continue.

In doing all this Tennyson also retains the stately quality of the traditional elegy. In the face of inner doubt he remains integrated, and this is partly what produces the remarkable effect. The sequence does not begin in the middle of grief, but with the sombre hymn to the god of immortal love. In this opening the matter of our earthly ignorance is emphasized before the grief that occasioned it is known to the reader except in the title:

> Our little systems have their day;
>   They have their day and cease to be;
>   They are but broken lights of thee,
> And thou, O Lord, art more than they.
>
> We have but faith; we cannot know;
>   For knowledge is of things we see;
>   And yet we trust it comes from thee,
> A beam in darkness; let it grow.

The first line of the second stanza here has sadness as well as a statement. Yet the addressed 'Lord' is not sceptical, simply indefinite; and the imperative mood of the final three words 'let it grow', suggests a stable position, a calm. 'Calmly' was the adverb in the first line of poem 78 quoted above, followed there by the beautiful ambiguity of 'fell', suggesting both the calendar day that had come but also the silent snow round the house. The sequence's entire movement, and its emotional charge and adumbration of that, does not come from its rise and fall, for there is none. Rather it comes from the overall progress forward in hesitant stages, going forward at times, then back retracing one's steps over old ground; occasional moments of the past glimpsed returning, and then again the appearance of a possible way ahead. Yet even the hesitation is orderly. There is puzzlement, but presented as in the mind of a full and whole personality.

This movement is the 'undertow' element in the English line, here possibly at its most explicit. The feeling of single waves slowly coming in and then receding but with the overall result of a flowing or ebbing tide over a great stretch, is no doubt an easy image. Yet one of Tennyson's few well-known first-person lyrics 'Break, break, break' has it, as does that other epochal Victorian poem of declining faith, Arnold's 'Dover Beach'. Tennyson's sequence actually embodies the sea's movement, with whole tide, medium current and separate small waves all moving in and through each other. There is the cycle of events through season and anniversary which return, and the departure from familiar places like the family home at Somersby (poems 100–103), which don't. It occurs on smaller scale too, when two or three poems in a group carry a theme forward and then leave it, as in the three 'geological' poems 54–6. But most of all it is in the rhyme scheme a-b-b-a, which for many readers is the poem's signature and haunting presence. The small drag back at the end of each fourth line when one is still half-expecting the quatrain, has a slow sad impotence. In the terms we have used already, mind and emotion are themselves worked and moved and drawn out as the poem's medium of existence. It is as though to attend to one's own failing and doubt is itself visceral, as Wordsworth's was when expressing emotion itself as verbal movement.

The fourth line is often a tentative conclusion, a sigh, a small resignation, a pause for more brooding thought, or a sense that no more can be added. The small brake on flowing spirit becomes memorable, and in the line from the poem 78 cited earlier, 'the quiet sense of something lost', the Wordsworthian touch of 'something' takes on stasis. Small antitheses appear: 'Or dying, there at least may die', 'The violet comes, but we are gone'. These feel like little stages reached in the search. The mind's work is being done, and the poet is committed to a probe into himself not by choice wording but as a brooding seen transparently through words as liquid as water.

And, as so commonly, grief at profound personal loss stirs memories of one's own similar feelings in the past. Notably these are loss of home, innocence and childhood. If loss means fear, melancholy and doubt as to the future, these same feelings bring recollections of when that has most deeply happened before. It is the first occasion of that which will have been most strongly imprinted. Whether this works because appropriate language for it is available, as Paul de Man believed[9], or whether that language is first called up by associated feelings, will be decided according to one's critical standpoint. In her valuable book on Tennyson, Marion Shaw has suggested the view that Tennyson is recalling infancy and the loss of the mother. The male must work through this experience to retrieve manhood. The image of marriage and widowhood which recurs in *In Memoriam* is cited to support this view, for example the close of poem 9 and the opening of poem 13. There is a similar motif in 40 and 41. When the poem was published anonymously in 1850 there was speculation by some reviewers that the author was a war widow.

Marion Shaw cites one of the sequence's best-known stanzas, from poem 54:

> So runs my dream: but what am I?
>   An infant crying in the night:
>   An infant crying for the light:
> And with no language but a cry.

She suggests that the excitement and risk of the poem are that Tennyson has the courage to express this latent regression to infancy. Tennyson knew he must resist it and stay with the male language of order, having first however entered the female world of feeling and gentleness which only the remembered mother of infancy can provide. The work of grief being over he then returns to maleness, and the poem can fall silent. The poem ends with a marriage; a woman is handed over by one man to another, so that male dominance is quietly reasserted[10]. The brooding and doubt of the poem, as with all English-line poems, has to be overcome; integration is retained but at a price.

The view seems to slightly overstate the case, insofar as the language of infancy is not merely 'no language but a cry'. As Kristeva put it, it is the verbal wandering among infant playthings which would grow into the language of modernist poetry and Joyce. But Tennyson never sounds simply annoyed or bewildered, infant-like, as when a mere possession has been removed. Even the earliest poems in the sequence could hardly be attributed to the hysterical disturbance associated not with depression but with hypermania. Rather, those early responses are what one would expect from a poet going through melancholy toward self-knowing. Most of all, however, the poem contains the usual feeling of threat, not to possessions but to nature. In *In Memoriam* the loss-of-Eden theme comes out as fear at how new sciences, here geology and astronomy, were destroying the Victorian age's sense of a stable world. Poem 3 dreads a blind mechanism in the movements of heavenly bodies, and poems 55 and 56 the implications of the fossil record. Less directly but still clearly, the emerging biology is faced and feared in poem 50. From that point of view the cause of Eden's loss is coped with as neither psychological nor political, but as what the natural world menaces us with, male and female both. This wider perspective of ecological damage enters English-line poetry for the next hundred years.

The strength of the poem seems highlighted when one arranges round it the main groups drawn from Tennyson's other poetry. There are the equally melancholic songs such as 'Break, break, break', 'Tears, idle tears' and a main example, 'Mariana'. There are the narrative group which would include the English pastorals such as 'The Miller's Daughter', 'The Gardener's Daughter' and 'Audley Court', influenced no doubt by Crabbe whose 'homely tragic stories' (Hallam Tennyson's phrase) Tennyson much admired. There are the sadder but more exotic and out-of-England poems like 'Oenone' and 'The Lotos Eaters', and there are the English but now mythologized *Idylls Of The King*. But there is also the smaller but significant group containing *Maud*, 'Locksley Hall' and some others. Here we encounter the question of the dramatic monologue. These poems contain a direct facing of marital and/or sexual predicament but in the voice of a person apparently not the poet, and in a tone of hysteria or frenzy. Marion Shaw supports her argument by pointing out how many loves and marriages in Tennyson's narratives are between childhood sweethearts who are thus in a quasi-sibling relationship. This is true of both these poems as well as, for example, 'Enoch Arden'. One must briefly ask then what is the connection between that focus on infant-love relationships and the movement toward an originally infant language which those poems – *Maud* most deliberately and indeed aggressively – seem saturated in, as *In Memoriam* obviously was not.

For in *Maud* Tennyson does use a more sumptuous vocabulary stemming, if one adopts Kristeva's view, from a thrust in infancy not later transformed. A number of critics remark on the infantile quality of the hysterical preoccupations of Maud's lover without much elaborating the point[11]. But here it is made into invective. Maud's brother, whom the narrator hates, wears a 'jewell'd mass of millinery' and her wooer has 'barbarous opulence jewel-thick', almost as though in emphasizing the precious stones to attack the rich wording itself. The alliteration may trace back to the Anglo-Saxon kenning, but it also curses and spits: 'Why do they prate of the blessings of peace?'; 'the languid fool,/ Who was gaping and grinning by'. The word 'babble' is itself frequent. Bitter hatred has to take solid language to hurl at the enemy like handfuls of mud, for the loving copula of 'to be' and the highlighting of quiet conjunctions and prepositions would have taken out aggression. Despite the occasional contempt (for example, I xiii 2 line 465), the landscape is still England, it is home. It is not exotic, and the poem is still one of mind. But it is not a mind the narrator seeks to understand by any work of knowing.

It is not certain why Tennyson wrote *Maud*. Some critics see it as a defence of England's actions in the Crimean War, others that Tennyson wanted to show that he was not tied to a first-person melancholic prototype. In short, this was a clear example of what Langbaum and Carol Christ argued about the dramatic monologue. But these two critics put slightly different emphases on the matter. Langbaum suggested simply that Victorian poets needed the dramatic monologue so that they could write first-person Romantic poems while seeming to conceal that. Carol Christ suggests that the poet cannot so have it both ways. She states that 'the fact that the poet does not present himself as a guide to experience or judgement in a dramatic monologue creates a crucial difference'[12]. Rather it is that the form allows the poet to present a different voice, a different pyschological story altogether. So, for example, Browning's stories have the deranged, the exotic, the scholastic and the excited. Ancient manuscripts are discovered, cups are poisoned, speakers are painters and/or cheats. None of this interests the English line poet. The English line poet only wants to know what that inner throbbing song is trying to tell him about himself, his sense of loss, his sexuality, his doubts and fears and his place in society and the world. In *In Memoriam*, as well as Tennyson's shorter lyrics, the feeling of self, quest, voice and undertow are uncompromising.

In poetic voice at least, Matthew Arnold is in some ways the most characteristic of these poets. His profound melancholy and despair, his ubiquitous image of the sea as undertow and as round the island home perhaps, and his settings, often, in English places and their institutions like Oxford, Dover, Rugby and the Lakes which were familiar to him and where his deepest securities lay, all bear this out. But they seem to prevent him from doing anything other than sadly face the great changes of mid-century Victorian England, 'this strange disease of modern life', which he felt like a personal burden. His admiration for what he called Wordsworth's 'healing power' was deep and sincere, but he could not himself offer to heal.

Even when Arnold's poetry is mythological and classical the greyness of tone seems to reflect his own depression. In fact unlike Tennyson and Browning he usually speaks in his own

voice with neither dramatic monologue nor narrative. Even
when he does use those, a psychological weight is unloaded
into characters seldom cut clean from each other or himself.
He too, however, if less markedly than Tennyson, is a 'halfway' case, for the poetry is impregnated by his reading in
continental philosophy and the far eastern sacred texts,
Senancour, Spinoza, Goethe and the *Bhagavad Gita*. Often, as
in 'Empedocles on Etna' and 'The Scholar-Gipsy', this halfway
quality is enacted by a clear split, in the poem's tonal nature,
between one or more of its sections. Early visits to Switzerland
and a passionate love for a German friend Mary Claude are
the basis of some early poems. But Arnold also more or less
gave up poetry just after mid-century when he was about
30. He turned to his second career as critical and cultural
commentator of the state of England, pleading with his
countryman to be less insular and internalize the mainstream
of continental literary and cultural tradition[13]. Most current
historicist criticism is deeply sceptical of the Arnoldian view
of 'culture', however, and seeks to dislodge it. The point is
highly relevant to the present discussion.

'Dover Beach' shows many of these tendencies. It is probably
Arnold's best-known poem. One is surprised, looking back at
it, to see how much of its 37 lines is an evocation of the sea
itself. We hear its

> grating roar
> Of pebbles which the waves draw back, and fling,
> At their return, up the high strand,
> Begin, and cease, and then again begin

This is much like the movement of *In Memoriam* again, as
though that tugging undertow surfaces explicitly as the
response of the Victorian English poets to their increasingly
oppressive times of doubt and despair. Here though the sea's
cadence is also permanent:

> With tremulous cadence slow, and bring
> The eternal note of sadness in.

Formal distractions in the poem from the sea's constant move-

ment are the reference to the ancient world ('Sophocles long
ago/Heard it on the Aegæan' – he didn't, because the Mediter-
ranean is not tidal), and the renowned parallel with 'The Sea
of Faith' which 'Was once, too, at the full'. The deliberate
quality of the parallel, as though the two things exactly match,
is emphasized by the commas each side of 'too' and the capital-
izing of the phrase itself. Yet the thrust of the poem is clear
and uncompromising in the way it connects deep melancholy,
mind and feeling under the words themselves, and the
unequivocally negative conclusion. Sophocles heard

> the turbid ebb and flow
> Of human misery; we
> Find also in the sound a thought,

while the sea of faith gives off only 'its melancholy, long,
withdrawing roar'. As a result the undifferentiated water, like
the language the English line poets use, is powerful because
it is that undertow itself. It is remarkable that this secular poet,
sensitive to what is being lost in non-transcendental terms,
should use this very image of the drag of the tide to express
it, and feel so bleakly as a result, that the world which could
have seemed both dreamy and beautiful

> Hath really neither joy, nor love, nor light,
> Nor certitude, nor peace, nor help for pain;
> And we are here as on a darkling plain
> Swept with confused alarms of struggle and flight,
> Where ignorant armies clash by night.

The Wordsworthian joy has gone. Yet the poetry, otherwise
so pessimistic, is saved as poetry by the correlative of the
realized sea, a theme used for its longed-for boundlessness in
'The Forsaken Merman', where the voice speaks from the sea-
bed itself. Equally in 'The Buried Life', a kind of extended
version of 'Dover Beach', our lives in the modern world are
seen as buried by that world's 'din of strife', its 'thousand
nothings of the hour'; and J. Hillis Miller has asked pointedly
how Arnold can insist, as he seems to, that the 'stream' which
flows under that life can be the 'grounded' language that

expresses it. Miller points out that 'Water threads its way through all of Arnold's poetry'[14] even though its metaphorical translation varies from place to place.

Ignorant armies clash, if not by night, certainly in a desert haze in 'Sohrab and Rustum', a story of just under 900 lines in Homeric mode, based on a Persian myth Arnold first found in an essay by the French critic Sainte-Beuve. Here the 'half-way' quality strikes more strongly. The setting and detail are of the ancient epics, but the voice and language are Tennysonian. Along with Milton, Tennyson was much on Arnold's mind in this period, as he said[15]. Arnold breathes, broods and resonates through it with somewhat the same balancing-effect that Wordsworth reached in the story of Margaret (*The Excursion*, Book I). The clue is in the story, for it is of a battle resolved in the end by a single-combat duel between a young warrior Sohrab and an older Hector-type veteran of many wars, Rustum. Unbeknown to both until it is too late, and although on opposing sides, they are father and son. Rustum fights reluctantly until the increasingly confident boy taunts him into more vigorous action. But then Sohrab sustains a death-wound, and lying on the ground reveals who he is. Rustum's grief, sitting by his son's body on the sand, closes the story, the camera pans back into the Victorian infinity and we are left with the majestic River Oxus sweeping on for ever into the Aral Sea.

The narrator has apparently an all-knowing wisdom in the sense that, as far as it goes, the poem seems to claim universal allegorical status. But one then recalls the eminence in Victorian education and more widely of Arnold's father Thomas Arnold, headmaster of Rugby, the century's most famous school which Matthew himself attended. Immediately, of course, deeper meanings suggest themselves. Gabriel Pearson sees the same division, between inner and outer, found in Arnold more generally. Rustum's aggressive calling out of his own name, '*Rustum!*' (line 516, Arnold's emphasis), early in the fight seems to be Arnold's unconscious recognition of the 'Nom Du Père' or name-of-the-father as Lacan terms it[16], by which the son is called to recognize his social responsibilities and, in context here, his duty to eschew poetry's luxury.

The poem's classical quality is seen only through the film of nostalgia for the truths that (an Oxford) classical education could give. The extended Homeric similies, the natural scenes, sand, animals, birds and river, and the complete absence of viciousness or even aggression in these two armies, are given their connotations in being really a psychological shimmering in Arnold's own mind, and past. The language is of that feeling, both in dialogue

> I seek one man, one man, and one alone–
> Rustum, my father; who I hoped should greet,
> Should one day greet, upon some well-fought field,
> His not unworthy, not inglorious son.
> So I long hoped, but him I never find
>
> (lines 49–53)

and in physical description:

> He spoke; and all the blood left Rustum's cheeks,
> And his knees tottered, and he smote his hand
> Against his breast, his heavy mailed hand,
> That the hard iron corslet clanked aloud
>
> (lines 661–4)

Here blood, body and armour can't escape out into any sense of words as having autonomous origin and history, or as more than local symbol for they are wrapped still in the mist of subjective melancholy which projected them there. It is surely a moving poem, but Arnold's own self as 'not unworthy, not inglorious son' is in it as Tennyson is not in 'Dora' or 'Enoch Arden'. We feel closer to an overtly first-person poem like 'Resignation' which evokes two walks in the English Lake District. Probably in 1833 when Matthew was eleven, Thomas Arnold bought the house Fox How there, to be close to his friend William Wordsworth for several months each year, and where the young Matthew sat (literally) at the old poet's feet.

The poem 'Empedocles on Etna' is again a classical story retold, but it too illustrates the Arnold duality. The central section, a monologue by the brooding isolate Empedocles himself, is more or less geologically faulted away from the poem's other two parts which surround it. Suddenly it is Matthew

Arnold speaking about, surely, his own personal search to
understand science and psychology in a ravaged industrial
England. The message comes as before:

> Look, the world tempts our eye,
> And we would know it all!
> We map the starry sky!
> We mine this earthen ball,
> We measure the sea-tides, we number the sea-sands; . . .
>
> We shut our eyes, and muse
> How our own minds are made.
> What springs of thought they use,
> How rightened, how betray'd
> And spend our wit to name what most employ unnamed.
>
> (Scene II, 317–21, 327–31)

What is happening is that Empedocles is on the verge of
suicide on top of the volcano, and the old philosopher Pausan-
ias and the young singer Callicles are trying to soothe him
from further down the mountain-side. Empedocles ends by
throwing himself down the crater, but this businessman-off-
the-office-block piece of action is all that happens in the poem,
and Arnold withdrew it when his 1852 collection was reissued
in 1853. The poem is very closely related to the *Preface* Arnold
wrote to his poems at the time, where he said that too much
modern poetry was internal and that the presentation of action,
according to the classical dicta of Aristotle, was required. It
was the suicide that drew Arnold's attention to the story's
poetic potential in the first place. But since, as both Hillis
Miller and Frank Kermode point out, the suicide in the poem
is hardly action, except as parable[17], the implication has to be
that Arnold recognized that he could not write this action-
poetry himself. He later stopped writing poetry altogether.

The same theme, and its double-edged writing, is found in
'The Scholar-Gipsy', the poem where Arnold is most explicitly
personal about the whole matter. Again we find a fable made
first-person by Arnold's use of it to project his own struggle.
Comparably to 'Empedocles', the poem has a clear break of
caesura halfway through, at line 141 to be precise. Hitherto

the echoes of previous poets, especially Keats' odes, are over-whelming if not a little suffocating. Gray, Milton, Clare, Wordsworth, Shelley and Keats follow in succession (at 67 and 70 'heats' and 'retreats' seem to be almost pleading to rhyme with 'Keats', the autumnal luxurious glow is so pronounced), and the story is told of the seventeenth-century Oxford scholar drop-out who 'went to learn the gypsy-lore'. This mysterious vagrant has something of Wordsworth's solitaries but nothing of their privation. He is even phantom, half sprite of the woods, one feels, and various sightings by village girls (line 90) do not confirm whether he is real, ethereal or imaginary. We might say he symbolizes Romanticism itself, much as Keats' strange figure on the granary floor symbolizes autumn in his poem of that name. But at line 141 Arnold suddenly crashes forward into his simple and dusty language of the modern world, later called (line 203)

> this strange disease of modern life,
> With its sick hurry, its divided aims,
> Its heads o'ertaxed, its palsied hearts, was rife . . .

That could be late twentieth century. In the lines just before the line–141 switch, Arnold had been in effect with Gray, at

> Some country-nook, where o'er thy unknown grave
> Tall grasses and white flowering nettles wave,
> Under a dark, red-fruited yew-tree's shade.

(The second line is possibly behind one of Edward Thomas's best-known poems, 'Tall Nettles'.) But what Arnold then does, in the rest of the poem, is to express a true melancholy, by begging the scholar-gipsy not to return. He does not say 'come back, we need you' any more than 'we've left you behind, you are obsolete'. Rather he implores him to 'Wave us away, and keep thy solitude! . . . Fly our paths, our feverish contacts fly!' And though stoically borne no doubt, the injunction is rather more a resignation and, most markedly, a desperate plea *not* to return, to one who already has absolutely no prospect of doing so. And since the scholar-gipsy cannot return anyway, Arnold is simply and rhetorically emphasizing how desperate his and England's plight has become. He offers no solutions, and these passages go to the edge of the maudlin for that reason. The plea cannot be against a real likelihood, or have real edge, and so again is wholly a verbal movement or throbbing of emotion itself.

It is an impressive but alarmingly tense poem. The difficulty perhaps was that in idealizing Oxford, making it yet another countryside which has lost pastoral innocence even with all its cited real local names (Cumner, Fyfield, Godstow Bridge and the rest), the headiness grows too much to bear and has to be unloaded in the extended simile of the final stanza. When Arnold really arrived home, later in life on a visit to Rugby, the resulting poem had a more even gaze, calm if still melancholy, because the elegy, while for his father, seems to be for his own poetry as well. England's condition has now to be faced.

> Coldly, sadly descends
> The autumn-evening. The field
> Strewn with its dank yellow drifts
> Of withered leaves, and the elms,
> Fade into dimness apace,
> Silent; hardly a shout
> From a few boys late at their play!
> The lights come out in the street,
> In the school-room windows; but cold,
> Solemn, unlighted, austere,
> Through the gathering darkness, arise
> The chapel-walls, in whose bound
> Thou, my father! art laid.
>   ('Rugby Chapel' 1–13)

Whether Arnold faced it successfully or not is a different story.

6

Emily Brontë, Christina Rossetti, Elizabeth Barrett Browning – Gerard Manley Hopkins

It now has to be considered whether it was possible, before now if ever, for women to have written this kind of poem, and if so in what sense.

In the last 200 years English-line male poets, and some others, on occasion wrote poems about a singing woman. There are for example, Wordsworth's 'Lucy Gray', Keats's 'La Belle Dame Sans Merci', Tennyson's 'The Lady of Shalott', 'Mariana' and 'Tears, Idle Tears', Hardy's 'The Ruined Maid' and so on down to Wallace Stevens's 'Idea of Order at Key West'. The most telling is perhaps Wordsworth's 'The Solitary Reaper', in which the poet hears a women singing across a field. But he cannot make out the words. In then asking 'Will no one tell me what she sings?' the poet could be read as saying that he does not know what, from a woman, is being sung even when it is so like his own poetry and those in the English line who succeed him. The characteristics are all there: she is 'solitary' (inward, first person), and he hears 'a melancholy strain' (melancholy) either of 'old, unhappy, far-off things' (memory of the past) or 'familiar matter of today' (the ordinary and familiar), in a song that 'could have no ending' (boundlessness). Not surprisingly then does a feminist critic like Christine Battersby say that 'The romantic conception of genius is singularly harmful to women'[1]. Yet one might say not so much romantic as Miltonic, since in the myth of Adam and Eve woman is the first target of temptation; awakened by the phallus (serpent) she offers man her luscious breast (apple) and he surrenders, blaming her thereafter. Our emphasis here is away from romanticism alone and toward maleness more widely, for these poems listed above do hear, if not with comprehension, the distant woman's voice.

Wordsworth's unconscious brooding as to whether there could be women poets and of his kind, is clearly a question for criticism now. It is deeply complex, because psychological and socio-political matters interrelate. To start with, if as Anne Rosalind Jones puts it[2] the male's domination is in effect phallic, we have to say that this is hardly true of the male English line. Their dilemma, perhaps, was that they were first drawn away from the infant-language potential by their fathers real or notional, then subliminally realized what had been done to them, but could not go back; hence the melancholy in the voice. As a result their writing flows, and the image is not only of the phallic pen (for example the tree) but more often water, a sort of colourless ink which endlessly seeks where to write itself and is suspicious of the solid word or 'poetic diction' it might have been expected to use by philistine authorities.

Our question then is whether one or other of the roles the woman may find herself in is the same thing from the other side. One possible feminine scenario is based where 'writing the body' lacks, after all, the *jouissance* or body-playfulness which comes either in pregnancy (the amused anarchic absurdity of having this graft on you), or else the playfulness connected again with the infant itself. The mother experiences this, both by her proximity to the infant and by having remained with her own mother herself, not drawn out by the father (or education denied to girls) into the public language where you can't just play with words for their own sakes but must use them soberly and in serious, authoritative, moral fashion. In both these cases then motherhood is a component, as are sex and love. And the unmarried woman, or the woman with unrequited love or a love that for some reason she cannot respond to, may not have that *jouissance* or be unable to take it forward into a poetry of its own founding.

If all that such women had instead was the male model of poet to follow, then it might be that some women found that its presence, and their unsuitability gender-wise for it, simply led to a deeper longing for it or some female equivalent. Rossetti, Brontë and Barrett Browning all heard and sporadically have the Wordsworthian voice. The enquiry is then not only whether writing the woman's body is compatible with that, but whether indeed that ought to be her desire.

Equally, whatever the woman's first position, the matter also becomes political. How to write, but also how to be allowed to write, or to resist that impulse. As with the male predicament, the female one also is multifarious. Susan Gubar recounts a story of a convent in which several bed-sheets hang on a wall in picture-frames, each stained with (hymeneal) blood; one though is unstained, the 'blank page'[3]. But, Gubar points out, there are lots of ways it could have stayed unstained. Virginity unscathed or virginity long pierced, or holding your man off by endless distracting stories, by running away, or even by finding the male was already impotent anyway. These are themselves all stories, hence woman's traditional power as novelist. But the moral of this one is that although 'women's writing' becomes an issue both as distinct from men's (a gender matter) and as a right (a political matter), nevertheless, as Janet Montefiore puts it, it is risky 'to lay a kind of grid of feminism over the map of women's poetry'[4]. For the gift of language may be found behind many of these routes out, and all the roles of nun, madwoman, working woman, lesbian and whore-who-never-marries may escape the patriarchal family and community which seem to deny the woman poet's voice. It is not just a matter of how to write without a pen. Do you have ink but no pen, bleeding from every aperture hymeneally, menstrually or at childbirth? Or do you have a page but no pen, the blank page itself, that on which men write and procreate as they like while she is denied that creative gift? Either the unphallic body, whether blood or page, itself must do the writing, or that too – with motherhood in happy egalitarian marriage perhaps – must be left behind, and men taken on and upstaged on their own ground, their tradition used by women with equal success.

Emily Brontë's poetry was much admired by both Tennyson and Arnold, as indeed was that of her sisters[5]. Along with their purity, integrity and elemental power, many of Emily

Brontë's poems have a set quality, as though they are mounted
on stones in front of her house on the Yorkshire moors. This
doesn't detract, but one wonders about it:

> So hopeless is the world without,
> The world within I doubly prize;
> Thy world where guile and hate and doubt
> Where cold suspicion never rise;
> Where thou and I and Liberty
> Have undisputed sovereignty.

That stanza is from 'To Imagination', the referent of 'thy' and
'thou' in the poem. It is admittedly less elemental than most
of her poetry, but even so the slight distance between the
firmness of what is said and any overflow of feeling in the
saying it, is notable. Here is a different kind of example:

> I'll not weep that thou art going to leave me,
> There's nothing lovely here;
> And doubly will the dark world grieve me
> While they heart suffers there.
>
> I'll not weep, because the summer's glory
> Must always end in gloom;
> And, follow out the happiest story–
> It closes with a tomb!
>
> And I am weary of the anguish
> Increasing winters bear;
> Weary to watch the spirit languish
> Through years of dead despair.
>
> So, if a tear, when thou art dying,
> Should haply fall from me,
> It is but that my soul is sighing
> To go and rest with thee.
>
> ('Stanzas')

If that were Housman, and the voice is similar in a number
of ways, you would feel sure that he had his life's love,
Moses Jackson, in mind. Here there is no referent, and Brontë

specialists have never found evidence of a love affair in her life. But even if we invent someone for the 'thee' to refer to (perhaps the 'unknown guest' in 'And Now The Housedog'), the poem gives no passing detail or flicker of a scene that once happened. There are such appearances here and there in the poems, but broadly this effect is present: namely, of a poem being made or entered from the outside, as though a poetic form, or even 'poetry' itself, is waiting to be given substance as a formal undertaking coming from a commitment.

This was possible even within an outstanding body of firm, passionate, individual poetry, because the 'young woman's accomplishment', even up there in that bleak landscape, was probably Emily's necessary route. Yet at the same time she already had and was one with the material which the poems were to be made of. It is as though from the start she grasped tight hold of clear categories, grief, love, scorn, passion, the moors, rocks, sky, her body, tears, rain, and evoked them and her passion through them, direct. Her observation is at one with her passion, and she notes the passion and the objective world, skylark, snow, home and hearth, real or imagined lover, at the same levels if intensely and at the same time. Consequently the things which deeply hurt the male English line poet, although all present in Emily Brontë, do not need to be pored over self-consciously. Even an obviously personal piece like 'All Day I've Toiled' moves away from exploration. She has spent all day in 'learning's golden mine', but the rest of the poem is about the 'peace' that 'lulls' her in the evening outside. Clearly influenced by Wordsworth (the Lake District and Yorkshire Dales being similar enough and not far apart), she echoes him often, if fleetingly, in actual phrases. But the need to release what is suppressed came to have a different outlet. With the male English line poet, the pressured poetry wells up, spontaneously overflows. Emily Brontë's blank page is always already the merge of the blank (in that sense) inner self and the blank landscape outside. Like Clare in his 'Address to Plenty', she in 'Stanzas' longs for home when already there. She wrote only the one terrifyingly powerful novel, *Wuthering Heights;* the page did not need to diversify into many stories.

Emily Brontë wondered briefly why she was denied 'The glorious gift to many given/ To speak their thoughts in poetry', and we can if we like hear 'men' in 'many'. It fits, but the missing element is only that mourning, brooding, worrying, searching self-consciousness at the centre of Wordsworth, Arnold and Larkin which ironically may have come from the male's need to dominate the landscape while depending on it. Home, the grey landscape and the first-person are there. The influence of individual precursors did not make her anxious. Uncertainty is not compulsive, for her melancholy is already an exact fit with the landscape.

Rossetti, though rather later (born in 1830) does have in parts of her work the same reduced vocabulary, the same blank page, as Emily Brontë. Most people agree that Christina Rossetti's nonetheless rich body of poetry is about renunciation, but here the freedom of many readings is at once a challenge, for we need to decide just what was being renounced. Spiritually-minded critics emphasize the *vanitas mundi*, the world's emptiness, in her work. But feminists such as Susan Gubar and Sandra Gilbert stress the rejection of a freedom Rossetti would have preferred, that from the patriarchy which forces one to end up 'the wife, the nun, or, most likely, the kindly useful spinster'[6]. Our interest is in how answers to such questions throw light on the poet's affinity, as far as it goes, to this English line.

Broadly that affinity might seem little. She was the sister of a pre-Raphaelite, they were of quite recent Italian descent, and she is acknowledged to have written in the tradition of Dante, Augustine, Petrarch and Herbert. What is interesting is the preoccupation, in what can roughly be called a middle period, with death and melancholy in natural settings, and most intriguingly with the Eve story and particularly the luscious juicy fruits that appear in the extraordinary *Goblin Market*, but elsewhere too. It seems that both those fruits in the early years, and the quite different godhead approached later after her renunciation, put a blockage – one she chose with open eyes – to the boundlessness of the Wordsworthian-Arnoldian kind she would otherwise have been left with.

In 'Goblin Market' two young sisters are tempted by goblins to buy cornucopias of fruit, and these have clear sexual connotation. One sister succumbs and suddenly goes grey-haired, and is rescued and restored by the other, and they both later, when married, warn their own children to eschew such temptations. This oversimple precis will serve to highlight what one suspects most people remember: the extremely sensual descriptions of the wicked goblins, their molesting of Lizzie, but most of all the fruit itself and the eating of it:

Apples and quinces,
Lemons and oranges,
Plump unpecked cherries,
Melons and raspberries,
Bloom-down-cheeked peaches,
Swart-headed mulberries,
Wild free-born cranberries,
Crab-apples, dewberries,
Pine-apples, blackberries,
Apricots, strawberries;–
All ripe together,
In summer weather,–

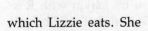

which Lizzie eats. She

. . . laughed in heart to feel the drip
Of juice that syrupped all her face,
And lodged in dimples of her chin,
And streaked her neck which quaked like curd.

and then tries to make Laura eat, much as Eve did Adam:

Hug me, kiss me, suck my juices
Squeezed from goblin fruits for you,
Goblin pulp and goblin dew.
Eat me, drink me, love me;
Laura, make much of me.
                    (lines 5–16, 433–6, 468–72)

These propensities are found elsewhere, if less so, in 'Another Spring', 'An Apple-Gathering' and 'Eve', although the latter is a more inward and regretful poem. It is that erotic sensuality surely, whatever it may imply, that Rossetti renounced, leaving her free some years and many, many poems later to write her *Monna Innominata* sonnet sequence in language like this:

> Yet while I love my God the most, I deem
>   That I can never love you overmuch;
>   I love Him more, so let me love you too;
>   Yea, as I apprehend it, love is such
> I cannot love you if I love not Him.
> I cannot love Him if I love not you.
>
> (Sonnet 6)

Not a physical object in sight, indeed almost a blank page hardly touched. Yet what intensity is evident in the word 'love' nine times in six lines. It is as if while this is clearly 'simple language' in one way, nevertheless love is now a strong clear-cut category, the blocking-object to an ordinary-language over-flow.

So why was Rossetti so admired not only by Hopkins, which is immediately understandable, but also by Larkin with Rossetti among his Twelve Poets (see p.176) on the shelf behind him? Why also of all people, Robert Frost, for whom according to his biographer, Lawrance Thompson[7], she was one of his 'secretly cherished favourites' because of her 'blending mysticism with passionate sensuousness'? One can see these qualities perhaps in Frost's famous if more pragmatic poem 'After Apple-Picking'. But there is also Edward Thomas's poem 'The Owl', which so closely parallels Rossetti's 'Up-Hill' in its weary, puzzled arrival of footsore travellers at a country inn at night. The remarkable thing is that the first word in Thomas's poem exactly opposes Rossetti's title: '*Downhill* I came, hungry, and yet not starved . . .' (my emphasis). Rossetti is moving up to the gates of a spiritual city, so to speak, but has not yet got there. Thomas responds to the gravity of this earth. The poem's tone is one of his least vulnerable, most grave.

The answer it seems is a tie between the sensuous, the spiritual and the linguistic. In renouncing forbidden fruit early on, Rossetti renounced poetically at least an aspect of the Eve in her, taking Eve there as feminists take her in one reading. And by doing that she is left with the pen-less blank page which the English line poets also long for, always desiring the same lack. Since with Rossetti it did not reach the hardening up of language at the other end of the continuum either until rather later, in the spiritual exact certainty of 'love' or (bisexual) God, it was left in between for a while, with only its own senses of loss in the past and death in the future. In short, between the earlier more sensuous period and the final one of full devotional writing she entertains the language of the English line poets. Her desire here is neither for fruits to hand nor for heavenly certainties she already knows of; her desire becomes unattainable.

In a couple of ways she was well equipped for this admittedly chronologically inexact period. As A. C. Benson wrote not long after her death, her poems are always likely to draw on a background of 'gardens, orchards, wooded dingles, with a churchyard in the distance . . . the dewy English woodland, the sharp silences of winter, the gloom of low-hung clouds, and the sigh of weeping rains'. All features of her grandfather's cottage in Buckinghamshire no doubt, as Benson suggested and which she often visited. Ruskin found the 'pathetic fallacy' element, as he himself termed it, in this poetry, condemning Rossetti's metric irregularities and rejecting her poems out of hand, although he did concede her power of observation and passion[8]. But Rossetti was also of the nineteenth-century religious persuasion that believed in 'soul-sleep', that is to say a sleeping period after death and up to the final resurrection of the saved. As McGann has shown, this is probably the reference of 'beds' at the end of 'Up-Hill', and it informs several other poems[9].

And from these two features, the natural familiar background and the soul-sleep belief, the relevant poems can now be seen. 'Up-Hill', 'Dead before Death', 'Dream-Land', 'Rest', 'After Death', 'Mirage', 'Despised and Rejected', 'Long Barren', 'If Only', 'Dost Thou Not Care?' and others, in greater or less measure have the unfocused reference, the yearning, and the linguistic and physical liquidity of the English line poets. Anthony Harrison detects in 'An Old World Thicket' the precursorship of Wordsworth's 'Ode: Intimations of Immorality'[10], but the tendency is diffuse across much of the work. A few lines from 'Shut Out' show how the fact of unseeing makes

the vocabulary less sharp and reduces the enjoyment of what
could have been more fully seen:

> From bough to bough the song-birds crossed,
>   From flower to flower the moths and bees;
>   With all its nests and stately trees
> It had been mine, and it was lost . . .

> The spirit was silent; but he took
>   Mortar and stone to build a wall;
>   He left no loophole, great or small
> Thro' which my straining eyes might look:

> So now I sit here quite alone
>   Blinded with tears, nor grieve for that,
>   For nought is left worth looking at
> Since my delightful land is gone.
>   (lines 5–8, 17–24)

It could be the early Robert Frost.

Rossetti suggested that Elizabeth Barrett Browning was too
happy. 'Had the Great Poetess of our own day and nation
only been unhappy instead of happy, her circumstances would
have invited her to bequeath to us, in lieu of the "Portuguese
Sonnets", an inimitable "donna innominata" drawn not from
fancy but from feeling'[11]. It is no sin to be happy, nor disquali-
fication for some poets, but fancy and happiness hardly seem
to square with melancholy and a deliberately understated language. So one wonders how Barrett Browning achieved a loss-
of-nature poem in *The Lost Bower*, or could have modelled her
longest work *Aurora Leigh* on *The Prelude*.

The Lost Bower is a handy reminder that Barrett Browning
(1806–61) spent virtually all her life until her mid-twenties in
Herefordshire. Yet the signs of the later witty urbanite are in
this poem. It is a first-person nature poem with, however, no
mournful voice. The poet recalls going out into the woods near
her home as a young girl. She presses on through thorn and
thicket, encouraged in that task by remembering how poets
from Langland to Wordsworth had done the same thing. She
comes across a bower which, though natural, seems wonder-
fully to be hospitable and gentle, as though nature was 'weary

of rough-doing'. Ivy, eglantine and roses form a room with windows and entrance. Yet when she seems to hear a most beautiful gentle music, she insists no bird could be credited with such a sound, and she determines to be the fairy of this bower herself. On future days she can never find the bower again. In later years she recalls this first loss of her life, but concludes that her own prayer and spirit can adequately preserve it, and that 'All is lost . . . and *won!*'

The essential point is that, albeit without any great hostility, nature is being rejected rather than espoused as a source of the poet's inspiration or creativity. Rather, she carries her words under her arm out to the bower with her from the sophisticated world she already knows. The rhyming in the poem is highly and skilfully artificial. Barrett Browning seems to go out of her way to make the rhymes ingenious. Daily – valley; said I – lady; near it – spirit; come there – summer; hushing – cushion; fairies – Ave Marys; and dozens more, like her future husband did in 'A Grammarian's Funeral' almost simultaneously, although probably she did not know this. 'Near it – spirit' is of course the first rhyming pair in Shelley's poem 'To a Skylark', and *The Lost Bower* employs Shelley's form of four short lines and a double-length fifth line as well. But the result of this crafted rhyming in Barrett Browning is that nature does not enter the unconscious to haunt it, but is held just gently at arm's length and so turned into allegory. In the central stanzas the birds are held incapable of making the sounds she hears in herself; 'never lark . . . never nightingale so singeth . . . never blackbird . . .' all birds subjects of odes by the great romantics for just their song's power, even Shelley's, whom here too she subverts. The loss of the bower at the end is no sorrow, though it is something the poet has to face. She has escaped any claim of nature to be her poetry's source, and reversed the traditional (male) allegorical meaning where finding the bower or garden is sexual entry into a woman. For she is herself the woman taking that role, and nature never threatens her. The woman is making a cast for a woman's poetry, to be found in her woman's self, inspired by the 'lady' the bower reminded her of when she was there; the muse she will never need. With light-hearted mysteriousness, exact easy phrasing and psychological import, *The Lost*

Bower has strong claims to being a major, neglected nineteenth-century poem and one of considerable interest to current criticism, feminist or otherwise.

The rippling fancy of the poem highlights another feature. In the middle of *The Lost Bower* there is an untypical moment:

> I rose up in exaltation
> And an inward trembling heat,
> And (it seemed) in geste of passion
> Dropped the music to my feet
> Like a garment rustling downward – such a silence followed it!
>
> (lines 211–15)

Having metaphorically dropped her dress for an instant and revealed her nakedness – very quickly covered again – there is a 'silence'. This silence at moments of real vulnerability turns out to be important in her poetry. There is little sense of silence elsewhere in either this poem or in *Aurora Leigh*, her famous work of 1856 which has become something of a feminist manifesto. Yet in between had come not only the *Sonnets from the Portuguese* but also the sonnets of 1844, which were closely connected to the death by drowning of her brother 'Bro', holidaying with her in 1840. Angela Leighton has perceptively written that this biggest single grief in Barrett Browning's life was something she could not articulate. In real terms it too stayed silent. 'The words [in the 1844 sonnets] remain at a long distance from that deep dumbness which most truly expresses the speaker's feelings' . . . 'the shame of this actual powerlessness cannot be overcome by the power of words'[12]. What the poet articulated was the numbness itself.

This insight seems to me paradoxically to go to the heart of *Aurora Leigh*, a poem of the reverse kind in which there is even a talking-heads atmosphere much of the time. Although there is ostensibly only one speaker, it is a mixture of many sources. Donald Thomas, Robert Browning's biographer, has said that *Aurora Leigh* 'seemed to be a compound of books by other men and women'[13]. In the rejected and eloped daughter of Edward Barrett, nakedness (sexuality), silence and deep feeling go together, and words do not go down into that dark place nor come up from it. Rather, her skill and gift lay in the

directing of public words to their places by quick-fire orders.
Her view about the woman as artist was therefore held as a
public responsibility and response. This would make it, on
the face of it, quite unconnected with 'English line' poetry,
where Tennyson could expurgate his grief by a poem of the
length of *In Memoriam*, as Barrett Browning both recognized
and said.

How then could *The Prelude* have been a major influence in
the making of it, even if *Jane Eyre* is the other parent with the
voice of Robert Browning in the background? Kathleen Blake
sees formal similarities between the two poems. Both record
growth of the poet's mind and death of the mother and father;
have modern socially detailed settings; turn toward nature and
self-doubt, and so on[14]. Barrett Browning visited Wordsworth
in 1836, hung his portrait in her room and praised him greatly
in her own writings. But these two main formative works were
very recent. *Jane Eyre* appeared in 1847 and *The Prelude* in 1850.
They had probably had little time to be absorbed into either
Barrett Browning's poetic consciousness or society's more generally. The suggestion is that they were not so absorbed and
that she, like Robert, did not write in that way. Rather, just
as she went into the bower but found she herself was source
of the inspiration she found there, so here she goes to the
English line in order to show that poetry is not the prerogative
of males. The Brownings had lived in Italy for several years
by the time the poem was written; it begins with her upbringing in the Malvern hills but goes on to the urban literary salon
and drawing-room debate. The poem's success and failure lies
in this feature of it. The poet's difficulty is that, having decided
to opt for an overt campaign for women's poethood, she the
poet must herself also be seen to be one, and in a poet of that
kind the two things do not sit easily together. She constantly
tells us things which we sense ought to have been felt. They
may have been felt, but the feeling seems to have come when
she sees what she has written:

> We women are too apt to look to one,
> Which proves a certain impotence in art.
> We strain our natures at doing something great,
> Far less because it's something great to do,

Than haply that we, so, commend ourselves
As being not small, and more appreciable
To some one friend . . .

                              (*Aurora Leigh* V 43–9)

Like any writing of this kind it is highly readable, with
moments of power, entertainment and debate on every page.
But those pages are blank ones held well out in front of the
poetic mind, and they get written on by the skilled manipulat-
ing pen getting them there from all directions. Elizabeth Barrett
Browning's task was to produce both a manifesto for women's
poetry and a woman's poem seen to stand in true descent
from the tradition it would both honour and subvert at once.
Her success lies, certainly, in a remarkable poem *Aurora Leigh*,
but more so in setting going a debate as to how her aim could
be achieved.

Gerard Manley Hopkins, who was brought up an Anglican
and became a Jesuit priest, was born in 1844 and died in 1889.
I place him in this chapter mainly out of convenience, for as
said in the first chapter, he stands rather to the side of these
'English line' poets. His interest is thus for comparison and
this can be discussed briefly. There are, as it happens, two
formal ways in which Hopkins is comparable to these women
poets. He was unmarried like all of them except Barrett Browning, and he places his deepest faith in a world away from
identification with the natural, like all of them except Emily
Brontë. But in their case a need to swerve from what we are
calling the English line was a necessity of cultural and sexual
politics. Despite his work in the slums of Liverpool and Glas-
gow and his notorious communist or 'Red Letter' to Bridges[15],
this does not seem to have been Hopkins's motive, which
was genuinely theological. This action possibly meant too a
deflection of loyalty from his own father to a God the Father
now differently aligned, as alternative genitor of a world
which, nevertheless, turns out still recognizable as the one in
which Hopkins was reared. Evidence for a homosexual tendency cannot be ignored, although it was hardly consistent or

dramatic enough to give us more than background gloss on some of the poetry's occasional features.

One might feel, in fact, that Hopkins has no place in the present discussion. His individual-word preoccupation and his placing of ultimate trust not in 'the mind of man' (Wordsworth) but in a construct of civilization – whatever its ultimate source – namely the Catholic Church, made him seem a forerunner to the Modernists. For many he was an important and exciting discovery. This is so marked that F. R. Leavis, in organizing the Modernist canon he was to present in his seminal book *New Bearings in English Poetry* (1932), gave a full chapter only to Hopkins in addition to those for Eliot and Pound. Leavis saw Hopkins as in the line of Shakespeare not Milton and as a verbal innovator of the first order. And, far from presenting a poetry of ordinary language, 'Hopkins is really difficult, and the difficulty is essential'[16]. But this difficulty is the 'oddity and obscurity' which Hopkins's friend and first editor Robert Bridges found in his work. Housman complained to Bridges about Hopkins's poetry, and added a remark which shows Housman's attitude to English-line poetry clearly enough: 'Originality is not nearly so good as goodness, even when it is good . . . (Hopkins's) manner strikes me as deliberately adopted to compensate by strangeness for the lack of pure merit'[17]. A few lines from Hopkins can illustrate what they are all referring to:

> Earnest, earthless, equal, attuneable, vaulty, voluminous . . . stupendous
> Evening strains to be time's vast, womb-of-all, home-of-all, hearse-of-all night.
> Her fond yellow hornlight wound to the west, her wild hollow hoarlight hung to the height
> Waste; her earliest stars, earl-stars, stars principal, overbend us,
> Fire-featuring heaven . . .

That is from 'Spelt from Sibyl's Leaves', and the title is instructive. It is 'spelt', suggesting a close verbal attention not born from a flow of mind and feeling themselves out through words drawn in naturally. Most important, a quotation from the Latin poet Petronius about the Sibyl was used by T. S. Eliot as masthead at the start of that prototype work *The Waste Land* to signal his intentions. In ancient legend the Sybil was the prophetess at Delphi. She gave her prophetic counsel in the form of individual words written on numerous leaves, which she then scattered in the air for her suppliants to assemble or 'spell' for themselves. Among other things, this stands as a metaphor of Modernism's tenet that the individual word not sentence flow (as Frost contemporaneously declared) is where language stores its referential riches.

Hopkins's own essential beliefs were, first, in God as the author of creation, so that creation is not 'boundless' but a finite structure of clear entities. Second, that those entities each have clear sacramental uniqueness, a uniqueness that separate words stand for. Hopkins called it 'thisness', a translation of the Latin 'haecceitas' of Duns Scotus, the mediaeval divine who is also a central influence in Hopkins's thought. And since words stand for real entities in the created world, they therefore cannot merge imperceptibly into one another. Hopkins was not a precursor of Ferdinand de Saussure.

One acknowledges all of this, and indeed it is clear that it radically disconnects Hopkins from what we are calling the English line. Yet through much of his poetry Hopkins never quite escapes traces of the same traditions of intellect and emotional response which formed those of the English line, and it is instructive then to see him, albeit briefly, in that light.

Although a Jesuit priest, Hopkins was born and raised an Anglican, went to an English public school and inherited just that liberality which enabled him to take a firm stand against his parents' anguished pleading when, just 22 years old, he decided on conversion to Catholicism. Like his other lifelong mentor John Henry Newman (who received him into the Catholic Church) he was apparently a happy child and eldest of a very large family. He came under the sway of Oxford and later of the Welsh countryside, and a number of poems mention both places. So indeed do his two poems on shipwrecks, of the *Deutschland* and the *Eurydice*, where place-names from the Thames and English Channel are cited, and even 'Sydney Fletcher, Bristol-bred . . . Of the best we boast our sailors are'. When he is in Dublin as a professor of classics in later years, the power of home and the familiar comes over him in the 'desolate sonnets', and it is painful:

> To seem the stranger lies my lot, my life
> Among strangers. Father and mother dear,
> Brothers and sisters are in Christ not near
> And he my peace/my parting, sword and strife.
>
> England, whose honor O all my heart woos, wife
> To my creating thought . . .

When in Wales confronting the natural world, it is its known beauty that strikes him, and his sense of inadequacy before it is close to that of Wordsworth in the 'Ode':

> Lovely the woods, waters, meadows, combes, vales,
> All the air things wear that build this world of Wales;
>   Only the inmate does not correspond.
>   ('In the Valley of the Elwy')

And while certainly, unlike Wordsworth, Hopkins then immediately asks God to 'complete thy creature dear', the sentiment does not articulate a full theology of that process. In the best-known of the 'desolate sonnets' of the Dublin period, the image of black despair is again Wordsworthian not hellish:

>   O the mind, mind has mountains; cliffs of fall
> Frightful, sheer, no-man-fathomed. Hold them cheap
> May who ne'er hung there.

In a famous passage Wordsworth too 'hung there' (*The Prelude* 1805 I 347), felt the 'mind's abyss', and the fear in nature as well as its beauty.

Indeed Hopkins attested, in the strongest terms, to his unreserved sense of the seminal importance of Wordsworth's 'Ode' as a poem of shattering first-person experience of the kind Langbaum mentions for Tennyson and Arnold, and this turns out relevant for our argument. The following comes from a page and a half on the subject: 'I feel now I am warm and my hand is in for my greater task, Wordsworth's ode; and here, my dear friend, I must earnestly remonstrate with you, must have it out with you. . . . There have been in all history, a very few men, whom common repute . . . has treated as having had something happen to them that does not happen to other men, as having *seen something*, got a shock, whatever that really was. Plato is the most famous of these. . . . In Wordsworth when he wrote that ode human nature got another of those shocks, and the tremble from it is spreading. This opinion I do strongly share; I am, ever since I knew the ode, in that tremble . . .'[18]. Clearly Hopkins's poetic sensibility was still wide open to the kick-start of powerful internal feelings despite his curiously single-word way of expressing them. These 'desolate sonnets' are just one such example from his work.

If then the poet internalizes a natural world as familiar as well as accepting, however fully, a doctrine legitimizing it, the poetry will bear a stamp of that, which of necessity is in part ideological. However much the poet also has a compulsion to jagged verbal separations as a sort of poetic loosener by which he can attach the mind to what he believes creation to be, nevertheless the actual vocabulary itself may not be esoteric. Its use may be, but not its terms. Hopkins never remotely approaches the internationalism of Pound, who (possibly answering Leavis) summarized Hopkins's poems as 'in their day unduly neglected, as more recently unduly touted'[19]. Pound's verse reads as though words themselves have more energy than do the simple lives we lead which make us draw on them:

> et sequelae
>
> Le Pardis n'est pas artificiel
>   States of mind are inexplicable to us.
>   δακρύων   δακρύων   δακρύων
>   L.   P.   gli onesti
>   J'ai eu pitié des autres
> probablement pas assez, and at moments that suited my
>   own convenience
>   (from Canto LXXVI)

By contrast in his best-known and, in their divergent ways,

most powerful poems such as 'The Wreck of the Deutschland' and 'Spring', Hopkins innovates certainly, but with the known well-worn vocabulary that signifies worlds already familiar, already the places where he lived, before sacramental connotations as to their roles in God's creation are imputed to them.

> Nothing is so beautiful as Spring –
>   When weeds, in wheels, shoot long and lovely and lush;
>   Thrush's eggs look little low heavens, and thrush
> Through the echoing timber does so rinse and wring
> The ear, it strikes like lightnings to hear him sing;
>   The glassy peartree leaves and blooms, they brush
>   The descending blue; that blue is all in a rush
> With richness; the racing lambs too have fair their fling.
>
> ('Spring')

In 'The Wreck of the Deutschland' Hopkins's authenticity gets its fullest expression. The battle of nuns and sailors with the raging sea comes over also as a battle in Hopkins to tie his human response to the elemental world with a plausible description of it theologically:

>   They fought with God's cold –
>   And they could not and fell to the deck
> (Crushed them) or water (and drowned them) or rolled
>   With the sea-romp over the wreck.
> Night roared, with the heart-break hearing a heart-broke rabble;
> The woman's wailing, the crying of child without check –
>   Till a lioness arose breasting the babble,
> A prophetess towered in the tumult, a virginal tongue told.
>
> (stanza 17)

The resulting language does indeed make us see the familiar world anew, and we have to put aside our subjective melancholies while doing so. Hopkins does not press the work of knowing,.which his Church takes care of, nor is there bewilderment at an unknown, for that is God, firmly claimed and stated. Yet, however innovatively one uses language, a major dimension of the language's innovative opportunity is gone if the individual words are always drawn from the setting of the writer's familiar world. Only what is nearby is named, and one's own feelings about it just slightly start to well up, whatever doctrine declaims about it beforehand. Unlike Shakespeare, Eliot and Pound, the individual words Hopkins chooses already have a relationship with each other by everyday usage. Their common association thus prevents the sharp edge of juxtaposition that would keep them apart at a strong level of meaning, as in the passage from Pound cited earlier. His innovations are brilliantly successful, but technical rather than semantic. This is no doubt why Pound in the end thought him overrated, although of course Pound was asking a lot and for a much wider programme. Hopkins's success, like that of Dylan Thomas, lies in the refreshing power he brings to a familiar language. Perhaps in reverse the critic J. Hillis Miller has put Hopkins's position as to language as succinctly as may be: 'For Hopkins, all things come together within language only to disperse'[20].

Intriguingly, Hopkins found himself greatly interested by the American poet Walt Whitman (1819–92) of whom he wrote – despite strong reservations of a different kind – that 'I always knew in my heart Walt Whitman's mind to be more like my own than any other man's living'[21]. Whitman too had a cornucopia of words still held integrated by the explicitly first-person voice which holds his long poem 'Song of Myself' together. Whitman acknowledged the poet and essayist Ralph Waldo Emerson as his master and was himself a strong influence on the whole later American tradition. In brief summary, Whitman's personal mood of energy moves him outward to a boundlessness, but there is an equally outward love of and relish for all things which takes need away for melancholic inward enquiry. To read his poetry is an exhilarating experience.

Part III

7
Thomas Hardy

For the English line we are identifying, the first quarter of the twentieth century was a major resurgence. There were of course chance factors, but it is still the clearest group of nature-based, plain-speech, inward poetry since the time of Wordsworth himself. No other group has appeared since until the 1950s and early 60s, when in Larkin, R. S. Thomas, Hughes and the early Heaney it looked as though a sort of rural version of the 'Movement' of the 50s might be forthcoming. That idea is still not wholly discountable for that period, although the three named poets still living have all long moved to other things. The dangers of canon imposition hover always, yet one discerns here by criteria of the mode of writing itself, a clear group, no group, and then a shadowy group, in three broad successive periods. For the earlier twentieth-century period one can first delineate some main considerations.

The poets are Hardy, Housman, Edward Thomas, Frost, and Owen a halfway case. Hardy and Frost would seem to qualify as major figures. Such poets make a continuity and a bridge from Romanticism itself to the present day, and enable one part of the current critical reaction to the Modernism of T. S. Eliot and Ezra Pound as the dominating presence in early twentieth-century English poetry. Prior to this reaction Donald Davie (though hardly with approval), Edna Longley and others had begun to suggest that Hardy in the one case, and Thomas and Frost in the other, were as important a poetic link as were Eliot and Pound[1].

Yet the position is complex, and it has long been seen in hindsight that a great struggle and indeed battle was going on for poetic legitimacy and supremacy. First, some distinctions between the poets themselves. Three of these poets, Hardy, Housman and Thomas, are notable for having other parallel and larger literary careers accompanying their poetic ones. Three of them, Housman, Owen and Thomas, wrote small

one-off (or two-off) bodies of poetry, somewhat like Gray and
Hopkins did. Two of them were war poets and were killed in
battle after extremely brief poetic careers. And most significant,
three of them, for the first time in this line, were either not
wholly or not at all English in birth and/or ancestry. Both
Thomas's parents were Welsh. Owen's father was, and Owen
was born in Wales and lived most of his short life on the
Welsh border. The position of Frost in this line seems one of
great significance, for he is for the first time a poet right away
from these shores who quite independently makes many of
these poetic attitudes his own. The intonation is a North
American one, so that through its association with a New
England work ethic the melancholic compulsion to knowing
tends towards a more positive laconic reflection.

This resurgence thus has another side to it. The broadly
straightforward English/middle-class prototype of the nineteenth century begins to be modified by the presence of other
cultural and national energies. The change begins to demonstrate this line's structural limitations, and even perhaps bring
on its termination, at the same time as it sets it up in sharper
profile as a clearly identifiable group of poets. It is too early
now to write the history of how a particularly English poetry
has been slowly attenuated by the arrival of American, Celtic
and now Caribbean influences both cultural and political,
making for the curious diversification within a poetry which
had hitherto seemed so homogeneous (this of course is quite
aside from the Modernist intervention itself, which aimed to
substitute a different poetry altogether). One noticeable feature
is that vernacular itself tends to be rich – ceases to be 'ordinary'
or 'familiar' – simply because more than one, perhaps several,
vernaculars can now be used at once, proliferating more questions per sentence, more imaginary futures, more scenarios.
And the conclusion more generally is that the poetry traced
in this book is ending, as political groups proliferate, there is
an international perspective, we become less country-conscious
than planet-conscious, and a world-attitude of authenticity and
openness to a quite inconceivable future makes nostalgia for
the past a luxury unless it turns into positive plans for saving
the earth at all. In this light Frost, Owen and MacNeice, as

much as Eliot and Pound if less obviously, modified poetry's future course.

However, that is to anticipate the later period. Historical factors and their accompanying ideologies were instrumental in precipitating the earlier twentieth-century group, and they were as far-reaching as were the features of a hundred years before, which derived from the French Revolution. First was the cluster of new scientific and technological factors associated not only with new evolutionary science but also with electricity, car, air transport, technologized medicine and numerous other allied things. Second was the Great War of 1914–18 which changed British domestic and political life for ever. Eliot's remark about the effect of the rhythm of the combustion engine on poetry is only a tiny dot in all that could be and has been said. How could a poetry of landscape meditation, ordinary language and inner depression expect to sound vibrant, purposeful and an authoritative poetry for the new age? To many, of course, it failed precisely in failing to do that very thing.

The literary battle, however, was wider than that. The reactions to Romanticism and Victorianism were now followed, in as disparate poets as Pound and Edward Thomas, by a reaction to what had itself been an anti-Romantic, anti-respectable Victorian reaction: late nineteenth-century so-called decadence[2]. Eliot and Pound took the continuity right back further than that, Eliot to the seventeenth century, Pound to Provençal and Italy. But this very emphasis on 'the mind of Europe', as opposed to what our line's poets might have called the mind of nature, may itself seem an over-reaching which was exactly what enabled this (narrowly defined) English line to proceed unmolested. Hardy remarked to Graves that in his opinion *vers libre* could come to nothing in England. 'All we can do is . . . write on the old themes in the old styles but try to do a little better than those who went before us.' Furthermore Hardy generalized the point: 'There is no new poetry, but the new poet comes with a new note'[3]. It suddenly sounds a quietly confident suggestion that the undertow poetry of the 'natural community' has only, ever, got to wait. Down to our own time, that is, when the very planet itself seems suddenly limited, and the world as electronic nervous system may be too great a force for even the ordinary voice, the earth under your feet and the inner unattained desire to overcome and poetically survive.

Thomas Hardy of Dorset (1840–1928)[4] was a major poet, one who remade and yet fully continues this kind of poetry, and who stands in it chronologically and structurally halfway between Wordsworth and Larkin and the poets still living now. His influences are wide, and his own notebooks and other writings show clear, if often implicit, influence of Wordsworth (especially the Preface) and *In Memoriam* as well as Browning, Shelley and Swinburne. He attested to the value he had found in Arnold's criticism.

He is particularly remarkable for having first pursued a career as architect and novelist; he did not publish his first book of poems until he was 58 years old. Hardy always wanted to be a poet first and foremost, and in fact wrote a fair proportion of his poetry in various phases in his earlier life. However it has been estimated that of his 900 or so collected poems probably fewer than 200 were written before his mid 50s. Thanks to a very long life, he nevertheless carried out in effect a full poetic career until his death in 1928 when he was 88. So, as far as his poetry goes, we can nearly see back to Hardy's world. Anyone now 60 was born only a little after Hardy died, and the world he touches on in his poems contains many details not in Victorian poetry let alone the Romantics: the car, telegraph wires, photographs, the esplanade on the sea-front with ladies with parasols and men bathing. Hardy was already 58 when his first book *Wessex Poems* was published in 1898, and the sense of an older time dead and gone pervades his poetry. Later books have poems on the sinking of the *Titanic*, the First World War and other events on this side of the Victorian age, when most of his poetry was published. And yet this change itself seems to elongate the same continuity with the past as before. We have said that a 60-year-old now would only just fail to overlap Hardy, but he himself once observed, with satisfaction, that Wordsworth could have looked into his (Hardy's) cradle and Gray into Wordsworth's[5]. It could have happened between many poets of course, but in

Hardy's poetry there is an imaginative bare sense of that long time's empty sweep and its dominance of human life.

There was both a shift from and continuity with the older tradition, though it is always clearly recognizable. On the one hand Hardy evinces an ironic detachment from his work's stories, scenes and contents, which might appear to do away with any surviving romantic and Victorian solipsism altogether. Yet the melancholic tone remains, and although the landscape is now bleak and unconsoling to the individual, it survives with a unity and integration which makes it seem reliable in the sense of permanent. This landscape seems always the same: a fair, a field, inside a pub, walking in a country lane, an old woman's house and her furniture, on a path by the sea, in drizzly rain, on a railway train, in fields with a milkmaid, trees on a windy day or in snow, and so on. It is of course Hardy's 'Wessex', which he painstakingly and lovingly created in a dozen novels. Furthermore the people in each poem seem to use, work or fit with that landscape uniquely and incidentally on each occasion. A widow sits hearing the rain and reflects on the fact that she no longer worries about her dead husband. Lovers walk in a rainy lane and the poet wonders who they are. Birds in a field are angry at finding no seed. The poet sees oxen in a stable on Christmas Eve and wishes he could believe in Christianity. A man is arrested on a country railway station and a small boy can't help him. The poet finds the burnt sticks left from a picnic camp fire in a previous year and reflects that the others who were there are dead. These incidents always put the human touch or fingerprint on nature that Hardy always insisted he looked for. Yet 'nature' still seemed to survive it, and indeed was given more meaning by it. The poems only occasionally leave this need to mingle people and landscape, to see more of the blank universe of which it is a part.

This landscape is seen rather than felt, and the poet does not, like Wordsworth, draw heart from the underlying natural world. Rather his emotion lies in his sense that this rural world, always there, does not provide answers, and that we live in it without understanding it. Consequently the apprehension is nearly always visual. There is no 'visionary gleam', and hardly a visionary dreariness. Rather it is, at first sight anyway, visual dreariness, the visual sense detached. The result is that the wider mysterious realities of time and space are merely where things occur; they are not themselves felt to be the source of what occurs, and therefore many poems are in effect isolated within them, brief moments, fleeting incidents. The titles of some of Hardy's collections, like *Moments of Vision* and *Human Shows*, make clear his own visual compulsion, as does one of his best-known poems 'Afterwards', in which he reflects on whether he will be remembered as someone who 'noticed such things'.

Apart from some of the ballad stories like 'A Trampwoman's Tragedy' or explicitly philosophical workings through positions as in 'The Absolute Explains', large numbers of Hardy's poems take place in a single scene, briefly and even fleetingly witnessed. In 'A Night in November' dead leaves blow in through the window of the poet's bedroom. When one touches him in the dark he thinks it is his wife's hand, until he remembers that she is dead. In 'The Garden Seat', a rather eerie poem of only twelve short lines, the seat's legs are seen to sink into the soft lawn as people sit on it, but when people who previously sat on it return, it stays firm, because they are weightless ghosts. Possibly the most explicit case is 'On the Departure Platform'. It begins:

> We kissed at the barrier; and passing through
> She left me, and moment by moment got
> Smaller and smaller, until to my view
>   She was but a spot;
>
> A wee white spot of muslin fluff
> That down the diminishing platform bore
> Through hustling crowds of gentle and rough
>   To the carriage door . . .
>
> Then show again, till I ceased to see
> That flexible form, that nebulous white;
> And she who was more than my life to me
>   Had vanished quite . . .

She is hidden behind the crowd, then reappears again, 'a wee white spot of muslin fluff', and finally vanishes altogether. In

'The Phantom Horsewoman' Hardy is more explicit about the nature of this 'seeing', its quality and its eyesight. The poet himself is object of surmise by others who witness his bewildered staring across the sand on the beach:

> They say he sees as an instant thing
>> More clear than to-day,
>> A sweet soft scene
>> That was once in play
>> By that briny green . . .

But this is a 'phantom of his own figuring', and

> Yea, far from that shore
> Does he carry this vision of heretofore:
>
> A ghost-girl-rider.

This is one of the *Poems of 1912–13* about the death of Hardy's wife Emma Gifford, and his statement of it in terms of physical seeing of her, places where they have walked, her clothes and so on is obsessive.

In a large number of poems however, these moments of immediate vision are seen twice. Two viewpoints are given on one scene or incident. This is what J. Hillis Miller has called Hardy's 'double vision', the seeing of any event or matter from two angles at once, neither having priority[6]. One example was given at the start of this book, 'A Thought in two Moods'. The other thought in that poem, we notice, was reached independently by two people. Two other very clear-cut examples are 'In Church' and 'Life and Death at Sunrise'. In the first poem a clergyman preaches an impassioned and emotive sermon which wins his congregation's hearts for its sincerity and depth. Afterwards a girl sees him in the vestry through the half-opened door. He is going through the sermon again, in front of a mirror, with a smug smile on his face. In the second poem a horseman and a drayman pass each other going in opposite directions in a country lane at dawn. The rider says happily that his wife has just given birth to a boy. The drayman is bringing the body of an old man to his funeral.

A highly dramatic case is 'The Convergence of the Twain', which Hardy wrote for a programme of performances for the disaster fund in May 1912 for the victims of the *Titanic* disaster. The poem traces the two inexorable and independent courses, exactly balanced, of the ship and the iceberg to the very instant of their collision.

In every case the story or idea is seen from two points of view, not one, and furthermore the two seem to be evenly matched. The reader is left with neither dominating the other. And one can begin to see why Hardy's thought is drawn to this doubling-up effect on so many occasions. Hardy's visual landscape is so homogenous that these double-seeings do not seem to suggest a conflict-politics at root. Undoubtedly Hardy held strong political views about English society, in which he suffered humiliation more than once on account of his lowly origins and lack of formal education. Yet such politics commonly in poetry can fragment life altogether, as in *The Waste Land*, where in the end little is left static at all. But the conflict in Hardy's poetry is more metaphysical, and its materials by no means always political ones. If life consists mainly of these fleetingly seen impressions, how are we to evaluate them and reach any kind of philosophy of existence or of ourselves? Hardy's work, both poetry and diaries, is permeated with Wordsworth, yet he was suspicious of that poet's fuller apprehensions. He said once that his aim was to record impressions, not convictions. Wordsworth in his later years had excessively recorded convictions.[7] Hardy has poems of wider reflection, like 'God's Education' and 'The Absolute Explains', but they are seldom elaborations of these fleeting double-glimpses.

In some poems the fifty-fifty matching is attained by an equal distribution of content, as in 'In Church', where the two equal-size stanzas give the two versions of the picture. In others it is attained by the equal significance of two angles on the matter. In some poems, for example, the twist comes in the last stanza and the effect ripples back up the poem, redoubling the implications of what went before. In 'One We Knew' Hardy recalls his own childhood and his grandmother telling stories of life in her own even more distant past. The turn at the end comes when the poet reflects that to her they were memories, while to himself and his brothers and sisters they are history. A briefer example is 'She Hears the Storm':

There was a time in former years –
    While my roof-tree was his –
When I should have been distressed by fears
    At such a night as this!

I should have murmured anxiously,
    'The pricking rain strikes cold;
His road is bare of hedge or tree,
    And he is getting old.'

But now the fitful chimney-roar,
    The drone of Thorncombe trees,
The Froom in flood upon the moor,
    The mud of Mellstock Leaze,

The candle slanting sooty-wick'd
    The thuds upon the thatch,
The eaves-drops on the window flicked,
    The clacking garden-hatch,

And what they mean to wayfarers,
    I scarcely heed or mind;
He has won that storm-tight roof of hers
    Which Earth grants all her kind.

The 'double vision' is clearly signposted by the opposition between 'there was a time . . . I should have murmured' and 'but now . . . I scarcely heed', both sets starting at a new stanza. The point of the contrast however is kept to the end. Other poems with this clear double vision are 'A Thunderstorm In Town', 'Near Lanivet 1872', 'The Sunshade', 'Throwing a Tree', 'The Wind's Prophecy', 'The Children and Sir Nameless', 'Afternoon Service at Mellstock', 'The Walk', 'The Lament', 'At a Country Fair' and 'The Curate's Kindness', and there are many more.

Hillis Miller suggests the main theme of this duality in the poetry generally is the distinction between present and past. Certainly many poems carry this contrast. A very successful example is 'During Wind and Rain', where picnic scenes of happy young people are remembered years later. The refrain

in each stanza sees the garden where they met now rotting
and the rain running down their gravestones. 'Where the
Picnic was' is similar. But the dualistic elements are more
diverse than simply present and past. Harold Bloom says they
lament the 'hopeless incongruity of ends and means in all
human acts' and Dennis Taylor the ever-likely 'jarring discord
of mind and world'[8] instead of the continuous flow of life so
pronounced in Wordsworth and indeed Arnold, commonly
symbolized in their poetry by running water. Hardy's poetry
often refers to the sea, and to rain, but his watery imagery
seems to mean greyness and colourlessness as well as the
unity that science has to assume if nature is to be investigated.
Consequently the theme in these double-vision poems is various. It is past and present, what is and what might have been,
your thought and my thought, real and imaginary, quick time
and slow time, rich people and poor people, conceited people
and humble people, life and death, what we know and what
we don't. What completes an incident for one person is unfinished business for another. What we thought the whole story
a moment ago is suddenly reversed by a final factor. What
seemed the case about a living person seems the opposite
when they die.

Despite this duality the poems usually take place in one
scene or one incident. The significance is that, in showing two
aspects of this and offering no conclusion, a profound irony
is presented. Again we are encountering a common English-
line theme, that of knowing and not-knowing. The poems
enact an irony of not-knowing in a context where one feels
understanding and knowledge are what are sought. The melancholic sense of limited understanding, and the sad and
sometimes hopeless search for remedies which pervades the
English line poets, is equally diffused across Hardy's body of
poetry. Indeed one might say there is hardly a poem that is
not marked by its shadowy presence.

In 'At Lulworth Cove', for example, we hear of a man who
beached there a hundred years before, but the speaker did not
know it was John Keats. In 'The Fallow Deer at the Lonely
House' the deer's eyes peer in through the window but the
people inside by the fireside do not know it. This sitting inside
looking out was found in Coleridge as we saw and it also

appears in Frost. In 'The Darkling Thrush', set in a bleak twilight scene on the last day of the century, the poet suddenly hears the compelling tones of a thrush. The poem ends longing that this bird had 'Some blessed Hope, whereof he knew/ And I was unaware'. The contrast with the confidence that underlies Shelley's rapturous response to the skylark is marked. It is equally marked in 'Autumn in King's Hintock Park', where the swirling coloured leaves of Shelley's 'Ode to the West Wind' are swept up again and again by an old woman park-keeper (the refrain is 'raking up leaves') in sad ignorance of any inspiriting transcendental power they might bear. Shelley's well-attested precursorship of Hardy, one feels here, is a matter of an attitude he had to turn inside out, like a jacket, rather than renewing it but in his own mode. In 'A Light Snow-Fall after Frost' the poet ends thinking that although

> The road was brown, and now is starkly white,
> A watcher would have failed defining quite
> When it transformed it so.

In poem after poem the meaning, the actual nature of what is perceived or apprehended, is this not-knowing element, this leaving the matter as a sad blank as to our powers of understanding the world we inhabit and even seem to dominate. Hardy was led to these attitudes by being aware of the ambivalent benefits of science in the new world of aspiration to social amelioration. It gave him the reputation of pessimism. He denied this, in the Preface to *Late Lyrics and Earlier* particularly, and certainly his reading in the social meliorists of the century such as Spencer, Comte and Mill was very wide.

But if his denial is to stand up to scrutiny, then it must be taken that he meant to say that social or any amelioration based on merely material provision is unlikely to be successful. A further human understanding of the wider existential situation is needed, and it is far from certain, in Hardy's cold cosmic world, that it could ever be reached. The disconnection between humans is shown not only by their mutually different stances towards any incident, but by the fleeting nature of those incidents themselves. It was as though all had become disconnected, and the collapse of the traditional world-view through biological and astronomical advances and by the disruptive effect of industrialization on communities has left the community inhabiting the same world as before, but now incomprehensible. This might be tied to what has been said about the role of blindness in the vocation of the poet. Hardy's acute physical perception itself seems to understand the presence of what cannot be seen; a sense that, not only are we blind, but the earth is too, like a dead eyeball, and perhaps the entire cosmos as well. Early in *In Memoriam* (poem 3) Tennyson had expressed the identical fears.

Blindness, greyness and colourless scenes and writing are endemic in English-line poetry. In a living world it would be as though, if one responds positively to flowers, or the other sex, or the sea, you feel they are somehow receiving the sunlight on them as well, so bringing out their colours, as Wallace Stevens always did. This colourful radiance is the point of Shelley's lines:

> Life, like a dome of many-coloured glass
> Stains the white radiance of Eternity,
> Until Death tramples it to fragments.
> (Adonais, 462–4)

But Hardy's poetry is black-and-white, or indeed grey, like the early photography with which it was contemporaneous. Colour is absent in all but a very few poems, such as 'A Thought in two Moods', 'A Light Snow-Fall after Frost' and 'The Sunshade'. This last poem makes the point well, for its double title (sun and shade) is spelt out in the story, in which the poet comes across the ribbed skeleton of a very old sunshade on the beach. He wonders whether its owner too is now in her grave, all her bloom gone like that of the sunshade's coloured panels. As I said earlier, Hardy's watery imagery of fog and rain seems to establish not only unity but also greyness; it irons out the clear colours of the spectrum.

This irony is not only uncoloured; it is also infertile. The dual vision of or two attitudes toward one incident can't marry, can't be understanding's parentage. And so the community cannot go forward. Again and again in Hardy's poems lovers and married pairs have no children, or we hear of none. When they do they are often illegitimate, or accompanied by an unnatural death. In the longer ballads 'A Sunday Morning Tragedy' and 'A Trampwoman's Tragedy' (both from *Time's Laughingstocks*) the complication of an unborn child leads to disaster. In the first of these the man leaves despite his betrothed's pregnancy. Conscience-stricken he returns, but by then she and the unborn child have died of the herb 'meant to balk ill-motherings' a shepherd has given her. In the second poem a pregnant girl flirts with another man – 'jeering John' – in front of her betrothed when they are in a group on a walk and have reached a tavern. Deliberately teasing him she hints that it might have gone further than this.

> Inside the settle all a-row –
>   All four a-row
> We sat, I next to John, to show
>   That he had wooed and won.
> And then he took me on his knee,
> And swore it was his turn to be
> My favoured mate, and Mother Lee
>   Passed to my former one.
>
> Then in a voice I had never heard,
>   I had never heard,
> My only Love to me: "One word,
>   My lady, if you please!
> Whose is the child you are like to bear? –
> *His?* After all my months o' care?"
> God knows 'twas not! But, O Despair!
>   I nodded – still to tease.

Here the irony is compounded, for this wretched lover now doesn't know whether his 'care' has failed, so that he has a prospective illegitimate child, or has succeeded, so that her child must be another man's. In anguish the lover stabs the flirting rival, and on the day he is hanged for murder the girl (in whose voice the story is told) 'drops his dead-born child'. The poem's lilting rhythm and second-line refrain are deeply ironic, for you want to sing it chantingly, making the agony of the story hover behind you like a shadow.

It seems there is a continuous allegory here between the sterile unions of lovers and Hardy's own world-view, which is congenital to the English line for much of its course. Hardy's marriage was deeply unhappy, he had affairs outside it, and a second marriage but no children by either of them. There is an impotent mood across the poetry, but not, it seems, through failure to reach women individually. The lack is of procreation or new life, and the writing contains the ambivalent question as to how much in the world he saw Hardy wanted such a thing. The histories of Coleridge's equally unhappy marriage to Sara Fricker, Clare's necessary separation from his family, Tennyson's fears of insanity in his wife's ancestry, Edward Thomas's distressing marriage too, Housman's homosexuality unrequited by the one lover he really wanted, MacNeice's marital separation, and finally Larkin's deeply ambivalent attitude toward the married state he did not wish for yet the loneliness that resulted – all these amount to a metaphor for an unproductive social organization based on the bourgeois family and its idealized bliss, and the world they inhabited seen newly by science as a dead thing in an empty planet with no development other than by routine organic laws. The expulsion of Adam and Eve from paradise's garden, that is from home, lies in the background.

All of this is doubtless connected with morbidity, which characterize Wordsworth and Tennyson too, as well as, it should be said, Browning. Early in his life Hardy was fascinated by public hangings. In one he witnessed, the woman's body was seen swinging and vulnerable, its sexual aspects in gruesome evidence. At first the executioner failed to tie down the condemned woman's dress to prevent it swirling up in the wind, and had to reascend the scaffold to do this properly[9]. This incident may have been unconsciously behind the half-funny, half-chilling poem 'In the Days of Crinoline' which appears in perhaps Hardy's most socially conscious collection,- *Satires of Circumstance*. An imperceptive country rector is gardening and sees his wife go off for a walk wearing 'a plain tilt-bonnet on her head'. He is secretly relieved at this plainness:

A plain tilt-bonnet on her head
She took the path across the leaze.
– Her spouse the vicar, gardening, said,
'Too dowdy that, for coquetries,
    So I can hoe at ease.'

But when she had passed into the heath,
And gained the wood beyond the flat,
She raised her skirts, and from beneath
Unpinned and drew as from a sheath
    An ostrich-feathered hat.

And where that hat had hung she now
Concealed and pinned the dowdy hood,
And set the hat upon her brow,
And thus emerging from the wood
    Tripped on in jaunty mood . . .

Having met her town lover and returned to the wood with
him, she goes home alone, the two hats restored to their
original places. Her husband the rector greets her with a brief
homily on modesty and 'as a recompense/ He kissed her on
the cheek'. (The kiss is usually the symbol of incomplete or
unsatisfied love in Hardy, the novels as well as the poems[10].
The kiss may seal the fact of a love affair but it engenders
nothing.)

Psychoanalytically the two hats under the dress might seem
to be phallic symbols for the two men's relative sexual powers.
But equally by their proximity to the womb they could stand
for the unborn children of either. That latter reading would
mean that the more glamorous hat (the one not under the
dress during the love-tryst) would stand for abortion. In a
community with rigid marital conventions liaisons outside marriage can only produce children destined, physically or socially, not to survive. As with the doomed hanging woman, it
is only morbid association that sees the body as both evoking
desire and deserving punishment. (Edward Thomas's poem
'As the Team's Head Brass', written in 1916, could have been
influenced by this poem. The Hardy collection containing it
appeared in 1914 and Thomas did review some of Hardy's
work, though apparently not this book. In Thomas's poem

two lovers also enter a wood, unnoticed by the ploughmen talking.) The two hats are clearly Hardy's double vision again, two attitudes to sexual activity, but in this case made strongly symbolic.

The question then arises of where such poetry stands in this English line. Such poets up to Hardy have felt nature, real or idealized, to be the source of emotional sustenance and philosophy for human beings. They have felt that distress comes when the inner self is cut loose from nature. They have felt that, with and from nature, there can be a very present ego which shapes its broodings themselves into language, making mind and feeling themselves the medium of the art. How can Hardy's detached ironies be such material, even if the strong features of the landscape, the melancholy of death and the language of ordinary people remain?

What happens is that, although ironic, Hardy seems to be haunted by the absence of direct melancholy itself. He still feels it ought to be there, and the poems convey this. His responses are ironic but not heartless. He is trying to keep the irony detached but is really throbbing with feeling himself. Irony occurs, not as a sort of instant entertaining wit, but as a resulting truncation of expansive response to the universe. That itself is a melancholic condition, but it can get the kind of throwaway melancholic expression Hardy gives it. The poetic expression of this melancholic irony lies in Hardy's stance toward death. He once made a remark which haunts the poems: 'For my part, if there is any way of getting a melancholy satisfaction out of life, it lies in dying, so to speak, before one is out of the flesh; by which I mean putting on the manners of ghosts, wandering in their haunts, and taking their views of surrounding things'[11]. By this bleak means Hardy can relate not only to loved people who have died, but also to a spiritual and non-material world such as he can only conceive it to be. It is as though only by being or feeling dead can Hardy rejoin nature, rejoin the natural world which scientists of the nineteenth century have themselves come to see as dead, as so much real estate or mineral floating through a godless empty void. The detachment of the neutral observer, like the camera, is a dead thing; the emotion in Hardy lies in the depth of his response to this sobering fact.

When Hardy's characters are dead, they are *already* dead. There are very few poems about the approach to death, or dying itself. This is well illustrated in an early poem, 'A Wife in London', subtitled 'December 1899'. A woman in her house in London receives a telegram to say her husband has been killed (presumably in the Boer War). The next day the postman brings a letter posted before the husband's death:

Fresh – firm – penned in highest feather –
  Page–full of his hoped return,
  And of home-planned jaunts by brake and burn
In the summer weather,
  And of new love that they would learn.

Yet another double-vision poem, but the poignant feature is that the death comes first. The arc or curve of classical tragedy would have been the other way round. The high hopes of the letter would have come first, all to crumble in tragedy and grief afterwards. Here it is reversed, and we are in not the tragic but the existential world. The woman's feeling is therefore not an optimistic joy brought crashing down, for since yesterday afternoon at least it was never up. We are forced to imagine her sitting reading the words as though *already* empty of feeling, for the words themselves, the hopes and glorious loves they express, are themselves already dead. And again, since the poem does not spell this out, we the readers are likely to be the more convinced of the truth, since to grasp the poem at all we have to supply the inference ourselves. The implication is that we can share such feelings which we might also call pessimistic.

Yet, surprisingly, in a world without pinnacles of worth to climb or aspirations toward a transcendent morality or godhead, this feeling can be one of intense relief. A huge burden is lifted. The broken-backed poems of the double vision avoid the oppressive poetic worthiness that sub-romantic imitations had displayed through multitudinous magazines of the Victorian era. Much later Larkin was able to write about his switch of allegiance from Yeats to Hardy: 'Hardy gave (later poets) confidence to feel in their own way. When I came to Hardy it was with the sense of relief that I didn't have to try and jack myself up to a concept of poetry that lay outside my own life'[12]. This sense of removal of burden occurs too in some of the poems Hardy wrote in which the house seems to contain a ghost, or the dead speak. They aren't necrophiliac in the ordinary sense. In 'Who's in the Next Room?' and 'The Ghost of the Past' the ghosts, such as they are, are surviving unnamed presences who offer companionship. Hardy seems to join with them in their pastness, their goneness. In 'Channel Firing' the noises of guns are heard in the English Channel as naval vessels prepare for the war Hardy prophetically guessed at. The skeletons in the churchyard regret man's folly while God – feeling hardly adequate himself – is sympathetic to their need for rest from human troubles.

'Friends Beyond' is the most explicit case. One by one the dead characters who 'lie in Mellstock churchyard now', from William Dewey and Tranter Reuben to 'the Squire and Lady Susan', express this release and the new serene and curiously open-eyed calm it brings:

> 'We have triumphed: this achievement turns the bane to
> antidote,
> Unsuccesses to success,
> Many thought-worn eves and morrows to a morrow free of
> thought . . .
> Fear of death has even bygone us: death gave all that we
> possess.'
> (lines 10–12; 15)

One by one they list the possessions that no longer matter: corn, clothing, Lady Susan's rich brocades, lace, household keys, contents of bureau and desk, and they do not even mind if their wives remarry or children forget them. Another group of poems about death, if in a different context, is the *Poems of 1912–13*, written just after the death of Hardy's first wife Emma. They are not elegies in the normal sense. Rather, through his ostensible grappling with the bewilderment and remorse he feels at the unhappiness they had shared, and the suddenness of their final separation, Hardy seems to be able to draw on a sense that, now that she is dead, it is over and can be viewed in perspective. He can return to his beloved seeing; his images of her in her 'air-blue gown' at a party, riding on the sands, walking up the hillside or tending her rose garden.

Connected with all this detached, bleak, ironic but deeply sad poetry is the much-debated question of Hardy's language. This raises the question of the ways in which it is the 'ordinary language' these poets commonly aim at. Hardy's language is at varying times awkward, rustic, puritanically simple, loosely-slung and throw-away. As one very short poem begins, 'Any little old song will do'. The phrase seems to echo one from a very fine and typical poem 'The Contretemps'. A man and woman, complete strangers, run into each other on a foggy lamp-lit bridge at night and nearly embrace each other, each thinking the other to be the lover or mistress they had arranged to meet there. They decide they might as well continue the unexpected match anyway, for where all is venture 'One pairing is as good as another'. But there is an even closer sense of 'throw-away'. In 'A Wife In London' the wife gets the letter after the husband is dead. Letter becomes litter; it is worthless at least as far as prediction is concerned. It is characteristic of Hardy never to make entities into symbols very calculatedly, as Joyce does with his 'throwaway' leaflet in *Ulysses*. Rather, litter returns to the soil or gets used up. Hardy is the first writer to be major in both poetry and novel, and we know that many of his poems are already fragmentary in origin, in being scenes or incidents first collected for novels but then not used. It was the Modernist Ezra Pound who perceptively recognized Hardy's poetic achievement and accurately located its sources: 'Now *there* is a clarity. There *is* the harvest of having written 20 novels first'[13]. The poems are the litter, beer cans, crisp bags, they rot back down into the earth whence they came, the small carelessness or defects of Hardy's poetic vision.

Then there is Hardy's supposed clumsiness. He invents words and inverts grammar awkwardly, often to get a rhyme. But the clumsiness is deliberate. As John Carey put it of some of Donne, 'though he liked joining things he also liked the joint to show'[14]. In 'The Five Students' each stanza recalls how at a different season of the year the original group of five

friends is diminished by one, presumably by death. The first
and last stanzas read:

> The sparrow dips in his wheel-rut bath,
> The sun grows passionate-eyed,
> And boils the dew to smoke by the paddock-path;
> As strenuously we stride, –
> Five of us, dark He, fair He, dark She, fair She, I,
> All beating by . . .

> Icicles tag the church-aisle leads,
> The flag-rope gibbers hoarse,
> The home-bound foot-folk wrap their snow-flaked heads,
> Yet I still stalk the course, –
> One of us . . . Dark and fair He, dark and fair She, gone:
> The rest – anon.

One might say 'hoarse' should be 'hoarsely' and that 'Yet I
still stalk the course' is an inappropriate phrase used for its
rhyme only. Yet it barely seems to matter, for stanza and
indeed poem make no attempt at concealment. What strikes
one is the several pairs of hyphenated words, some of which
at least could have been replaced by single ones – 'halyard'
and 'people' for 'flag-rope' and 'foot-folk' for example. But
most of all there is the very stark, jerky refrain, which makes
for a countdown from five to one only, presumably the poet,
by the end. And in not seeming to mind what it looks like
the poem anticipates much modern design, where buildings
leave their girders and central heating pipes intentionally visible, and stitches are not hidden on jeans or indeed much
informal clothing. The language is not only somehow provisional; its work-processes are apparent, just as when in agri-
culture or the building trade cattle-troughs and bales of straw
are left about and piles of breeze-block and sand can't be put
away every night.

But the individual word is also craggy, and this is another
aspect of the matter. Tom Paulin puts this language of Hardy's
in a tradition he sees as Northern and consonantal, having 'a
fricative, spiky, spoken texture', a 'populist delight in rough,
scratchy sounds'. These are solid words – not just 'thought

and feeling' – but they retain physical ordinariness instead. They feel like bits of flint, broken gate-posts, bits of stubble. It is as though Hardy is defying them to be 'poetic' in an over-refined sense. Ralph Elliott has done an exhaustive study of this language, finding either Saxon roots or Hardy's own coinages in such words as: flexuous, fulth, orts, chine, outskeleton, fellow-like, a breath-while, indwell, dolorifuge, liberticide, 'checkless griff', bandy, boaming, stoor, nabs[15]. These features, along with the strange loosely-slung feel of the poems, allowed Hardy to avoid any sense of the too-accomplished. Again this last anticipates the loose edges of modern urban life too, its casual slipping from coffee bar to provincial bus-station to digs to motorway, its broken-up strenuous music.

Much light is thrown on all this by certain remarks Hardy himself made about poetry and his aims in it. He said once that poetry must be made of what is ugly, of nature's defects. But this also meant that to seem to achieve naturalness poetry's language must not be too fine or polished. 'The whole secret of a living style and the difference between it and a dead style, lies in not having too much style – being, in fact, a little careless, or rather seeming to be, here and there. It brings wonderful life into the writing'. 'The ultimate aim of the poet should be to touch our hearts by showing his own, and not to exhibit his learning, or his fine taste'[16]. Numerous critics have recorded this strange sense, that Hardy's poetry at first seemed so bad and then turned out good. Virginia Woolf wrote, 'It is on the face of it so bad, yet it achieves its aim so unmistakably'. Eliot curtly dismissed Hardy as too much a dweller on emotion not intellect, yet could say too that 'at times his style touches sublimity without ever having passed through the stage of being good'. Leavis acknowledged the same more fully. 'It might reasonably be concluded [on this evidence that Hardy] couldn't possibly be a distinguished writer of any kind. Nevertheless, it is an unusually dull patch when half-a-dozen pages don't yield instances (of) a decided expressive strength and clarity.' And firmly and sharply Katherine Anne Porter: 'What could be duller? What could be more laboured? Except for this in my memory: I have seen it. I was there'[17].

Larkin, Hardy's most uncompromising champion, felt such

remarks were patronizing. Yet one hears perhaps in these
critics as much the voice of bewilderment, which is at least
honest enough to acknowledge a success it would really have
preferred to be impossible. It is all most reminiscent of the
same kind of response to Wordsworth. John Stuart Mill called
Wordsworth 'the poet of unpoetical natures' and the feminist
Harriet Martineau decides in her autobiography that 'with all
their truth and all their charm, few of Wordsworth's pieces
are poems'[18]. And yet in both cases the context shows quite
undeniably they both had the greatest regard for Wordsworth's
poetry and indeed personal indebtedness to it. Hardy has
made a comparable impact, although it is the legitimacy of
clumsiness and awkwardness rather than Wordsworth's firmer
egalitarian claim to subjectivity and elevation that is his work's
justification.

This quality of the language, like bits and pieces where 'any
old word will do', on a level untidy landscape where nothing
particularly dominates, of field, bridge, path, church and barn,
is possibly behind another feature on which many later poets
have remarked. This is the sameness and evenness of the
whole. Both Larkin and the contemporary poet Vernon Scan-
nell have noted that you can go up and down the 900 or so
collected poems and still find a new surprise, one you hadn't
noticed; just the same as before, but with some different twist
or scene or touch. This is the invariant personality that the
main English line poets of this kind usually seek to express,
although Tennyson and Arnold, as was said, are distracted
from it by their classical and mythological dispositions. In
Hardy the level sameness is projected on to the level landscape, seen and witnessed. His integration of fragments, half-
understood scenes, familiar and unexceptionable landscape,
death, sadness and curiously dog-eared yet true language is
the mark of the twentieth-century world that we have
inhabited.

Donald Davie has said that Hardy's poems do not transform
their material, and so take out from poetry one of its most
honourable traditional functions, that of showing a world truer
and more real than the one we know from commonsense,
statistics and the everyday[19]. Yet Hardy surely has been the
central force in virtually establishing another equally central

function. Hardy renders back the world in which we do live, but includes in it what seems to be its deepest collective mood as that is not ordinarily visible to most people. The ironic melancholy and the deeply unsatisfied desires turn into a haunting music, and that has always been a main characteristic of the English line poets.

8
A. E. Housman, Wilfred Owen and Edward Thomas

A. E. Housman was a classics don of acerbic and sometimes hurtful wit who wrote a small body of poetry of almost pure feeling. He was born in 1859 and brought up in a respectable country home in Worcestershire, the son of a solicitor. At St John's College, Oxford, having got a first class in the first part of his degree examinations (Moderations) he failed his finals (Greats), a result scarcely credible in terms of his real abilities, despite what we gather of how he went about classical studies as an undergraduate. At Oxford he conceived a homosexual love for a fellow-undergraduate Moses Jackson; this love was reciprocated but through Jackson's unwillingness almost certainly never sexually requited, and all his life Housman never got over it. Housman then worked for ten years in the Patent Office in London; but next, as the result of doing brilliant classical textural criticism and emendation in the evenings and publishing the results, was elected Professor of Latin at University College, London, in 1892. Housman stayed at this post until 1911, when he was elected Kennedy Professor of Latin at Cambridge and Fellow of Trinity College there, where he remained for the rest of his life. His poetic fame rests on two short works: *A Shropshire Lad*, published in 1896, and *Last Poems* no less than 26 years later in 1922, and one famous lecture, 'The Name and Nature of Poetry', delivered in Cambridge in 1933. Other poems were edited and published by his brother Laurence Housman after Alfred's death in 1936[1].

Housman is the poet of pain; he also said that to him poetry is of feeling not intellect, and that it is physical. In his lecture he said of part of Milton's 'Lycidas' that it reduced him to tears without his knowing why. It may be that the lack of range and size which many people feel limit the quality of his poetry, is essential to it. The diminutive character and the overwhelming intensity of the poems are aspects of the same thing. Pain could be seen as an experience which usually has very small instrumentation. The pain from a needle point is as great as that from being hit by a brick or stone. That is a crude analogy which can generate many countering examples, but it does point us in the direction our responses to Housman are likely to have to take.

Pain from a needle point is, perhaps, a comparable experience to that of feeling a shiver down the spine, water in the eyes or goose pimples on the flesh – all examples that Housman himself famously gave of poetry's effect in 'The Name and Nature of Poetry'. Though varying in degree of pain, all are recognizable, local, single and highly physical experiences. A comparable if less painful one is taking a tot of Scotch. In describing Blake as 'the most poetical of all poets' Housman characterized Blake's songs as 'poetry neat'. His own poems have such an effect:

Shake hands, we shall never be friends, all's over;
    I only vex you the more I try.
All's wrong that ever I've done or said,
And nought to help it in this dull head:
    Shake hands, here's luck, good-bye.

But if you come to a road where danger
    Or guilt or anguish or shame's to share,
Be good to the lad that loves you true
And the soul that was born to die for you,
    And whistle and I'll be there.
                          (*More Poems* XXX)

This very personal poem is like so many of Housman's poems. Its plain language, with only eight words of more than one syllable in the entire poem, makes the sharp pain all the sharper; 'born to die'; the way 'danger' enters a small thrill because of its previous half-rhyme 'over'; and the 'whistle' at

the end, as though to an abject dog. But it all hangs round
three words: 'Be good to . . .'. He doesn't say, don't worry,
I'll be there, but *please* let me be there, even in danger. Many
of his poems quickly reach their moments of finality, as this
does: 'Shake hands . . . all's over'. They sometimes emphasize
their own brevity, as in 'Tell me not here, it needs not saying'.
Many of his last lines are sharp passings away of events,
feelings or ideas, never to return: 'That hanged himself for
love', 'But you will die today', 'And cannot come again'. The
plain terms suggest a deliberate lack of expansiveness, cliché
coming in naturally as though to tie that feeling to common
human experience, as here: 'the lad that loves you true', 'born
to die for you'. As so often in such poetry, this means that
'puns' (always an inadequate word for this in such mode,
suggesting as it does clear-edged verbal jokes) even when
common, are latent, part of a more general ambiguity. Until
he was dissuaded by a friend, Housman wondered whether
to publish his first book anonymously under the name 'Terence
Hearsay'. The surname is a double pun, both echoing 'Housman' and also saying that it is an echo: 'Housman' is 'heard
said'. But the pun is seldom tied to so specific a noun. In the
well-known poem 'Loveliest of trees, the cherry now', the
cherries are cherished, and in the last line in winter they are
'hung' with snow. The same morbidity there as Hardy's about
hangings can scarcely fail to be heard since Housman's own
preoccupation with death, including that by punishment and
in war, lies blackly underneath the whole work. There is
another quiet pun in this poem 'Shake hands', for it seems
that where 'whistle' is like calling a dog, it is also wistfully
accepted by the poet.

Another feature, curiously common in these poems, is the
mood of injunction; in strict grammatical terms, the imperative
mood. He has a tendency to *tell* the person addressed what
to do, how to feel, what attitude to take. But as with many,
the power of the present poem lies in the ironic contrast
between these injunctions to shake hands and to whistle, with
the sad sexual servitude that is beneath them. The poems
enjoin stoicism, courage or just seeing. Arguably a puritanical
reduction is present in this, but the Victorian and Edwardian
don and schoolmaster in the Victorian class system is also

being turned inside out, and indeed commonly a reason for the command follows it. In the ubiquitous quatrain, there are commonly two lines of command and two of proverbial support:

> Leave your home behind you,
>   Your friends by field and town:
> Oh, town and field will mind you
>   Till Ludlow tower is down.
>   (*A Shropshire Lad* III)

A third characteristic of Housman's poetry is the obsession with death. Yet the word 'death' is very rare. Command, end of love or its unfulfilment are repeatedly marked but by a lying in the grave which is itself expressed not directly but by poetic innuendo. The most prevalent, not surprisingly, is the (inexplicit) comparison with lying in the dark with lover or mistress, a deep coupling of love and sleep with death which is at the heart of Housman's own obsessions and perhaps his homosexuality. Again, as with Hardy, one sees this English line's decreasing wish for procreation in an increasingly populated world, a theme in Larkin and later in others. By the poetic innuendo or unsaying, the fertile seed is turned away from its apposite final resting-place just as the poetic statement of lying in the grave is turned away from saying that thing itself:

> Lovers lying two by two
>   Ask not whom they sleep beside,
> And the bridegroom all night through
>   Never turns him to the bride.
>   (*ASL* XII)

> When I shall sleep with clover clad,
> And she beside another lad.
>   (*ASL* XXVI)

This coupling or absence of coupling is verbally matched by the many small tensions or oppositions, usually taking a 'couplet' each themselves. They express the tensions Housman felt in his own life: public life and illicit love, emotional poetry and intellectual textual criticism, life and death, scholarship and nature, what was and what now is gone. The form 'A but B' in the third and fourth lines of the quatrain is extremely frequent:

> The heart of man has long been sore
> And long 'tis like to be.
>   (*Last Poems* XXXV)

But the different characteristic in Housman is the huge risk he takes of saying nothing at all by drawing back and back from any familiar natural world and so risking self-extinction in the obsession with the grave. In 'The Name and Nature of Poetry' Housman himself said that poetry is, in effect, about nothing: 'Even Shakespeare, who had so much to say, would sometimes pour out his loveliest poetry in saying nothing'. Edmund Wilson, in what is still one of the best essays there is on Housman, suggested that the poet's classical scholarship allowed nothing to grow; it was 'the discovery of things that are already there'. This entails that the knowing/not-knowing tendency through the English line is present in Housman only as a bitter absence, itself part of the universal tragedy. His elaboration is monosyllabic, and like Lewis Carroll's *Alice* his poetry lives in a looking-glass world 'either sexless or with an unreal sex which turns only towards itself in the mirror of art'[2]. One may contrast this view with Larkin's more sympathetic one, that 'as Housman himself said, anyone who thinks he has loved more than one person has simply never really loved at all'[3]. Today we take a wider perspective altogether, but it does remain that the focus was down on to a pin-point, and one has to ask what has become of the gentle, fertile natural scene which normally is the dwelling place of the English melancholic poet. For despair at the state of the cosmos, along with dangerously simple language, are likely to depend on a solid ground underfoot for their normality. The risk or fear of extinction, as in Arnold, Edward Thomas or Larkin, grows as the terrain recedes.

The point to be made about a book called *A Shropshire Lad* is that Housman barely visited Shropshire in his life and certainly never lived or perhaps even stayed there[4]. The signing of the poems with Wenlock Edge, Bredon and Ludlow – where incidentally he is buried, such had been the effect of the poetry on English readers – is an artifice. But this itself has possibly been misread. Perhaps the best-known poem and the one that says it all is this (I use Christopher Ricks's text but prefer the textual alternative 'That' for the first word of stanza 2):

Into my heart an air that kills
   From yon far country blows:
What are those blue remembered hills,
   What spires, what farms are those?

That is the land of lost content,
   I see it shining plain,
The happy highways where I went
   And cannot come again.
                (*ASL* XL)

One sometimes feels that all Housman's poetry is written against those 'blue remembered hills'. Yet Housman almost never turns to face them directly. His few nature poems, like the hills, are often the ones most remembered, yet they are so elusive and recede out of sight. The answer may be that the lost world of childhood, the lost paradise, was *already* lost to Housman when he was a boy in Worcestershire. He is said to have looked out to the Shropshire hills from a hilltop near his Worcestershire home, and that was the nearest he ever got to them. This is comparable to the great distances across time in much of Hardy, where again what is recalled is often itself a further recalling of something even further back. Housman's singleness of vision which so dangerously narrowed his output down to a single love, a single image of the unspoken grave, a single tot of strong Scotch, was just saved by this distant memory of an even more distant scene, evoked in a few startling images which parallel in all probability his sense of what they really stood for.

As a result his memory has a terseness which makes it epigrammatic, though in grey and sombre fashion. His pure feeling is also a precision of feeling. The danger is that we are seduced into these very arresting poems, into their darkness

and vacuum, with seduction an apt metaphor. Eliot liked
Housman's definition of poetry as a 'morbid secretion'. Apart
from Christopher Ricks[5] there is little body of criticism on
Housman now. This may be changing (both Ricks's essays are
recent), but there is possibly a sense too that to seek too much
explanation of this poetry is to chase shadows. The poetry is
evocative, but it is rather like war-letters sent home by home-
sick soldiers and discovered posthumously. It is written in the
basic lexicon of sadness, loss, love, tears, trees and graves,
but with exact execution. The absence of a real Shropshire may
be a disablement too, for the poetry cannot go beyond a certain
magnitude.

   This is Housman's strength and limitation. He could hardly
be called original, and as his remark to Bridges about Hopkins
shows, preferred not to be. In his poetry there is no blood,
kisses, love-making or quarrels or small domestic detail. It is
as nearly, perhaps puritanically non-referential – those blue
remembered hills just surviving on the horizon – as personal
poetry could be. Housman intended it that way, and said so.
He remains in some ways the most extreme of the English line
poets.

In August 1916 Wilfred Owen, a soldier aged twenty-three and
dead two years later, bought a copy of *A Shropshire Lad*, no
doubt intrigued to read poetry apparently from his home
county. The incident is symbolic. Housman hardly ever went
to Shropshire, and never enlisted, yet was obsessed by both.
   Wilfred Owen is similar to Hopkins and Dylan Thomas in
the present context in being somewhat marginal to the continuity we are tracing. The common ground of the three is that
whatever thoughts, perceptions or feelings such poets have,
get swirled up into a language which is already in place,
already static, before their ideas connect with them. Owen's
sensibilities took him direct to the powerful external entities
by which the psyche could seem to be symbolized: blood,
gold, selected flowers and birds and seasons, strong physical
struggle, blonde hair, Beauty, Eros, Greece and Rome and
God. These are seen as though in sunlight, as though their
accurate nature in cosmic truth can stand up to the fullest

white light like that which ends Dante's *Paradiso*, a poem Owen used and greatly admired. Suffering itself, of which Owen was to see plenty, is redeemable and worthwhile as being comparable with that of the great sufferers, Jesus Christ and the martyrs. Owen's mentors are the Bible, Dante, Shelley, late nineteenth-century decadent poetry, and above all, at least in Owen's earlier years, John Keats. Owen's famous 'Anthem for Doomed Youth' echoes with the last stanza of Keats' ode 'To Autumn' at every phrase.

Yet, as Dominic Hibberd puts it in his recent absorbing book on Owen, Keats's allusions in Owen's poem 'are meant to be noticed, revealing the battlefield as a demented parody of the Romantic landscape'[6]. The piteous and horrific experience of the First World War trenches and hand-to-hand fighting which he personally underwent – as did the comrades he came to observe more and more compassionately – dragged his poetry into a different arena. It had to account for this new factor of experience. The main break was clearly Owen's bad shell-shock experience of 1917, leading to his meeting with the rather different Siegfried Sassoon in the military hospital in Craiglockhart in Scotland. Sassoon introduced Owen to Hardy's poetry, Sassoon himself saying he admired Hardy 'more than anybody living'[7]. Since the younger Owen rather hero-worshipped Sassoon, it may be that this was what led him to look at a different kind of poetry as a serious model, although it was certainly more than a matter of reading Hardy.

As a result the characteristic greyness and colourlessness begin to appear. Even when action survives, in Owen's poems it takes place under a fateful shadow. The full spectrum to which such a poet normally resorts turns to the grey tone of French and German mud. Even when unnamed, mud seems always there. It takes the edge off colour and sunlight, burying the notional angels and gold and swords of a different poetry, and introducing and mingling the tears and familiar soil of the poet who is inward. The well-known and aptly-named 'Futility' can be read in effect as about a failed attempt to evoke the sun in its transcendental power as source of truth and healing, to revivify a dead comrade:

Move him into the sun –
Gently its touch awoke him once,
At home, whispering of fields unsown.
Always it woke him, even in France,
Until this morning and this snow.
If anything might rouse him now
The kind old sun will know.

'Even in France', even down here on earth in ordinary non-mythological places on the map we know and are actually at. Owen attempts to plead with the sun in a new guise of family friend, 'the kind old sun', rather than the martial sun, source of light, that burnishes shields and ignites the fires of victory. The next couplet sees a faint hope from the sun in the secular evolutionary terms Owen found in the poetry of Hardy and Tennyson he read in the winter of 1917–18:

Think how it wakes the seeds, –
Woke, once, the clays of a cold star.

But that too fails and he can only burst out angrily with a scathing condemnation of the sun altogether: 'O what made fatuous sunbeams toil/To break earth's sleep at all?'.

Mud spreads across the coloured poetry's surface. The somewhat arch 'Apologia Pro Poemate Meo' begins it:

I too, saw God through mud, –
    The mud that cracked on cheeks when wretches smiled

and elsewhere mud kills individuals as in 'The Last Laugh': 'Till, slowly lowered, his whole face kissed the mud'. The fullest treatment comes in the chilling poem 'The Show'. It was written as a result of Owen's attestedly increasing obsession with the idea of a landscape crawling with wounded bodies, seen as from a great height. Again the starting otherworldly perspective turns out to be a way of looking down on a vast Hardyesque terrain on which tiny humans painfully creep. The cratered landscape, shrunk by perspective, is grey and quite sunless, and on it seem to move 'thin caterpillars, slowly uncoiled' which 'vanished out of dawn down hidden holes'. This is the landscape of Hades and the underworld, yet strangely recognizable as what an aerial photograph would actually have shown over the fields round Beaumont Hamel, where Owen had had that terrible period of shell-shock in spring 1917.

Owen did not abandon his first idea of poetry. Hibberd shows how Owen's preoccupation with the entry of the doomed into hell dates at least as far back as 1911–12[8]. This mythological projection of war's nightmare survives into two of his most powerful poems even though they are also visionary and apocalyptic, 'Strange Meeting' and 'Spring Offensive'. These poems are two of Owen's most memorable achievements, as indeed they are of twentieth-century poetry. Standing over against the English line, as they do, they emphasize all the more that line's limitations. Yet the circumstance of war did continue to draw Owen towards the habitual preoccupations of the English line poets. He uses such language, for example, in poems of hospital or the wounded.

In dealing with the wounded in the hospital poems, the poet still does not enter their terrified lonely minds. But for example in 'Mental Cases' he does convey, if in residually Dantesque fashion, what the minds do to the bodies when under the worst duress. This seeing from the outside has its own symbol. The poems are stamped with the recurring image of blindness. Repeatedly eyesight is threatened, as here where 'panic/Gouged these chasms round their fretted sockets' and 'their eyeballs shrink tormented/Back into their brains'. In 'A Terre' (subtitled 'Being The Philosophy of Many Soldiers') the bedridden speaker is 'blind, and three parts shell', and in 'Dulce Et Decorum Est' the soldiers who were bent double like sacks 'all went lame; all blind'. The poem 'The Sentry' (at one point called 'The Blind' but altered probably at Sassoon's suggestion) is the most elaborate case, describing a gruesome incident in a dug-out which Owen himself witnessed and which was one of his most traumatic war experiences.

Blindness turns out to be widespread in these poems. In 'Exposure' the landscape of war is very exactly rendered: 'Watching, we hear the mad gusts tugging on the wire' (his own grotesque Eolian lute perhaps). We are watching, yet only hear; and as a result, while detail on detail is accurately added,

each stanza still ends in the unknown and unpredictable. 'But
nothing happens.' 'What are we doing here?' 'But nothing
happens.' The sunlight being cut out, nothing is seen, not
because we cannot see at all but because the things to be seen
have gone grey and do not radiate. The poet therefore turns
to inner knowing and learning, to blind prophecy. In 'Anthem
for Doomed Youth' the sestet and last line seem to seal the
lesson of the entire blinding horror, now as allegory too:

What candles may be held to speed them all?
  Not in the hands of boys, but in their eyes
Shall shine the holy glimmers of good-byes.
  The pallor of girls' brows shall be their pall;
Their flowers the tenderness of patient minds,
And each slow dusk a drawing-down of blinds.

The switch is from the traditional candle to the more modern
(drawing-down not drawing-across) effacement of the only
way bar words that humans can make relationships; by body-
language, here eyesight. It could well be that this compulsion
is an unconscious recognition of the physical but also mental
faculty that Owen himself would most miss. He recognizes
that his own search-for-knowing is philosophically and subjec-
tively lacking. He acts as though there is a sort of created
vocabulary of the cosmos, by which the poet needs to find
what words ring with what, to bring out realities which have
been caught up into such language. But his new experience
of mental suffering in the bodies of others was a realization
that his own bodily embodiments in words do not express
what others can feel without words, or prior to words. Owen
does not fully write this English line poetry, not quite, for his
own profound satisfaction with the word takes away desire,
of which his poetry shows none. But he has taken a step, in
this response to the mud and to the unseeing which began
when Wordsworth switched from seeing to hearing and feeling
in 'Tintern Abbey' and went on with Hardy looking at a world
with acute vision but by that very fact seeing a boundlessness
which would not be pierced.

Behind this whole story is the strange character of Wilfred
Owen himself, as the biographical work of Stallworthy and

more recently Hibberd has shown[9]. When Owen wrote 'Above all I am not concerned with Poetry' he was making a commitment not stating a fact. This self-styled disciple of the truth-beauty that (at least for the revered Keats's Grecian urn) is 'all you need to know', was profoundly shaken by its actual embodiments in the trenches where there was all mud and no sunlight. His poetic salvation emerged because he found, in the war and its horrors, a new aspect of the poet's traditional word-choosing power. Dug-outs, slimed corpses, smashed legs and modern artillery had their substance which nouns and adjectives could extract from them and put into a new symbolism, just as permanent, for the future. It was possibly the final blow to any surviving 'poetic diction', and for this reason Wilfred Owen stands more importantly in modern poetry than is sometimes suggested. One could hardly get more uncompromising actions than those at the Sambre Canal or Savy Wood.

It is just possible that Wilfred Owen met Edward Thomas. Late in 1916 Thomas arrived at Hare Hall Camp in Essex where Owen was already posted. They probably never knew each other, but during that period, no doubt by chance, Owen bought a copy of Thomas's book on Keats.

Both men were killed in the war, but with this difference, that while Owen was in his early twenties, Edward Thomas was already thirty-seven years old, married and with family, when he enlisted in the Artists' Rifles in 1915. Comparably to Hardy, though with sharper transition in Thomas's case, Thomas turned to poetry only after a long professional career writing prose, and much of what could be said about Hardy's post-novel situation applies to Thomas also. Like Hardy, Thomas found much of his poetry inherent in the prose he had already written, although in his case it took circumstance, and probably the friendship of Robert Frost, to prize him out of his diffidence. But because, unlike Hardy's, Thomas's body of poetry was small and late it is tempting to overlook the deep and prolonged thought he put into poetry's nature during the earlier years. Thanks to a number of critics however, notably Edna Longley, Thomas is, as she wrote back in 1973, 'at last coming into his own as a major twentieth century poet'. Her list of later poets who acknowledged his influence is impressive: Auden, Day Lewis, Alun Lewis, Ted Hughes, Philip Larkin and the West Indian poet Derek Walcott. One might add W. H. Davies, Walter de la Mare and Robert Frost himself as well as several other later poets all of whom have written poems to or about Thomas[10].

What Thomas had lacked and needed, was an opportunity to clear a space in which the poetry could come to the surface. This 'clearing a space' is characteristic of many of the poems. Thomas's professional life, of reviews, articles and book-length studies, exhausted him, paid him very little, and doubtless was one cause of the strain he found in marriage. Yet Thomas's biographer George Thomas has also argued that Thomas was already moving toward the writing of poetry earlier[11]. It was hidden down in his prose works (as Frost realized, and pointed out), and the suppression of it had been a deeper matter than simply strains in personal life. Edward Thomas's literary reviewing and criticism, hack-work as his friends sympathetically thought it, contains deep within it an on-going struggle to throw off the presence and weight of late nineteenth-century 'decadent' poetry, associated with the pre-Raphaelites and Wilde and Swinburne. This trend originally stemmed from the work of the critic Walter Pater, who had been a major Oxford literary figure up to his death only about ten years before Thomas went to Lincoln College, and whose presence in Oxford was still an influence in Thomas's time there. To cut this story short, Thomas did not throw off the 'aesthetic' influence of Pater until he wrote his own book on Pater in 1913, and his travel book *In Pursuit of Spring* the next year. In the latter book Frost claimed he found several embryonic poems which only needed to be written out in poetic form, keeping the cadence.

Pater's language is choice, precise, scrupulous – all Pater's favoured critical terms[12] – but Thomas came to feel that it was unnatural; one could never imagine it being spoken; it could never be heard as a person's voice. This view again is reminiscent of Wordsworth's Preface of 1800, and Thomas clearly echoes that work at various points in his prose writing. In fact, at first Thomas did not take our 'English line' poets as his real poetic forebears. But this was because of his high rating of a body of prose writing which also deals with a familiar natural world: namely, the countryman's writing of such as George Borrow, Gilbert White, William Cobbett and Richard Jefferies. This attachment may throw light on Thomas's one uncompromising espousal of an English-line poet: John Clare. Clare was 'a real poet, however small, and actually an agricultural labourer out and out. . . . He possessed a similar, fresh sweet spirituality to that of Jefferies, a similar grasp and love of detail. . . . No man ever came so near to putting the life of the farm . . . into poetry. He gives no broad impressions – he saw the kite, but not the kite's landscape – yet his details accumulate in the end, so that a loving reader, and no one reads him but loves him, can grasp them'[13].

From this passage one can go to the heart of Thomas's own poetry. For he too writes about his immediate landscape in minute terms, and to be down almost inside it himself seems an emotional necessity. His poetry of speech is hesitant, frail, vulnerable and, like the reviews we referred to above, somewhat elusive, deliberately undecided. The word 'if' is very frequent in Thomas. As such it is a good example of a common tendency in these poets, where the small connective words are what do a lot to enact the movement of mind itself, rather than the outer objects mind apprehends. As Freud said, these are the words – 'if, because, just as, although, either-or' – that dreamwork can't capture directly[14]. It is another kind of poetry, surrealistic or Modernist more widely, that enters dreams and so puts less weight on these words, in that connections in dreams are abrupt and unmediated. These tiny hesitancies in Thomas are matched by the tiny things in nature on to which he projects those feelings. A bird's chance note when you were thinking of something else, a twig blowing across, an odd clump of nettles in the farmyard, a jam-jar set for a wasp-trap, rain on your hand, a leaf on a gatepost, a herb by the back door. In the poem 'It Rains' there is a microscopic density:

> It rains, and nothing stirs within the fence
> Anywhere through the orchard's untrodden, dense
> Forest of parsley. The great diamonds
> Of rain on the grassblades there is none to break,
> Or the fallen petals further down to shake.

But, unlike with Clare, this cannot remain separate for long from the poet's own deeply moved, uncertain inner emotion:

> And I am nearly as happy as possible
> To search the wilderness in vain though well,
> To think of two walking, kissing there,
> Drenched, yet forgetting the kisses of the rain:
> Sad, too, to think that never, never again,
>
> Unless alone, so happy shall I walk
> In the rain . . .

It may well seem depressing, simply to draw all back to a reminder of oneself, as critics have sometimes said. But Thomas sings his puzzlements into an equilibrium; the stretched rhyme of 'well' after 'possible' becomes reassuring. Also, apart from a sad reference to his own inadequacy for marriage, what Thomas had done here is to latch on to rain as his own single symbol, just as the sea was for Arnold and Wessex for Hardy. Thomas finds from that support the chance to get some small breathing-clearance both in his mind and in the garden or field. He clears a space, finds somewhere to be alone in a clearing. This clearing of a small patch is most marked at the start of a famous poem, 'Adlestrop':

> Yes. I remember Adlestrop –
> The name, because one afternoon
> Of heat the express-train drew up there
> Unwontedly. It was late June.
>
> The steam hissed. Someone cleared his throat.
> No one left and no one came
> On the bare platform. What I saw
> Was Adlestrop – only the name
>
> And willows, willow-herb, and grass . . .

The frequent full-stops let in silences, little gaps of space and time, and even a throat is cleared, as though for solitary articulation. In 'Old Man' the poet pauses by a door and sniffs a herb, which removes more pressing things from round him to allow in a deep, dark meditation. In 'The Wasp-Trap' three stanzas of rather puzzled admiration for the moonlight then lets him see the jam-jar hanging: 'long may it swing/From the dead apple-bough,/So glistening'. And in one of his most successful poems 'October' (in which incidentally there is a line clearly indebted to one from Wordsworth's sonnet on Westminster Bridge) Thomas lists in meticulous detail the leaves, twigs and bird-sounds of the small autumn scene. Again it clears space for him to continue, as though with relief at something eased: 'And now I might/As happy be as earth is beautiful . . .'.

Within this cleared space Thomas became the most explicit of these poets about the tie-up between pleasure and pain. The equilibrium just referred to in 'It Rains' turns out to be widespread. In many of his best-known poems the balance is exact and deliberate:

Either in pain or thus in sympathy
('It Rains')
Without pleasure, without pain
(refrain, 'The Gallows')
Endeared, by gladness and by pain
('I Never Saw that Land Before')
And yet I still am half in love with pain,
With what is imperfect, with both tears and mirth
('Liberty')
Or must I be content with discontent
As larks and swallows are perhaps with wings?
('The Glory')
Yet naught did my despair
But sweeten the strange sweetness, while through the
wild air
All day long I heard a distant cuckoo calling
And, soft as dulcimers, sounds of near water falling,
And, softer, and remote as if in history,
Rumours of what had touched my friends, my foes, or me.
('Melancholy')

The happy-sad emotion had its fullest statement in Keats' 'Ode On Melancholy'. Thomas had the highest regard for that poem, but it is a question of just what is being balanced. For

Keats it was that joy leaves as it arrives, as both the 'Ode On Melancholy' and, inversely, the 'Ode On A Grecian Urn' show. But for Thomas, as for the American writer Ralph Waldo Emerson (a major influence on Frost), it is that nature is longed for and loved, but somehow always over the next hill, and finally found nowhere. So his poems always end in an area cleared for movement toward the boundlessness these poets so often express, to nearly nothing, or 'the night' as one of his last poems ended by having it. Elizabeth Wright, following Freud, has suggested that the death instinct 'arises from the organism's wish to return to desireless stable state'[15]. The remark recalls Wordsworth's 'I long for a repose that ever is the same' ('Ode to Duty'). It is happy and sad at once, because without something to desire there is despair, yet with it, it is always unattainable if nature is its object. For Thomas this exactly balanced position may have become a source of obsession.

Thomas finally cleared the spaces he needed. As with Hardy, Housman, Larkin and the writer of *In Memoriam*, the poems were once more a 'morbid secretion'; for a long time he published none, and showed them only to a few friends. Then he got a room to work in, got clear of reviewing to write poetry, went to the Gloucestershire countryside with Robert Frost and worked out just what he found poetry had to be. In the end he went to the open space of the battlefields of France, where his restlessness seems to have ended, writing itself quietly stopped, and the calm of a 'desireless stable state' settled, finally in death, over this somewhat sharply unhappy man.

9
Robert Frost

Although Robert Frost was born (in 1874) in San Francisco, he was in all important respects a New Englander, and his mother took him back to Massachusetts when he was eleven and his father died. Frost's father was born and raised in Massachusetts and his mother as a Presbyterian brought from Scotland to live in Ohio when she was twelve. Mainly from his mother, the future poet inherited the New England tradition of Bible-reading, teaching and puritanical work, and one sees across his writing the influence of Emerson, the Concord romantic who lived in the country with an Eolian harp at his window, and Henry Thoreau, who built himself a hut in the woods near Emerson's house at Walden Pond. Thoreau lived there at subsistence level for about two and a half years. Behind both these is yet again Wordsworth, whose views about poetic diction Frost clearly used in elaborating his own theory of why 'the sound of a sentence' matters to him more than the evocations of substantial words. (A number of Frost's poems echo Wordsworth, especially *The Prelude*[1].) But Frost's poetry is certainly touched by Milton too, and he made approving remarks about Hardy and Tennyson. Another major influence in Frost's thinking was William James, American disseminator of the philosophy of pragmatism. Frost's poetry, loosely speaking, is about woods, water and snow in the New England countryside and the hard-working people who live there and their quiet reflections on life. It is inward and meditative, and it is written in the simplest language. But there is, to say the least, more to it than that.

Since neither Frost nor his parents were English, it is all the more to be asked why he emerges so clearly from other outstanding twentieth-century American poets as closely comparable to the British group already discussed. Frost went to Dartmouth College and to Harvard, withdrawing from both, and spent most of his life in a slightly unsettled but always discernibly consistent mixture of university lecturing, writing and farming. He owned small farms variously near Salem and at Franconia, New Hampshire, and near Arlington in Vermont, both New England states. He taught for periods of varying length at Pinkerton Academy, Amherst, Ann Arbor, Harvard, Dartmouth and elsewhere, although many of these appointments left him large amounts of free time for his own writing, home life and travelling. After the death of his wife Elinor just before the Second World War he travelled more widely and consolidated his image as something of an American institution. He read a poem at John F. Kennedy's presidential inauguration and in his old age visited Khrushchev in Russia, on a putative diplomatic cultural mission. Frost died in 1963[2].

From 1912 to 1915 however he had spent his one period of any length outside the USA, namely in England, which he visited for the purpose – always carried out uncompromisingly, sometimes ruthlessly – of cultivating contacts and furthering his career as a poet. His first two books of poetry *A Boy's Will* (1913) and *North Of Boston* (1914) were both first published in England, and much of their contents written there. These collections made Frost's literary reputation, and he returned to America to find himself famous.

It was in the spring of 1914, in Gloucestershire, that Frost most came to know Edward Thomas. They had already met in London the previous autumn; but at that time Frost had not really been aware of Thomas's status as a critic, and a previous remark about the Georgian poet W. W. Gibson is a silent comment that the friendship with Thomas had not really got going[3]. This state of things so changed that in the summer of 1914 Elinor Frost could write home to her sister, about Thomas, that 'Rob and I think every thing of him. He is quite the most admirable and lovable man we have ever known'. In 1917, after Thomas's death, Frost wrote to a friend, 'Edward Thomas was the only brother I ever had . . . I never had, I never shall have another such year of friendship'. A more important statement in literary terms comes in 1921 when Frost wrote to an American lecturer Grace Conkling. In his letter Frost, perhaps characteristically, seems to be guarding his own reputation. He insists that whatever he and Thomas had in common already existed before they met; yet also that he,

Frost, was the one who convinced Thomas that he should write poetry. 'I bantered, teased and bullied all the summer we were together at Ledington and Ryton.' Yet the sincere wish is apparently present too, to insist that all he did was show Thomas that he (Thomas) was a poet already, potentially an outstanding one. And Frost reconfirms the friendship without reservation: 'We were greater friends than almost any two ever were practising the same art'[4].

All this is interesting in evaluating not only Thomas but Frost. The Frost-Thomas friendship symbolizes but also shows how, given certain temperamental affinities and other common ground, the attributes of these English poets could be transferred to, or already stem from, different backgrounds, even though the broad picture of the English liberal bourgeoisie during and after the Industrial Revolution is the central background historically. The letters between Thomas and Frost in the first part of the friendship show the detailed similarity of their view of poetry, feeling, sentence and speech. At least some poems by Thomas could have been Frost; for instance parts of 'Man and Dog', 'The Chalk Pit' and 'Wind and Mist'. The story makes possible an assessment of how far there was indeed a Frost-Thomas manifesto even if implicitly, as Edna Longley argues[5], as there was an Eliot-Pound one. In the summer of 1914 Thomas published three reviews of Frost's *North Of Boston*, all three unreservedly enthusiastic. Thomas's reviews were undoubtedly a large contribution to Frost's resulting early success.

The now-famous opening sentences of Thomas's first review have been taken to announce a new beginning: 'This is one of the most revolutionary books of modern times, but one of the quietest and least aggressive. It speaks, and it is poetry'. Again and again through these reviews Thomas emphasizes that the poetry's strength lies in its simplicity and proximity to speech. It is 'more colloquial and idiomatic than the ordinary man dares to use even in a letter', and Frost has 'gone back, as Whitman and as Wordsworth went back, through the paraphernalia.of poetry into poetry again'. Again, as invariably with these poets, the remarks give just the touch of suspicion of words themselves, except insofar as by words we feel and hear mind and emotion, which is what matters most to the poets, and what they want to shape. Thomas confirms this. 'With a confidence like genius, (Frost) has trusted his conviction that a man will not easily write better than he speaks when some matter has touched him deeply'. But most interestingly perhaps is raised 'the thrilling question, What is poetry?', and the book will be enjoyed, says Thomas, 'even by those who decide that, at any rate, it is not poetry'. Shades of Mill and Martineau again, and it is noteworthy that Thomas cites the case of Wordsworth here more than anywhere else in his body of criticism. The concluding sentence of the review reads like a deliberate answer to Pound's precept that poetry should be at least as good as prose: 'It is poetry because it is better than prose'[6].

Until recently Frost has not been very well known in Britain, and Thomas's star too only came into any ascendancy about twenty years ago. This English line in effect survived down through Hardy, and Donald Davie's book on that poet and his influence mentions neither Thomas nor Frost in its index. We can accept this readily enough; it does certainly seem that Hardy has the greater stature than Thomas – after all, he had more time. But the Frost-Thomas partnership did occur, albeit briefly, and the link in this particular continuity does seem, if in hindsight, to have been tightened by it.

Again it is important to decide about this, for Frost's own reputation has gone up and down variously. He suffers currently from a kind of dual attack, based on increased biographical knowledge of his personality, and the collapse since his death of his image as wise, genial poetic countryman. In 1957 the poet Sylvia Plath wrote home from Cambridge (England) to her mother in America saying that 'we heard dear, shrewd, funny, lovable Robert Frost read yesterday afternoon . . . Ted [Hughes, Plath's husband] loved him, and I feel the two of them have much in common'. The image today could scarcely be more different. Karl Miller lists items from the index to Lawrance Thompson's standard biography of Frost: brute, charlatan, cowardice, enemies, escapist, fear, hate, insanity, jealousy, punishment, puritan, rage, rebel, revenge, spoiled child, vindictive, war. Wallace Martin summarizes Thompson's picture as 'a selfish, egotistical, cunning, paranoid, manic depressive . . . baffler-teaser-deceiver, charlatan, myth-maker and pretender in pursuit of the ideal' who nevertheless still generated the public figure 'that readers learned to love, and that discerning critics always distrusted'. On the other side, and despite these distressing characteristics perhaps not compatibly, we have the 'spiritual drifter' idea of the American critic Yvor Winters. Winters saw Frost as someone unable to make up his mind where he morally stood, and therefore without the firm and intelligent rationality which was Winter's own criterion for the hallmark of worthwhile poetry[7].

All the more then is the question raised as to his 'quietest and least aggressive poetry', as Thomas called it, its almost total lack of violent content, and its ceaseless exploration of silent, measured, seasonally rhythmic implications in what he apparently saw in snow, forest, brook, and men and women where he lived. It is what Robert Poirier's exactly titled study of Frost calls 'the work of knowing'. Some writers, such as MacNeice, have touched on a sinister element in Frost's poetry, which Auden saw as violent but latently so[8]. The sense is there, but one feels it is contained within the solid presence of a rural New England that could still be taken for granted.

Work and processes of work are written right across Frost's poetry. This work is not, as such, hard physical labour, the sustained discipline of philosophy, or 'working for community goals', though all three and others are present. Rather it is a puritan application as existence. There is a level expenditure of energy by which we inhabit both the earth and our minds and bodies at all. In poem after poem the characters, or Frost himself, are immersed in physical tasks such as clearing snow, chopping wood or mending walls or picking fruit; reflecting as they go about neighbours they have seen, or working through a difficult matter in or just outside marriage. In 'Blueberries' and 'After Apple-Picking' the gathering of the fruit is inseparable from the welling-up of controlled reflection as to what is entailed in it or follows from it. The same is true in 'Mending Wall'. There the question of how the gaps in the boundary wall appear, and how to get his neighbour to see that it is important, are tasks that share a rhythm with that of picking up large stones for the repair job. But this stuff of work is not Frost's 'topic' in some overt sense, and the reader gradually comes to see that the writing of poetry is itself a process generated, it seems, as work too. The poet is an integrated individual when that overall mind-emotion-body process is allowed to run.

Small pieces of this work seem to come urged up into place as the very rhythm of the writing itself. In 'Home Burial' for example, an anxious unhappy wife suddenly realizes that her husband upstairs is obsessively looking out of the window at the small graveyard area where their child is buried. Both attachment and hostility come out of their desperate attempts to explain how they feel to each other. The wife at one point attacks him for his insensitivity:

> If you had any feelings, you that dug
> With your own hand – how could you? – his little grave;
> I saw you from that very window there,
> Making the gravel leap and leap in air,
> Leap up, like that, like that, and land so lightly
> And roll back down the mound beside the hole.
> I thought, Who is that man? I didn't know you.
> And I crept down the stairs and up the stairs
> To look again, and still your spade kept lifting . . .
>
> (lines 72–80)

The remarkable thing is the way that her watching of his physical work process is itself a piece of work at understanding. She is trying to *work* out what his work is doing. This example points to the darker underside of the work, but many examples have a straightforwardness in their engagement with it. Characters seem to be alert to a need to draw out, for themselves, a homely folk-wisdom as far as it will go without needing the formalities of philosophy. In 'The Mountain' the speaker meets a man with an ox-cart, and asks him where his village is. The answer comes:

> 'There is no village – only scattered farms.
> We were but sixty voters last election.
> We can't in nature grow to many more:
> That thing takes all the room!'
>
> (lines 24–7)

Three of the four lines are elaborations of the simple answer. It is as though the villager has his ideas about the mountain – 'that thing' – at his fingertips all the time, as though he keeps an on-going reflection as to it, himself, and their place in the world as a calming accompaniment to all his arduous activity.

Everything can carry its comment. Everything is considered as to what should be done about it. As Lacan put it in different context, actions including subconscious ones can then be raised to the conscious level by the everyday language, what Lacan called *verbe*[9]. For the language of work has to be the verb. In 'The Death of a Hired Man' husband and wife discuss how to treat an old man who has unexpectedly arrived wanting his usual employment. In 'Snow' the task is what someone should do when stuck in a neighbour's house four miles from home during an impending snowstorm. In 'Birches' the question, if more whimsically, is the best way a boy could get fun by swinging the thin saplings down to the ground and leaving go at the right moment. In 'The Road Not Taken' the question is of which path to follow through the woods. Even this famous and near-allegorical poem (supposedly speaking for Edward Thomas but fully compatible with Frost himself) is saturated with the question of a practical decision. But if this matter of work and application is indeed a through and through matter of existence itself, then the work that simply provides our physical subsistence is not the whole story. As we have said, relations in marriage, thought itself, and articulating ourselves to ourselves are all part of it too.

It is an interesting reminder that for some years Yeats was Frost's rather unlikely choice of favourite poet. One suddenly recalls how many of Yeats' poems, most of them early, touch on the matter of work[10]. Yeats' poem 'Adam's Curse' (itself of course work) points to a strand of the Miltonic tradition behind Frost's whole approach, which the poet both inhabits but also successfully escapes. Adam was expelled from the Garden of Eden for disobedience to God, and as a result condemned the human race to work and labour as the hallmark of their condition. Frost it seems accepts this work-bound condition, and lives in it and explores it by the act of doing it. But why was Adam expelled in the first place? Because he 'fell'; succumbed to woman; ate forbidden fruit which may be carnal; knew what he should not know from the Tree of Knowledge. But Frost's poetry is saturated with these entities. The tree, and many trees, constantly surround him; he wanders by and into the trees, plants them, chops them up, watches them through the seasons. In his best-known poem 'After Apple-Picking' the rumbling of apples into the apple-bin seems like a revelling in the indulgence of what elsewhere is forbidden. This poem is the one possibly most influenced by 'Goblin Market' by Christina Rossetti, who also wrote a poem called 'After Apple-Gathering'. Apples and other fruit figure in many of Frost's poems, 'Unharvested', 'A Cow at Apple Time', 'Mending Wall' a rather underrated poem 'Blueberries', and also 'Good-by and Keep Cold'. Attention by work is what distinguishes the last-named from the equally fruit-in-snow poem of Housman, 'Loveliest of trees . . .'. Marriage as an often strained land-tending partnership, occurs in the longer poems 'The Hill Wife', 'West-Running Brook', 'Maple', 'The Fear' and many others including some named earlier. And, as has often been remarked, the poetry is inscribed with seasonal falling; falling of apples, of leaves and of snow. Frost's own line, with its curious drifting voice, has its ending fall.

But there is an all-important difference from Yeats. It led Frost in the end, like Larkin later, not to adopt Yeat's principles. The difference lies in the fact that although these elements are present they never comprise an overt, known symbolic system such as Yeats sought. As Poirier puts it, 'A "system" for symbolizing, like Yeats's, is inconceivable for Frost because for him the power of voice in a sentence exists independently of words and necessarily changes their significance with each usage. . . . The shaping of sound in a sentence is the voice's way of exerting control over particular words that can become too intimidating, words like "God" for example, or "snow" '[11].

There could hardly be a clearer indication of how Frost's attitude is consonant with that of the English-line poets. His renowned formula of 'sentence sounds' was that it is the sentence, not the words in it, which is basic and the locus of essential language sound. In a long passage in a letter to a friend Frost wrote: 'A sentence is a sound in itself on which other sounds called words may be hung. . . . You may string words together without a sentence-sound to string them on just as you may tie clothes together by the sleeves and stretch them without a clothes line between two trees, but – it is bad for the clothes. . . . The sentence sound often says more than the words'[12]. All this is a matter of the actual talking we do in our own situation and familiar surroundings. Its result is that however 'symbolic' things come to be if they are often enough repeated – snow, apples, trees, the homestead – they can never congeal as symbol finally because they are also simply where we live. Frost's engagement with the place where he and his neighbours work and live – in Freud's phrase, work and love – means that work, thought, talk, poetry, eating, married life, everything, are all the one process which cannot have a clear foundation of interlocking parts pre-decided, for we inhabit them and could never see them objectively. Talking is working, apple-picking is working, marriage is a difficult working, looking at snow is working.

But from these broad considerations one can see where the richness of Frost's poetry comes from. As Poirier again puts it: since these solid objects abound yet none come to symbol fixedly, every poem can 'tremble with meaning', because so much is sought but also so much is available. Almost any poem of Frost's, and certainly many, can seem to contain many possible meanings. Possibilities include work-task-related, sexual, natural and rural, and poetic itself. The temptation to read the poems psychoanalytically is always near with Frost, because, presenting a world of solid things that are lived with, the Freudian possibility is always present that male and phallus and female and breast will be recalled by anything straight and by anything curved. In short there is a direct unmediated reference to instinctual life, resulting often in a straight sexual reading which Elizabeth Wright[13] calls a 'compelling fantasy, rather like a strange poem in its own right'. It is intriguing to consider some examples, although it could soon become reductive.

Norman Holland produced an interpretation[14] several years ago of 'Mending Wall' which highlighted certain lines:

He is all pine and I am apple orchard.
My apple trees will never get across
And eat the cones under his pines, I tell him.
He only says, 'Good fences make good neighbors'.

Holland suggests a strong unconscious sexual symbolism here,
with the neighbour fearing castration by a female. (My own
added observation is that 'pines' anagrams 'penis'.) The fear
is answered by a reference to a non-negotiable law, by which
exact zones of life are demarcated by right boundaries; by
walls. That is a very interesting reading. But as Holland himself
also pointed out, like any traditional psychoanalytical reading
it becomes merely reductive unless it is seen as one of the
poem's ingredients, not the poem itself. It is a one-eyed reading. If we shut that eye and open the other, however, we see
that the poem might also be about language and communication. The two farmers meet only once a year, and for the
sole purpose of repairing gaps in their party wall which have
mysteriously appeared in that period. For two-thirds of the
poem nothing is said except to cast a spell by which round
stones stay upright (curved rhythms stay in place). The neighbour can only make his one point: 'Good fences make good
neighbors'. This stirs the more loquacious poet to open up a
bit:

Spring is the mischief in me, and I wonder
If I could put a notion in his head;
"*Why* do they make good neighbors? Isn't it
Where there are cows? But here there are no cows.
Before I built a wall I'd ask to know
What I was walling in or walling out,
And to whom I was like to give offense.
Something there is that doesn't love a wall,
That wants it down." I could say "Elves" to him,
But it's not elves exactly, and I'd rather
He said it for himself . . .

Yet the poet does all the talking, for the neighbour cannot say
it for himself. He can only repeat his traditional proverb or
non-negotiable law (later called his 'father's saying') 'good

fences make good neighbors', and so the barriers remain up.
Talk and work are highlighted by the pun itself, for to 'give
offense' is a verbal act as well as to erect a partition.

It is comparable, if in reverse, in 'The Ax-Helve'. The
speaker is chopping logs on a snowy day when a neighbour
(there are few strangers in Frost) comes quietly up behind him:

> This was a man, Baptiste, who stole one day
> Behind me on the snow in my own yard
> Where I was working at the chopping-block,
> And cutting nothing not cut down already.
> He caught my ax expertly on the rise,
> When all my strength put forth was in his favor,
> Held it a moment where it was, to calm me,
> Then took it from me – and I let him take it.
>
> (lines 6–13)

This exquisitely observed moment prepares us for the lucid
depiction of skill and craftsmanship that comes later, when
the poet visits Baptiste's own yard where the ax-helves are
hand-made:

> Needlessly soon he had his ax-helves out,
> A quiverful to choose from, since he wished me
> To have the best he had, or had to spare –
> Not for me to ask which, when what he took
> Had beauties he had to point me out at length
> To insure their not being wasted on me.
> He liked to have it slender as a whipstock,
> Free from the least knot, equal to the strain
> Of bending like a sword across the knee.
> He showed me that the lines of a good helve
> Were native to the grain before the knife
> Expressed them, and its curves were no false curves
> Put on it from without. And there its strength lay
> For the hard work. He chafed its long white body
> From end to end with his rough hand shut round it.
>
> (lines 63–77)

The attention to work for work's sake, skill for skill's sake, are so known and concentrated on, that the sexual reading stays lower than it might have, even when we have it appear in consciousness. In the first passage, the Frenchman (i.e. of a nation renowned for sexual prowess) 'caught my ax expertly on the rise' but also 'held it a moment where it was, to calm me'; which can be read as a subtle victory in sexual competition, taking away the desired woman at the moment of the loser's desire (moment of erection). It is also generous and civilized in triumph, and with 'ex' skilfully following 'ax' so that 'sex' itself is subtly heard. Baptiste's many ax-helves, well made and understood by himself, would then be his many sexual exploits. Baptiste's wife stays quietly in the background, an unprepossessing figure, her verandah rocking-chair disturbingly rocking. But equally, the description of the work process itself cannot be merely held secondary, and the two, or more, readings merge very naturally into each other. Frost's sentence-voice holds the potential symbols in solution, letting them always be voiced by the very person – himself – who is experiencing these deeper-sourced imaginings.

Both these poems centre on work, like so many of Frost's poems. But in other poems, although work of communication may go on, physical work may be over and recovery needed. In Frost this is expressed by slower thought, sighing, drowsiness, and in the end sleep. The well-known poem 'Stopping by Woods on a Snowy Evening' yields the same richness of meaning, but this time in a first-person meditation with no dialogue or other countering character or presence. It is one of many such short lyrics, and runs (I share the view that there should be no comma after 'dark' in stanza 4):

Whose woods these are I think I know.
His house is in the village, though;
He will not see me stopping here
To watch his woods fill up with snow.

My little horse must think it queer
To stop without a farmhouse near
Between the woods and frozen lake
The darkest evening of the year.

He gives his harness bells a shake
To ask if there is some mistake.
The only other sound's the sweep
Of easy wind and downy flake.

The woods are lovely, dark and deep,
But I have promises to keep,
And miles to go before I sleep,
And miles to go before I sleep.

As with so many Frost poems, the tree of knowledge which
successfully led Adam and Eve to fall is here multiplied into
woods, to hundreds of trees, to much knowledge and in mul-
tiple forms, just as the 'ten thousand thousand apples' of his
near-exhausted hallucination in 'After Apple-Picking' tap the
senses and come 'rumbling in'. And as with other Frost poems
of richness, there is a fatigue in the voice, as though much
work has been already done this time. The repetition at the
end of 'Stopping by Woods on a Snowy Evening' is that nearly-
asleep state when we mumble a phrase to ourselves as we
drop off, or indeed 'fall asleep' as the last stage in the fall from
grace that Eden witnessed. The poem contains knowledge and
ignorance, light and dark, a brief halt in time ('stopping by'
not arriving at or passing through), death ('the darkest evening
of the year') and other more deeply hidden meanings, in the
middle of which rather than 'about' which the poet writes.

One such reading can conveniently be taken here ahead of
the others, as being related to work, sleep and poetry itself.
The poem is arguably about snow itself, and whiteness. This
would imply a counter to the richness it in other respects
contains, and implies a symbolic milieu in which both work
and the sleep it earns occur. In virtually all his poetry Frost
gives this whiteness priority over a spectrum of colour. In two
poems this is explicit, for he refutes Shelley's famous assertion
(quoted on p. 114) that life's 'many-colouredness' breaks up
eternity's singleness of white. The poems are 'The Trial by
Existence', lines 9–10, and 'Birches', lines 7–13. In the present
poem 'Stopping by Woods' the woods are admired, but that
is only stated. The snow is what is evoked. Its silence puts it
all about us, and only in hindsight do we see that the curious

elongated 'though' in the first stanza is not only leading up to the rhyme with 'snow' but also thereby somehow embodying the snow silently falling. The poem, like the woods, will 'fill up' with snow as it goes through; and 'the only other sound' (reminiscent of Coleridge's 'sole unquiet thing' in 'Frost at Midnight') leads into 'the sweep/Of easy wind and downy flake', the poem's most memorable physical, and I think sexual, experience. As a result the doubling of the final two lines suggests a drifting, just as snow drifts itself.

It would take much space to go into the meaning of this whiteness in Frost; possibly subliminally to do with his own name, its similarity to 'forest' too, and that of Elinor White, who became his wife in a marriage that was always uneasy. It may, again, be that archetype the blank page, on which sentences make a more general and so less incisive mark than words. Again the poetry of this line shows its slight distancing from palpable language, its preference for going through language to more diffuse, elusive feelings. In this respect Frost differs from the poets of Britain in that his departure from a colour spectrum is in terms of sheets of white, rather than dreary greyness alone. At one level this comes from the more extreme climate of New England, with its long winters of deep, heavy snow instead of the soft drizzle commoner in the British Isles. Whatever our politics or relationships, material conditions exist prior to human action on them. Yet both work and sleep, one might say, minimize richness and plurality; they are concentrated, absorbed states.

A similarly encompassing effect to that of the snow here is found in 'After Apple-Picking'. There the magnetizing lines round which the others seem to hang and to which it all seems to lead, perhaps Frost's whole oeuvre in hindsight leads, are the sudden relief:

> . . . The rumbling sound
> Of load on load of apples coming in.
> For I have had too much
> Of apple-picking: I am overtired
> Of the great harvest I myself desired.

Here, as in 'Stopping by Woods', sleep is only approached.

To enter sleep fully would be to dream, and that would engage with the symbolic word fully. This Frost's poetry will not do. He talks of dream, but always from wakefulness. Work is not possible during sleep, and all Frost's poetry is work. Frost has miles to go before he sleeps, and here, although at the start

> . . . I am done with apple-picking now.
> Essence of winter sleep is on the night,
> The scent of apples: I am drowsing off.

– nevertheless by the end he is still wondering about sleep, still awake:

> One can see what will trouble
> This sleep of mine, whatever sleep it is.

and ends with a joke.

This seems to embody a great wariness of the sleep which permeates the poetry of Keats, from 'Sleep and Poetry' through to the 'Ode To A Nightingale'. Keats's sleep does not result from the processes of work. The same thing occurs in Frost's 'The Oft-Repeated Dream' (in 'The Hill Wife'), where the tree at the window is feared, supposedly in dream but surely really in a husband's anxiety:

> It never had been inside the room,
>   And only one of the two
> Was afraid in an oft-repeated dream
>   Of what the tree might do.

If this – which incidentally could be Hardy speaking – is closer to Robert Frost's own married life, as it seems to be, the poem's ambiguity lies in that 'only one of the two' fears the tree's phallic power. Either the wife could be unfaithful or the husband could do violence. But either way the first line surely implies waking thought, not dream. Frost is always more likely to keep awake, keep watch. This is part both of the work and of the unattainability of the result. The poet needs to work at knowing but not finally know, and so live in a fallen state with the 'fruits' kept at a distance. It is as though, in Yeats's

phrase, neither perfection of the life nor of the work is possible. Frost's solution, as far as it goes, is to accept the opportunity and burden of work itself.

In confronting a single tree on its own Frost's fatigue is at
its greatest. It was to Wordsworth too, in the immortality ode:
'But there's a Tree, of many, one' that spoke of 'something
that is gone'. It is found elsewhere in Frost in 'The Oft-
Repeated Dream', with its marital charge, but evinced most
tellingly in the poem 'Tree at My Window':

> But, tree, I have seen you taken and tossed,
> And if you have seen me when I slept,
> You have seen me when I was taken and swept
> And all but lost.

Just possibly it is the tree of knowledge itself. We are left
hearing this extraordinary poet, extraordinary in that he
inhabited a familiar landscape of farms, trees and snow, where
mind is the medium if ever a poetry achieved that, and which
reminds us of a lost paradise which may have once existed,
or may not. As a result, attendant and puritan labour all the
days of our lives is our ordinary condition, and desire is firmest
as a longing to know or to express not-knowing at all points.
And always with that voice which in the end a critic can
only try to describe: a sideways, drowsy, laid-back, watchful,
elongated, laconic, thinking-out-loud, amused-absorbed, painful, worked, swaying, strangely enriched but always mellow,
drawling and always falling voice.

Part IV

10

Louis MacNeice and Dylan Thomas

But, in the words of the title of Robert Graves's book, it was also 'goodbye to all that'. Thomas and Owen were killed in the war in which Graves also fought. The other three survived for one, two and four decades each, but Housman and Hardy were well into the centre of their poetry careers by the time the war started, while Robert Frost returned to a New England 3000 miles away. The Georgian poets dispersed, and the inward brooding voice of the English poet in a moving but rainy, snowy or grey landscape is not found again, bar sporadically, until the second half of the century, today in the new context of our environmental and ecological concerns. MacNeice once wrote an approving review of Frost, but the English thirties poets had their own problems.

What were the post-war indigenous poets to do in the new situation? Owen's poetry in particular shattered the picture of a serene landscape; instead were the mud, snapped-off lifeless trees, dead horses and abandoned broken machinery, human bodies and hideous unreal trenches. But the war unleashed ideologies too. Marxism became articulated with the Russian Revolution of 1917, but so did Freudian psychoanalysis, for these upheavals were cataclysmic events in human understanding. It suddenly seemed as though the human animal could be seen inside out, with sociology and psychology bringing economic and social conditions to the forefront of human questions and the unconscious to the surface. The poetic response of melancholic song had been groping in the dark with experiences that the social sciences began to seem to know about more explicitly. This particularly affected W. H. Auden. Auden was of course influenced early by Tennyson, Hardy and others of the earlier years. But the factor which seemed to take him knowingly away from this kind of poetry was only partly the influence of Eliot. Auden accepted the influence of Freud, and the Freudian idea that the isolated unknowable self was not the rock-bottom source of feelings. In consequence no feeling need now be presented spontaneously but could itself be objectively, if still poetically, judged in a partly dispassionate meditation whose intellectual shape was itself to be the basis of the poetic rhythm. The first person, even the word 'I', is rare in Auden, certainly as referring to himself. Again and again his poems seem to be about the feelings the English line also have, but in his case seen from outside; feelings experienced by himself, but then in effect checked against the authority of Marx and Freud before a word is written. His more obviously feelingful poems are therefore often ballads or more public songs, as though the form is taken by external choice. One would not say simply that with Auden this English line ended; rather, that after his deliberate and cerebral change of approach such poetry would need a greater self-knowingness to survive at all.

And certainly the voice we have heard so far in this book could not have responded to the new twentieth-century world with the powerful extremity of the Modernist. Not only T. S. Eliot's early poems but then also later, and magnificently, *The Waste Land*, embodied the break-up of European civilization itself, the artefacts and literatures of centuries knocked to pieces and yet still discernible in their ruined state within it.What was any 'English line' poet to do? Indeed could there now be such poets? To put it oversimply, gradually the English-line voice divided. (Both new groups rather defiantly tried to fend off the Wordsworth influence – not always successfully.) The preoccupation with the landscape became archaeological, evoking its layered strata and the work of humans on it, in the poetry of David Jones, Basil Bunting and others, down to the work of Geoffrey Hill in our own time. These poets step deliberately outside the continuity as this book has seen it. The primal melancholic voice, on the other hand, always responsive to its own personal predicament, found its surroundings to be more and more suburban. It never really ceases its hope that some reliable 'nature', some permanent landscape, is out there somewhere down the arterial road (or motorway), but the anxiety grows. This continues down to

Philip Larkin and, around him, the less poignant verse of the 'Movement' poets of the 1950s.

Between the wars this voice is clearest in Louis MacNeice, an Anglo-Irishman born and brought up in Belfast but son of an Anglican clergyman and given an English public school and then Oxford education. Yet MacNeice was also a founding influence behind the Northern Irish school of poets associated with the present Troubles, a fact that underlines the growing dimension of the non-Englishness in this English line as the decades pass.

MacNeice's chief spokesperson in our time, Edna Longley, sets up a challenge many will recognize. 'One day, I dream, there will be books with titles like *The MacNeice Generation; Thirties Poets – The MacNeice Group; MacNeice And After*'[1]. These titles all refer to real books but with MacNeice's name substituted for that of Auden. The implied challenge Longley mounts to the hitherto dominant Auden hegemony has two aspects: the one of MacNeice's non-English birth and status, the other to his unprogrammatic, non-cerebral response to the between-wars period. On such a view, Auden somehow knew too much; his poetry is compelling and interesting, but the lyric voice did not take off, and the verbal fecundity could not fully grow either.

Especially in his central and possibly best-known poem, *Autumn Journal*, MacNeice uses a different terminology. Amazingly, this sad, nostalgic, up-to-town work, running to about 2500 lines in 24 sections, resorts incessantly to cliché; cliché knowingly and deliberately adopted. Immediately after the signing of the Munich Agreement MacNeice let loose this record of his own life. We get his middle-class Irish upbringing; boarding school and Oxford; reading and then teaching classics; his broken marriage; his philosophy and his political positions including a by-election; the round of London social life of theatre and cocktail party, lodgings, trains and buses. We get, too, the landscape, or the town-and-countryscape the 'natural community' now is, rain at windows, outlooks across estates, scraps of land, crowded streets, leaves in the gutters. And all in the now tired clichés of the time, a subject MacNeice himself had already engaged with in the poem 'Homage To Cliché' and later 'All Over Again' and 'Idle Talk' and com-

parable poems. This too despite the fact that he was as aware
of technical innovation as anyone, providing a painstaking list
of new techniques and urging his readers that 'it is important
among dead poets to read Gerard Manley Hopkins and Wilfred
Owen'[2]. In *Autumn Journal* the hackneyed phrases pour forth:
forty to the gallon . . . a place in the sun . . . newsboys drive
a roaring business . . . packed to the roof . . . zero hour
approaches . . . things look better . . . save my skin . . . if you
can call it winning . . . Glory to God for Munich . . . now we
are back to normal . . . all we can do is argue . . . what is
life . . . the dice are loaded . . . call no man happy. These
examples all come from two facing pages in the Faber 1979
edition of the *Collected Poems* (pp. 116–17 – the lines are
unnumbered). A slightly more poetic passage of description in
traditional sense runs (p. 127):

> The next day I drove by night
>   Among red and amber and green, spears and candles,
> Corkscrews and slivers of reflected light
>   In the mirror of the rainy asphalt
> Along the North Circular and the Great West roads
>   Running the gauntlet of impoverished fancy
> Where housewives bolster up their jerry-built abodes
>   With *amour propre* and the habit of Hire Purchase.
> The wheels whished in the wet, the flashy strings
>   Of neon lights unravelled, the windscreen-wiper
> Kept at its job like a tiger in a cage or a cricket that
>   sings
>   All night through for nothing.
> Factory, a site for a factory, rubbish dumps,
>   Bungalows in lath and plaster, in brick, in concrete,
> And shining semi-circles of petrol pumps . . .

Yet it still seems less like a poetic thrust than a Sunday paper
feature article aimed at capturing an area's atmosphere. The
casual plurals, the generalized present tense ('housewives bols-
ter'), the lists of items as though each is worth no more or
less than any other, these and other features run right through
the poem, along with slack general questions ('Who am I –
or I – to demand oblivion?', 'Why do we like being Irish'),

unattributed 'yous' and 'wes', empty defiance ('All I want is an elegant and witty playmate/At the perfume counter or the cocktail bar'), and crudely altered literary reference: 'Glory to God in the Lowest', 'spider, spider, twisting tight'. Woven through all this is a profound frustration, as though these intelligent and sensitive public-school products of the 1930s have seen through their situation and environment but then, without the sophistication or ruthlessness to buy their way in, going for a non-poetry of the cheap widespread print: middlebrow newspapers, radio and magazines. In the new democratic world inexorably coming, the English polite reserve tries to live alongside a new technology that penetrates every part of life. A couple of months before a second war potentially as hideous and terrifying as the first, it can only desperately and laconically recall everything of the one past continuity it knows. And it sardonically transposes this into a language now controlled by a technological-political machine that, seemingly, won't ever let it go free again.

And yet the poem can be read from the reverse side of the tapestry, making it delicious. Whether it is corruptingly so the reader has to decide. There are signals as to the nature of this success. There is the title itself, *Autumn Journal*, where the nostalgic and the everyday both signal the very poetic continuity the poem offers to defy. There is a section on cliché itself (XIII-XV): 'a core/Of fact in a pulp of verbiage' and 'Education gives us too many labels/And cliches'. But most of all there is the fact that, unlike cliché, the poem never once repeats, so that the mixture of piled-up stock phrases and deeper reminiscence and reflection become compulsive reading. Not word, not sentence, not even image, but cliché, is the poem's medium. 'Everyday language' takes on a new emphasis. The critic's question is clear. Has MacNeice written a poem of mere cliché, or transformed cliché into a poem? The poem has a putrefaction about it, yet from first to last it is authentic, and the redounding banality of its central statement, 'All that I would like is to be human' (XII), has a true despair at the failure of this between-wars period, already foreshortening to us by historical perspective, to generate a better voice for its waiting poets. 'Lovely banality' was one of Frost's terms of praise for Wordsworth, 'and that penetration that goes with it'. The tone continues.

One may claim that MacNeice has successfully expressed the poetic predicament itself, by an act of huge honesty and risk. But the question is of what sort of expression results, and what is being expressed. Both Edna Longley and Samuel Hynes capture with penetrating observations the poetic moment that *Autumn Journal* achieves. Longley concludes that it is 'an act of pluralistic conjunction, a series of links that evolve into a great chain'. Hynes's sentence is itself a chain, and again takes us back as far as Wordsworth: 'loss: the loss of a by-election, the loss of a dog, the loss of Czechoslovakia, the loss of love, all together composing the mood of the autumn of 1938'[3].

This sense of loss provides what for the earlier nineteenth-century poets we called the undertow. MacNeice recalls his wife after their separation:

> And my common sense denies she is returning
>   And says, if she does return, she will not stay;
> And my pride, in the name of reason, tells me to cut
>   my losses
> And call it a day.
>
>   (Section XI)

With bravado he seeks an uncertain high life:

> Give us sensations and then again sensations –
>   Strip-tease, fireworks, all-in wrestling, gin;
> Spend your capital, open your house and pawn your pad-
>   locks,
>   Let the critical sense go out and the Roaring Boys come in.
>   (Section XV)

He fights off a longing for his country:

> And God Save – as you prefer – the King or Ireland.
>   The land of scholars and saints:
> Scholars and saints my eye, the land of ambush,
>   Purblind manifestos, never-ending complaints,
>   (Section XVI)

– and ends, after the tacked on *poésie-des-départs* flight to Spain, with a section-long lullaby longing for sleep to obliterate everything (again, no dreams), before waking the next day in the next war. Here again desire for an unknown fulfilment constantly defers its result, and the result offered in the poem is artificial. Headline language and cliché render everything grey; yet the poet's subjective integration and indeed integrity is retained, for his courageous act in writing such a poem at all from the inside, means he confronts the welter of phenomena of this new world as one man. In the poem's very last lines the poet crosses his 'Rubicon – the die is cast' and enters a new boundlessness.

It is a long way from *The Prelude* and that poem's 'appointed close', for MacNeice's time does not allow him Wordsworth's tenacious moral grip against his guilts, nor is there Auden's firm sense of intellect. This 'sleep' is not Frost's open-eyed guarding against sleep, nor Housman's terse sad farewell to his mother: 'Sleep on, sleep sound' ('Parta Quies', *More Poems* (xlviii). But the sensitivity to virtually every nuance of his time, cultural, political and deeply personal, allows the reader a strange sense that everything MacNeice says is done to see how it sounds, and what the corruption of language by headline packaging and easy documentary summary is doing to the very minds of those poets who most of all try to word their feelings and thoughts. And it asks whether any 'everyday language' other than this is left by which that can be done. The undertow is the parallel irony, at an underground depth, that this is how anything said in his time will have to be said at all. It is poetry entering poetry's opposite, not now merely 'prose' or 'speech', but corrupted speech, and it is the first time large-scale poetry has entered it.

It is a laconic logical consequence of Wordsworth's declared manifesto of 1800, and it sets, and requires, a new method if this kind of poetry is to continue. We cannot say that *Autumn Journal* is primarily political or primarily personal; rather, it is a sad entry into the remaining language by which we must speak both. It is the language itself that would blind if not so saved, and it is in this sense that in MacNeice, too, the mind and emotion are themselves the poet's medium. We are in the age of Orwell as well as Joyce and Lawrence.

As its name suggests *Autumn Sequel* is a follow-up to *Autumn Journal*. It is double the length but a less successful poem. In his autobiographical essays and his autobiography *The Strings Are False* MacNeice grappled with the same matter with the same nostalgic recalling[4]. His difficulty was perhaps that he did not have the new critical equipment of the social sciences to carry out this critical project as Auden did, and therefore could only initiate progress by this honest taking of risk. In later, mainly post-war poems, he develops a short lyric where opposites work on each other; tautology and surrealism; the objective and the enchanted; the homely and the darkness below. Here one can only list, and recommend, some poems: 'Woods', 'London Rain', 'Soap Suds', the earlier 'The Sunlight on the Garden' and a sequence of four, 'The Park', 'The Lake in the Park', 'Dogs in the Park' and 'Sunday in the Park'. In these last four the trapping of a nostalgic landscape in the urban scene is again evinced, again in curious haunted mode, touching the surrealistic. The known and familiar have surrendered to cliché, and so while understanding may not be advanced, our awareness of that very limitation is. But to use cliché so commonly is itself melancholic, itself loss, for deep in the clichéd phrase is the fact of its familiarity and pastness, that, like autumn, it is language already fading. It was one way out of the linguistic quandary, while retaining an approachable language, which others were to use in the same period.

In October 1914, in all probability the month in which Edward Thomas at last began to write serious poetry, a baby was born in Swansea where Edward Thomas may even have yet again just visited[5]. This infant was the future poet Dylan Thomas, who, like Gerard Manley Hopkins, might seem an unlikely candidate for discussion here. But Thomas's poetry has the same tensions, if for different reasons, as does Hopkins's. And like MacNeice, Thomas stands in mixed relation to any 'English' line, not only because he was Welsh just as MacNeice was Irish, but because the nationality itself may have compounded the situation through both poetic sources and personal attitudes. Thomas again then, like Hopkins, is introduced here to illustrate how an exception can work; how a poet, undeniably different from most discussed in this book, still seems to echo and work from some of the same origins, even if with markedly different results.

In 1951 when he was living in West Wales, Thomas wrote to an enquiring student. Thomas said: 'I wanted to write poetry in the beginning because I had fallen in love with words . . . . What the words (in nursery rhymes) stood for, symbolized, or meant, was of very secondary importance. . . . These words were, to me, as the notes of bells, the sounds of musical instruments, the noises of wind, sea, and rain, the rattle of milkcarts, the clopping of hooves on cobbles, the fingering of branches on a windowpane, might be to someone, deaf from birth, who has miraculously found his hearing'[6]. It will be seen that this picture is exactly the reverse of Frost's when he said a sentence is what you hear through a closed door, or Wordsworth's when he heard the solitary reaper across a field. Frost and Wordsworth heard the sentence, the meaning, without the words. Dylan Thomas heard, and loved, the words without the meaning. Thomas proceeded to make an evocative poetry of words in which meaning was not always clear even when the words' pungent effect was present. With at least some rivals, for example the 'Movement' poets of the 1950s, this did not make him popular. John Wain wrote that 'the gnawing doubt remains as to whether (Thomas) really *cared* whether the poem meant anything precise or not'. Donald Davie made comparable remarks with even more exasperated emphasis[7].

Is it possible to love or even hear words without their meanings? The question brings to mind the word of the French linguist Ferdinand de Saussure, whose work has been so influential in criticism, and particularly deconstruction, in the last two decades. Saussure said in effect that there is not a word and a (pre-existent) thing; rather, *within* any one 'word', there is both a sound-image and a concept. The sound-image cannot fail to call up a concept, for without that it would not be a 'word' at all, but just a noise or some marks. One cannot have the one without the other. Saussure called the sound-image and concept 'signifier' and 'signified', and the terms have become widely accepted and used. But, since Saussure, these terms have been used with considerable extension as to what they indicate about poetry. Among other things, the point has been made that while the signified is always present – language cannot contain sheer meaningless word-things alone – nevertheless, as it has been put, the signified concept can 'slide about' under the signifying sound-image[8]. Any poet, in short, may treat the relation between the two as close or distant, single or variable. If it is distant and variable, the poet may be captivated more by the apparent palpable 'words' themselves, for the sound-image element will be strong and constant, the concept shifting. The associations will be present, but as those readily come in train, rather than (as with the English-line poets) according to a pre-experienced set of thoughts or feelings at first in verbal terms only dimly known and so always reaching beyond themselves.

This is what Thomas seems to have been suggesting to his student in emphasizing the sounds of words, like hoofs or musical note and, precisely, heard by 'someone deaf from birth, who has miraculously found his hearing'. On first consideration these recollections of words in infancy seem to put Thomas with those who Julia Kristeva lights on as verbally playful wanderers. Such poets enjoy and follow words where they take them, and not, as with English line poets, having them stuck with already fixed referents which will drive the poet back inward to value more greatly his hitherto unverbalized mind and emotion. The signifier and signified are inseparable, as Saussure suggested, but the question is of which calls up which. With the English line poets, the concept (drawn from mind and emotion) comes first and must call up the word. With different poets, as Thomas at first seems to be, the word is played with and enjoyed as to its sound-image, which seems only then to resonate with the concept it calls up: apple, chain, the sea. As Thomas put it himself, 'When I experience anything, I experience it as a thing and a word at the same time'[9]. The English line poets by contrast claimed to experience something more nebulous, and the word 'something' was itself one of Wordsworth's commonest. Because of such considerations – though not then in Saussure's terms – Thomas was greeted as a Welsh Modernist, a surrealist, in his own phrase as a 'Rimbaud of Cwmdonkin Drive' (his birthplace) and other things besides. In retrospect one might apply such ideas to Hopkins too.

Yet looking at Thomas's poetry it seems that, as with Hopkins, such a summary is true but only half the truth. In the poems for which he is most remembered, he does indeed play with words with dexterity and joy. Yet they seem to come from a common source and memory, and he is himself at the heart of them:

> Now as I was young and easy under the apple boughs
> About the lilting house and happy as the grass was green,
>   The night above the dingle starry,
>   Time let me hail and climb
>   Golden in the heydays of his eyes,
>   And honoured among wagons I was prince of the apple
>   towns
> And once below a time I lordly had the trees and leaves
>   Trail with daisies and barley
>   Down the rivers of the windfall light.
>
> ('Fern Hill')

Surrealisms ('once below a time'), language of the hierarchy of formal civilization not nature ('honoured', 'prince', 'lordly'), and impossible conjunctions ('the rivers of the windfall light') all still occur within and bounded by a unified natural setting. It is playful and verbally savoured, but still within a prescribed world, and the surrealist vocabulary seems to come from the child's notions of it, not from outside it. This setting is the small farm of Thomas's wider family in Carmarthenshire. More often, in fact right across his poetry, it is the language of the sea and shore, obviously of the sea-and-estuary village of Laugharne in West Wales where he lived:

>   It was my thirtieth year to heaven
> Woke to my hearing from harbour and neighbour wood
>   And the mussel pooled and the heron
>   Priested shore
>   The morning beckon
> With water praying and call of seagull and rook . . .
>
> ('Poem in October')

Water prays, the shore is heron-priested, the syntax is encapsulated and weird, yet the scene is vivid and unified. And there are other features of Thomas's poetry which draw him back from an out-and-out espousal of 'words, words, words, and each of which was alive forever in its own delight and glory and oddity and light'[10], that is to say, outside of natural syntax and inner feeling. His poetry centres on himself, on the ego. Many first-lines start there: the two we have just seen, along with 'I dreamed my genesis', 'I fellowed sleep', 'If I were tickled by the rub of love', 'I see the boys of summer in their ruin', 'I, in my intricate image,', 'This bread I break was once the oat', 'Then was my neophyte', 'I make this in a warring absence' and many more. Gwen Watkins has declared from first-hand knowledge of Thomas's supposedly closest friendship, with her husband Vernon Watkins, that 'I do not think that the friendship meant very much to Dylan'[11]. He was affectionate and lovable, but his own needs were his imaginative centre.

There is also the tendency to make identification between self and nature melancholy in cast:

> The force that through the green fuse drives the flower
> Drives my green age: that blasts the roots of trees
> Is my destroyer.
> And I am dumb to tell the crooked rose
> My youth is bent by the same wintry fever.

The first three lines are a symmetrical Wordsworthian identification with nature, the 'fitting and fitted' to which Blake objected. John Bayley even suggested that 'no other poet since (Wordsworth and Coleridge) has shared their interests so much as he'[12], a view which raises the eyebrows now, yet when Bayley wrote this Hardy, Frost and Edward Thomas did not have their present exposure. Finally the local and domestic ambience are made by the way Swansea and elsewhere shimmer behind the poems; and the ubiquitous presence of the father-figure, undeniably that of Thomas's own father schoolteacher D. J. Thomas, who effectually formed his small son's ear with his own readings out loud and his ample home library. Thomas's reputation for esoteric content and reference by a still incomprehending public, was uncompromisingly denied by himself: 'Nowhere, indeed, in all my writing, do I use any knowledge which is not commonplace to any literate person'[13]. He also denied what was often imputed to him, that his chief influences were the Bible, Freud, Joyce and the Surrealists. Thomas was not above throwing dust in the eyes of probing critics, yet this did not stop him declaring that his favourite poet by far was Thomas Hardy[14]. There is little reason to doubt his sincerity in this remark.

It seems from all this that Thomas never escaped, nor much wanted to, a womb-fixation which expressed itself in his poems about genesis, his unrebellious naming of his father and his centring in an almost watery suspension in the geographical areas where he was brought up. His biographer Paul Ferris has reported how these tendencies of Thomas lasted into adulthood; homesickness, latent castration-fear and cognate factors[15]. These dispositions lock him back into an obsession with pre-infancy which, although not Wordsworthian in poetic expression, nevertheless throws light on the wordplay Thomas does practise. Thomas's womb poems abound, 'I dreamed my genesis', 'Before I knocked', 'From Love's First Fever' and the rest. He proliferates womb, worm and tomb as connected rhymes and references. Donald Davie complained that the entities Thomas's congested nouns and adjectives refer to 'will not stand still, but fluctuate and swim like weeds in a stream'. Exactly how the embryo floats in the womb one would think, and the stanzas quoted above from 'Fern Hill' and 'Poem In October' have just that tendency.

None of this argues that Thomas was then a true Englishline poet merely covered over with thin layers of word-fun, or a wild Welsh poet suitably laundered for metropolitan consumption. My examples necessarily give only one half of the picture. Much of the time Thomas is opaque, verbally congested, syntactically minimal, and probably meaningless. He feels through and in words' tangibilities not their connectives; the poetry is full of sunlight as well as water; desire is blocked and often satisfied by a relish and investment in the words themselves. He loves to make an individual word rear up on its legs like a horse. And there is always that crucial *distance*, never found in Frost or Hardy, between the underlying emotion and the coding of that into exterior things: birds, chapels, Bibles, sea-shells, trees, flesh, night and so on. But, because the complement of vocabulary is from the same region of home, he lives it. Thomas's poetry, at its best, is a pungent lexical coding of a few obsessions. It is not dream but holiday childhood.

The wider question is therefore raised of Thomas's Welshness, and the implications of that for the twentieth-century development of what, as to its poets' nationalities, begins to look rather less an 'English' line. The effect of the Welsh language and its formal and alliterative poetic properties did undoubtedly influence Thomas, possibly mediated by Hopkins, as Walford Davies has argued in some detail[16]. Walford Davies also points out that Welsh culture and life is written into the poems in numerous subtle ways. But the other essential factor is that Auden and as we clearly saw MacNeice, increasingly found that their terrain was suburban, as later did Larkin too. Thomas also explicitly espoused the suburban. But it could remain romanticized, sunlit, because it was out in a region where an untouched nature could still seem to be taken for granted and be seen both sacramentally and domestically at once.

MacNeice, who evidently much admired Dylan Thomas[17] came from Ireland into England and in effect took on the poetic problem, as an Irishman, of rendering the newly laid-over English landscape. The poet Charles Tomlinson has called this the 'manscape'; the suburban world of roundabouts, pony-paddocks, garages, estates, playing fields and commuters, and some surviving farmland. Dylan Thomas did it the other way round; instead of secularizing the natural he idealizes both the natural and the suburban. The result was another ambivalent poet, comparable to Hopkins, without the latter's formal religious belief or scholarly approach to words, but with a remarkably similar verbal texture in the result. Both Thomas and MacNeice thus aided the English line's possible survival in a shift to north and west. Throw in Frost as well, and the scene for English-line poetry is at least in part moving off centre.

Finally, to suggest that it is off-centre is to raise a long-standing controversy about a group of post-Second-War poets usually known as the 'Movement', and the discussion of them that took place at the time and since. To be brief, it can only be suggested that the homelier Amis, Wain and Betjeman (although the latter was strictly of an earlier generation), lack in their poetry the element of self and self-search being co-extensive, which has been this line's main compulsion; while Davie, Enright and Gunn, all of whom have spent many years abroad, are always nearer the world of panoramic and trans-atlantic wit/seriousness and its more esoteric tradition. Succinct complaints about Robert Conquest's anthology *New Lines* (1956) were made in the introduction to Al Alvarez's seminal anthology *The New Poetry*, which attempted to reverse the Movement's influence. 'It was, in short, academic-administra-tive verse, polite, knowledgeable, efficient, polished, and, in its quiet way, even intelligent.' To romantics and non-roman-tics equally the prospect would be scarcely enthralling, but the topographical point is more relevant here. Again Donald Davie is the writer: 'We all know that England still has bullfrogs and otters and tramps asleep in ditches; yet because in the land-scape of Hughes's poems these shaggy features bulk so large, it may strike us as more an Irish landscape than an English one'[18]. It needn't, but Davie's force is clear, and it is why MacNeice and Dylan Thomas are given more prominence here. It is also why any new, now unmelancholic and now differ-ently English-line poetry is likely to run from poets like Basil Bunting, Geoffrey Hill, Charles Tomlinson and Peter Red-grove. However, if there was one last survivor from the inward English line from just before Wordsworth, it had to be Philip Larkin.

11
Philip Larkin

Philip Larkin (1922–85) is just possibly the final poet to place and partly ease pressing personal difficulties in a known landscape. It seems he feared death more than anything, and of these poets most recently died.

His work would appear to have all the components of the English line we have looked at. It is melancholic and laconic; sited in a recognizable and familiar landscape; written and indeed spoken in ordinary everyday language; preoccupied with domesticity, love and death; searching unavailingly for where true knowing may be found; inward and self-anxious; stamped with unfulfilled desires and longings; and casting back to a secure lost world which, in his case, he sardonically laments never existed. Indeed, he acknowledgedly follows much the kind of poetry we have been tracing. 'Within reach of my working chair I have reference books on the right, and twelve poets on the left: Hardy, Wordsworth, Christina Rossetti, Hopkins, Sassoon, Edward Thomas, Barnes, Praed, Betjeman, Whitman, Frost and Owen. True, I reach to the right more than to the left, but the twelve are there as exemplars'[1]. And yet his work is a paradox.

The paradox is seen first in his changing influences. Broadly he follows the twentieth-century poets already considered, Hardy pre-eminently. Of Hardy Larkin wrote 'may I trumpet the assurance that one reader at least would not wish Hardy's *Collected Poems* a single page shorter, and regards it as many times over the best body of poetic work this century so far has to show'[2]. When he wrote reviews, which was not often, he stuck to his favourites: Barnes, Owen, Housman, Edward Thomas, Betjeman. In places the poems echo Edward Thomas and Frost closely. For instance, the last line of Thomas's 'Old Man' is behind the last line of 'High Windows', while the last stanza of Frost's 'The Trial by Existence' very strongly pre-echoes the last stanza of 'Dockery and Son'. And yet in certain phrases other voices are heard. There was the three-year allegiance to the symbolist Yeats towards the end of the last war when Larkin was in his early twenties, and he had already undergone an Auden period, though this was mainly for Auden's 'ease and vividness'. There was also a friendship with Vernon Watkins (admirer of Yeats, friend of Dylan Thomas) as well as Kingsley Amis. Finally, according to Barbara Everett[3], Larkin much later went against all his previous principles by briefly espousing French symbolism. This emerges in 'Vers de Société' and other late poems. And the paradox is compounded by the recent publication of Larkin's *Collected Poems*, nearly 250 of them, far more than anyone had previously thought. In straight quantity that gives him more than double the number of poems the limited-output poets such as Housman, Thomas and Hopkins produced. There has been some disagreement about the value of this previously uncollected work[4], but certainly the new poems reveal a very personal Larkin trying to cope with sexual and other distresses of self-knowledge. This throws further light on the poetry's overall significance.

Yet there is a factor behind this paradox factor. It has been succinctly put by Donald Davie, writing about Larkin in the book cited earlier. 'It was English poetry (with Wordsworth) that in modern times first expressed ideas of elemental sanctity and natural piety; and it seems it must be English poetry which asks what to do with these ideas in a landscape where virtually all the sanctuaries have been violated, all the pieties blasphemed'[5]. Davie's view is that Larkin – and Hardy – lowered their poetic sights, but at least did so because they accepted that the messy, uninspiring world of supermarkets, housing estates, dirty beaches and generally shrug-of-the-shoulder standards is better than other more tyrannical political alternatives. A human dignity, if with Larkin's sometimes gloomy and defiantly four-letter language; the reek of the human. The resulting plain-spun poetry of personal feelings, reading the paper, lying in bed worrying about sex and death, going on train journeys and the rest, still manages to culminate in a few extraordinary poems which at times look out from this grey but secure and more human ambience. That is the paradox. Some of Larkin's greatest poems, 'Here', 'Dockery and Son',

'The Whitsun Weddings' and 'Aubade' are on the usual central subjects of landscape, knowing, love and death respectively, yet they are fuller and more elaborate than the shorter down-to-earth pieces. And there are curiously visionary signs, at unexpected points, in them and elsewhere. They move toward symbolism and are touched with light. One might begin by asking where these outstanding effusions grow from.

To start at the bottom, many people have castigated Larkin as being a nihilist, a whinger and a seller-short of poetry's true vocation. Harold Bloom states that 'meaning' and 'moaning' are connected etymologically[6]. He doesn't have Larkin in mind particularly, but the observation could have brought a sardonic response from Larkin himself. There is truth in this view, yet the progress of Larkin's work is surely missed by any such dismissal. Larkin's more nihilistic poetry is an emptying-out process which was probably essential preparation for his fuller epiphanies. One can see three characteristics in the lesser poems: solitude, disconcerting candour and this emptying out itself. Perhaps it is time for an example:

> They fuck you up, your mum and dad.
>   They may not mean to, but they do.
> They fill you with the faults they had
>   And add some extra, just for you . . .
>
> Man hands on misery to man.
>   It deepens like a coastal shelf.
> Get out as early as you you,
>   And don't have any kids yourself.
>   ('This be The Verse')

There are numerous poems like this, not all of them withheld until Larkin's death. At bottom he loves to cut nature-visionaries down to size with four-letter and scatological language as in 'Vers de Société', 'Sad Steps', 'Love Again' and elsewhere; and even without such lexicon poem after poem is at one level about the pointlessness of relationships and the ubiquity of boredom. Solitude is strongly and sadly evoked in many poems: 'Best Society', 'Vers de Société' again, 'Mr Bleaney' and 'At Thirty-One' are some of them. Davie wondered whether such work is written 'under pressure not from "the age" but only from some compulsion in himself'. This strength of inner compulsion is what most of the other 'Movement' poets lack; but its source is a non-source; an absence of that landscape and seemingly natural community where such poetry of the inner sadness had been written before. Without root in the community sex and self are left stranded. Loss now is nearly total.

So Larkin is isolated in himself and organically cut off from an altered landscape he still knows is there. But even the poems that do evoke the daily tangible world still have a once-removed feeling, a mood of disconnection. They are a stage away from those basics of what had hitherto seemed our natural places of habitation. To the cursory reader this might seem questionable. Aren't Larkin's poems full of marriages, hospitals, comfortable if indifferent interiors, the odd church, seaside scenes, books and lengthy lists of photographically-observed details from the contemporary scene? Indeed they are, but in so many cases it is not the thing itself, but the left-over shell of it when our ideals and roots have been destroyed, that is evoked. Countryside, home, marriage, religion and respect for the dead are what the traditional community was made of, it seemed permanently. But with Larkin, it is not roots in countryside but journeys across countryside; not home but lodgings or hotels; not marriages but weddings; not religion but church buildings; not mourning of the dead but fear of one's own dying.

Take for example home. Larkin lived nearly all his adult life in flats, and when he finally moved to a house in 1974 it seems he more or less stopped writing[7]. 'Friday Night in the Royal Station Hotel' is illustrative, and so is the much better-known 'Mr Bleaney'. In this poem the poet goes to live in some dismal and bare lodgings, where a garrulous landlady incessantly tells him about all the habits and relations of 'Mr Bleaney', the previous incumbent. Larkin ends reflecting that all this talk can't tell him about Bleaney's inner imaginative life, his fears, private jokes and loneliness. The poem is permeated with a kind of landscape-that-might-have-been:

Flowered curtains, thin and frayed,
Fall to within five inches of the sill,

Whose window shows a strip of building land,
Tussocky, littered. 'Mr Bleaney took
My bit of garden properly in hand' . . .

But if he stood and watched the frigid wind
Tousling the clouds, lay on the fusty bed
Telling himself that this was home, and grinned,
And shivered, without shaking off the dread

That how we live measures our own nature,
And at his age having no more to show
Than one hired box should make him pretty sure
He warranted no better, I don't know.

He 'doesn't know', and the search of the English-line poet for a missing understanding is still with us.

Even so, staying in lodgings and hotels seems more normal; perhaps because 'home is so sad' as one short poem has it, on the same subject from the other side. Home there is a left-over, 'shaped to the comfort of the last to go', and having in it only things like, in the last line, 'The music in the piano stool. That vase'. Yet the poem itself is sad, a longing for what could have been. Larkin never married, whether as he frequently said because he preferred the freedom of solitude, or whether as some poems seem to suggest a love, perhaps more than one, came to nothing[8]. Equally, while weddings are temporary, marriages last – or can – and mean children. Larkin avoids the company of children, and he glimpses weddings not marriages, out of the corner of his eye in varying circumstances.

Commonly it is a wedding ring or wedding photos in albums. 'Afternoons', 'Annus Mirabilis', 'Wild Oats', 'I am washed upon a rock' and other have this signature. Other poems touch on the wedding day subliminally as, surprisingly, does the poem 'At Grass', about racehorses past their prime. After years of being watched winning classics on major courses, the horses are quietly out in meadows at dusk. For they

Have slipped their names, and stand at ease,
Or gallop for what must be joy,
And not a fieldglass sees them home,
Or curious stop-watch prophesies:
Only the groom, and the groom's boy,
With bridles in the evening come.

So the poem ends. If the last two lines do hint at the wedding match, with the 'groom' and so nearly the 'bride' reached as at the end of a wooing when they 'in the evening come', the rest of the poem alters perceptibly, as though one had shaken a kaleidoscope. The fashionable Ascot-type scenes described earlier in the poem (again a landscape) suddenly seem like a society wedding. But the horses too are free at last from stares of friends and relations, and they 'gallop for what must be joy' and can go 'home' to hymen unwatched. The 'groom's boy' is the progenitive result, and it is indeed subliminal, denying Larkin's normal aversion to children and procreation. And, intriguingly, when the horses 'slipped their names' they did just what brides do, or till our time have done, when they leave their 'Maiden Name' behind. This is the title of another Larkin poem, in which all he has left of a friend when she marries is the other surname she then no longer used. There is also the equally deflected 'Wedding Wind', a poem still under the influence of Yeats, and in which the poet stays outside. The surely great poem 'The Whitsun Weddings' has an even larger consummation.

Wedding as symbol of marriage figures in the much-quoted 'An Arundel Tomb', where a knight and lady in stone effigy in a church (Chichester Cathedral in fact) are suddenly seen to be holding hands. The poem is one of two extended poems about or set in churches. The other is 'Church Going'. The title puns in the quiet syntactical way that this kind of poetry so often does; but the poem itself is subdued, a little anxious and considered, as though this particular church does not stir him sufficiently for his weighty topic, that of the church's past significance and present decline. This church 'was not worth stopping for'. Larkin sees 'some brass and stuff/Up at the holy end'; his conclusion is serious, but respectful rather than deeply felt. Arnold's Rugby chapel has faded.

These two poems are the nearest Larkin reaches to elegy (apart from the visionary 'The Explosion', the last poem in his last book). Fear of dying is not part of elegy. It drags Larkin down, in many poems; symbolistically, as at the end of 'Next, Please', again in a landscape, looking at the sea, and seeing ships you think are bringing good to yourself. But:

> Only one ship is seeking us, a black–
> Sailed unfamiliar, towing at her back
> A huge and birdless silence. In her wake
> No waters breed or break.

The dark image marks the absence of the supportive world which buries its dead as well as nurturing its living. It is 'unfamiliar', not of family, and no waters 'breed'. 'Birdless' is the chilling touch. You suddenly realize what ought to have been there. Death rather, in our world, is hidden away in institutions, and you are taken there in machines called ambulances (as in the poem so named), to large brick buildings with clinical wards. When waking before dawn, as in 'Aubade', the terror of death is doubled in size. This poem is an ironic allusion to the traditional 'aubade' or lovers' regret dawn has come, for here Larkin's fear of reproduction and increase make for a greater loneliness in face of death itself. 'Aubade' and 'The Old Fools' have curious and wonderful epiphanies of their own, here and there, but the black truth is faced, that in a world without God or an after-life to go back to from Wordsworth's pre-natal existence, there is nothing at all:

> And specious stuff that says *No rational being*
> *Can fear a thing it will not feel*, not seeing
> That this is what we fear – no sight, no sound,
> No touch or taste or smell, nothing to think with,
> Nothing to love or link with,
> The anaesthetic from which none come round.
>
> ('Aubade')

The reduced language of the English line evokes only nothing: no 'perchance to dream', nor the 'fiery floods . . . thrilling region of thick-ribbed ice' that Claudio dreaded death would bring in *Measure for Measure*. There won't be even the musty, homely skeletal comfort of Hardy's churchyard ghosts, pushing up weeds against the churchyard wall. It is the blackest reverse of the personal poetry of any rooted human when the sense of that community has gone, and it is difficult to see the English line surviving it.

One senses that Larkin saw the danger. For although 'The Old Fools', 'Aubade' and others are the natural partners of Larkin's younger poems of total solitude, in many others the familiar world and landscape, though receding, cling on as a desperate presence. It is hoveringly there in 'At Grass' and 'Mr Bleaney', but in many the setting, naturally enough, is the journey, by train or car. These poems too are a once-removed approach to the traditional communal world, but at least you can see that world, or its remains, from the carriage or car window. In 'Here' the poem's subject is a traversed landscape. The poet pictures a car driver from presumably the A1 going east across the Fens:

> Swerving east, from rich industrial shadows
> And traffic all night north; swerving through fields
> Too thin and thistled to be called meadows,

More scenery is described:

> And the widening river's slow presence,
> The piled gold clouds, the shining gull-marked mud . . .

before the car enters what must be Hull, past shoppers from estates who

> Push through plate-glass swing doors to their desires –
> Cheap suits, red kitchen-ware, sharp shoes, iced lollies,
> Electric mixers, toasters, washers, driers –
>
> A cut-price crowd . . .

and then through the old harbour district out on the east side to the flat land stretching to the beach:

> Here silence stands
> Like heat. Here leaves unnoticed thicken,
> Hidden weeds flower, neglected waters quicken,
> Luminously-peopled air ascends;
> And past the poppies bluish neutral distance
> Ends the land suddenly beyond a beach
> Of shapes and shingle. Here is unfenced existence:
> Facing the sun, untalkative, out of reach.

Many commentators on this, including Davie, have said that the supermarket customers or 'cut-price crowd' are seen contemptuously. But the shape of the poem suggests a larger vision than that. The town is sandwiched between the open landscape on both sides of it, and the poem mirrors this by beginning and ending with those open scenes. The final two lines are ambivalent and a touch mysterious, for as Andrew Motion points out[9] 'out of reach' can imply both unattainability and safety. Unlike the highly significant poem about knowledge 'Dockery and Son', this poem ends with none and with the statement, in effect, that it is not to be had. The poem like the land is compellingly flat. Yet the landscape remains; the flatness is its end and the poem's most secure and reliable quality. But the flatness is double-edged. Because the population are given no controlling action or purpose, a strange agnosticism hangs over the poem. 'Here silence stands like heat'. If it is not ominous neither is it optimistic. It is one of Larkin's most uncluttered and lucid landscape poems, yet the reason for that is in its suppression – for once – of questioning, to allow in the landscape's sheer immeasurable, detailed presence.

But in 'The Whitsun Weddings' – surely Larkin's major poem and one that stands comparison with the strongest poems this line of poetry has produced – the railway line goes back from the countryside into the city. The train going south from the Fens to London takes aboard more and more newly married couples on Whit Saturday, in the sunlight, in what finally amounts to a meditative hymeneal celebration. The newly-married couples come serially on to the train with the same staged movement as the spots of scenery that go past it. At first there is the 'street/Of blinding windscreens', 'the

river's level drifting breadth' and then 'the tall heat that
slept/For miles inland'. Then, much later, the train approaches
London where 'fields were building plots, and poplars cast/
Long shadows over major roads', till finally 'we raced across/
Bright knots of rail,/ Past standing Pullmans, walls of black-
ened moss', images tingling with sexuality as marriage consummation is reached. But all of this is paralleled by the wedding events which punctuate each stop on the journey:

> All down the line
> Fresh couples climbed aboard: the rest stood round;
> The last confetti and advice were thrown,
> And, as we moved, each face seemed to define
> Just what it saw departing: children frowned
> At something dull; fathers had never known
>
> Success so huge and wholly farcical;
>   The women shared
> The secret like a happy funeral;
> While girls, gripping their handbags tighter, stared
> At a religious wounding . . .

The poem ends, as it began, in stasis:

> We slowed again,
> And as the tightened brakes took hold, there swelled
> A sense of falling, like an arrow-shower
> Sent out of sight, somewhere becoming rain.

Larkin slots in the details with such astonishing and infallible
accuracy that one wants to quote every line; failing that, one
can only wonder what prompted Philip Larkin to bring virtually everything into his major poetic effort that his other
poems, and his own life, seemed to have concentrated on
rejecting. As with the brief sunlit memories of the decrepit
aged in 'The Old Fools', and his own dawn of curtains and
postmen in 'Aubade', and even the 'strong unhindered moon'
of the sobering poem of unwanted knowledge 'Dockery and
Son', this ending to the wedding poem has been described by
a number of critics now as an epiphany. It is a sudden sighting

of what Motion calls 'a release from the everyday because of a sense of the marvellous'[10]. It is as if the nihilistic aspects of Larkin's other poetry were a necessary purgation. It begins to move signally away from the main poetic idea of this English line's concerns.

And yet, it cannot be left there. The vision achieved by 'The Whitsun Weddings' and comparable poems is inspiring in its contrast to the truer, messier world, but it does not answer the prosaic questions Larkin went on asking about not weddings but marriage. The train journey ends apocalyptically and that is certainly uplifting. But it ends when the weddings end and the marriages start, and we are left to remember comparable marriages in the real world. Equally Larkin had also to face not a past England but a real present one. He confronts it, briefly but directly, in the poem 'Going, Going'. In that poem he comes right up to date with a bleaker sense that England is in practice being turned over to developers and bulldozers:

> And that will be England gone,
> The shadows, the meadows, the lanes,
> The guildhalls, the carved choirs.
> There'll be books; it will linger on
> In galleries; but all that remains
> For us will be concrete and tyres.

Until now we could 'always escape in the car', but the routes are diminishing annually, and Larkin has anticipated Britain's environmental emergency by nearly two decades.

Is that what we have left of Eden? This is hardly the place to answer, but as far as poetry is concerned the question is what there is left to say when such poetry can no longer resort to a rural world which, rightly or not, it remembered as home and by which it saw itself as nurtured. The value of the mournful poetry of the English line is that it has imaginatively accompanied, perhaps led to, psychological advances in the experience of self-consciousness and self-knowledge. This is most strongly expressed in Larkin's poetry in the poem 'Dockery and Son', which sadly space prevents us examining closely here as it surely deserves. Visiting his old university (Oxford) the poet learns that a current undergraduate is the son of one of his own contemporaries of years before. On the long train journey homeward the poet thinks about this, shrugs it off, falls asleep, changes trains, and turns it over further, but still hours later can't escape the questioning, in the end about life and death, into which he in his very different unmarried and childless state is plunged. As he says, if defensively: 'Why did he think adding meant increase? To me it was dilution'. But the inference here is that the element of a wider searching, of not knowing yet still wanting to know, is deep in the poet's thrust behind the poem. The parallel and contrast is with Arnold's 'The Scholar-Gipsy', where Arnold himself stays sadly in Oxford but recommends the knowledge-seeker to stay away. Here, Larkin himself goes away, but the more he gets away from conscious learning (Oxford) the more he is led into deeper waters.

As Michael Ignatieff put it recently, self-knowledge entails some melancholy, otherwise it is shallow[11]. And such poetry of bourgeois melancholy has only reached self-knowledge without mental breakdown by conceiving and relying on a reposeful landscape of 'nature', that which is naturally there, not man-constructed though always with the symptomatic threats of human hand built into it. If we are now increasingly cut off from this natural source, this poetry has to end. Larkin has expressed that ending, and found, if very occasionally, a kind of brief underlying glimpse of something larger and more transcendental. Some glimpses happen at such moments.

12

Conclusion

W. H. Auden's poem 'In Memory of Sigmund Freud' ends as follows:

> but he would have us remember most of all
> to be enthusiastic over the night,
>   not only for the sense of wonder
> it alone has to offer, but also
>
> because it needs our love. With large sad eyes
> its delectable creatures look and beg
>   us dumbly to ask them to follow:
> they are exiles who long for the future
>
> that lies in our power, they too would rejoice
> if allowed to serve enlightenment like him,
>   even to bear our cry of 'Judas',
> as he did and all must bear who serve it.
>
> One rational voice is dumb. Over his grave
> the household of Impulse mourns one dearly loved:
>   sad is Eros, builder of cities,
> and weeping anarchic Aphrodite.
>
>   (stanzas 25–8)

This passage, and the whole of this elegy on Freud, might be read as an oblique comment on how the kind of poetry this book has discussed should now be regarded. This would neither add to nor detract from one's aesthetic enjoyment of that poetry, nor even its power to meet our own needs. The greatest need is to find our depressions and melancholies named, and so given an articulation to match any comparable one of the human condition. But Auden's passage, and his whole poetry perhaps, suggests that the relieving expression of one person's melancholy – entailing a confessional quality – has been radically altered by the wider formulation of our condition by the human sciences. Any such poetry will now be and for some time has been written in a climate that already possesses a non-poetic account of melancholy, individuality, sexuality and loneliness, and their relation to or alienation from the natural physical world. As Freud himself put it, 'The poets have been there before me': Freud was not thinking of Wordsworth and the English line, yet the implication remains that – to switch to Marxist terms – the social and psychological conditions for this particular voice no longer hold, for its sources have made their appearance in consciousness. Auden's own poem, like much of his poetry, considers the matter with the authoritative tone of one who stands off the experience he has himself understood, and his poetry has this quality of *aufhebung* – abolish and transcend – in that by expressing this later understanding of the earlier he ends it; by ending it he expresses it. The poem's last references are classical; the individual melancholic condition, desperate for the reassurance of known fields, houses, water, roads and trees, enters civilization.

For a few weeks soon after it was published in 1988, Larkin's *Collected Poems* reached and stayed with the *Sunday Times* Top Ten list for hardbacks. Yet despite his popularity many critics feel that his and other comparable poetry is over. Looked at objectively, many factors may seem to be contributing to such an outcome. One is a displacement of our idea of the landscape itself. It is partly that the landscape is increasingly covered with human artefacts. But the result is more than simply the disappearance of lovely and reassuring scenes. The earth begins to seem like an artefact, and artefact by its nature leads to the outward, the exaggerated, the playful. The world also begins to feel less and less like a vast terrain where one can wander for ever and still find deserts, seas and mountains enough for all populations and activities. The idea begins to grip that where we live is a small spinning ball, a long way from any other. Equally it is not just despoilation of this environment by a growing use of electronic heat and burning fuel that bothers people, but also that this is changing the climate itself, perhaps permanently. The lost paradise these poets yearned for, taken away by industry and technology, is

where rain-forests and seashore were not hacked or burnt
down or covered with oil-slicks, and where birds, rivers and
mountains were wilderness, not bought and sold for profit. It
was where true understanding of reality, and everyday symbols for that, felt able to be found. Even in *In Memoriam* Tennyson feared only geology, not yet total pollution. But now, will
there still be autumns to write about in the future, to identify
with melancholy, where autumn was always home?

Ideas of England and Britain are similarly affected. As we
have seen, English-line poets decreasingly had to be English.
The changes in the landscape, broadly speaking, are – as yet
– less extensive in Wales, Ireland and Scotland. The poets who,
if any, at first seemed candidates for this line's continuation are
often of those countries or of the margins of England itself.
Seamus Heaney, R. S. Thomas and Ted Hughes are clear
examples. But, as will be suggested, all these three have long
moved toward considerably different themes and modes of
poetic expression so that their earlier work needs revaluation
in that context. Much could be said on this matter of British
nationalism and its relation to unEnglishness; Yeats's essay 'A
General Introduction for my Work' is still a most valuable
starting-point in examining the topic[1]. Large ethnic minorities
also mean the culture may be modifying altogether, with a
sudden consciousness of Islam in Britain the most recent example. There is also of course a large African-originated population, Europe comes ever nearer, and there could be an influx
from Hong Kong. These events arise in a post-imperial era in
which there is debate as to whether a wholly cosmopolitan
culture, containing in a few small islands something like the
global range, is or isn't preferable to a local and familiar continuation of the past. Equally, poetry in English is increasingly
written elsewhere on the globe and on different cultural foundations. American poetry has already influenced British poetry
for most of the century. The feeling of England as home, easy
enough for an island and when it had (paradoxically) the global
domination Tennyson and Arnold could assume, gets harder
when different cultural strands come to be present in it, living
in it in new and unfamiliar ways.

Equally the English language is no longer 'ordinary' anywhere, for there is no single dialect or mode of speech, even

if there ever was. We still sense deeply that poetry is a matter of voice, of saying or singing things, and the English line provided that legacy. But the voice is now more outdoor, more often to an audience and, in ways sometimes not too obvious, geared to the fact of performed music. Furthermore, words are more and more physically visible in small numbers. Headlines and ad slogans seldom contain more than five or six words, and these are usually united with colour, texture, visual artwork of all kinds, and typefaces hugely enlarged on hoardings or television. The word is displayed on computer screen, glossy paper, pulp paper, T-shirt, brand product and banner. This of course runs partner to the arrival and penetration by television itself into the intimate centres of personal life as well as nationally and politically. Anyone feeling they might be a poet today is likely to have become aware very early of language in public display, physical presentation or accompaniment by music or political context. As has often been said, the intricate pattern of human communications across the world, and any one country in it, is now more like a nervous system than a literature.

These factors are interconnected, along with that of the new role of women in society and the change of relationship between the sexes. Because of widespread divorce and separation the effect is not only on parents but on children. Equally the close tie to a sole tiny and perhaps stressful home and nuclear family is less often the individual's only experience. The poet's topic is therefore less likely to be a melancholic brooding on the inward self in uncoloured fashion. How that affects the poetic sensibility more generally might be hard to guess at. But clearly the experience of traditional parental attitudes by adolescent males is already much diluted. The pattern of language learning is less and less frequently a matter of infant learning from the mother and then later social adaptation by the father. Quite early in a child's life the sources from which language can be imbibed are highly diverse. Language as an inward matter survives, but is residual, the bit left over from public or community life.

The question arises then of how finally to characterize the worth of these poets in larger terms; that is to say, as more than only the individual occasion of the expression of a melan-

choly or depression which readers, feeling their own loneliness
and sadness has been shared and made universal, can look to
for reassurance. This can only be put briefly. The strength of
the poets we have discussed would seem in the last analysis
to be epistemological. Commonly this poetry is not, as such,
intellectual, but it is of great intellectual significance. The
element of knowing/not knowing is an element both of unsatisfied desire and of formal knowledge. The period of the massive
expansion of education in Britain and the west coincides with
the slightly longer period in which, as Foucault has argued,
we have sought knowledge in sexuality[2]. Indeed sexuality has
itself been thought to be the basis and locus of the energy
which desires a fuller cognition. At this point sexuality ties in
with its immediate environment, namely the family or family
group, and the emerging belief of the last 200 years that knowledge is not attained objectively but is psychologically and socially located. The longing for understanding of reality became
inseparable from one's own adequacy and status.

I would tie this to the Socratic idea that courage is knowledge. The great strength of the English line poets would
appear to lie in their courage. The search for real rather than
nominal self-understanding must entail an inward search that
goes so far to the frontier of self-examination that melancholy
and depression are always a risk. It is risky because it entails
convolution of the seeking self and the self sought. Any poet
already works without the palpable, solid material which other
artists use; the actual stone or metal for sculpture, raw sounds
for music, or pigments and colours for painting. And unless
they stick to 'ordinary' language even poets will attend to
words themselves as a sort of object. The words will become
more like pigment or other material, and the erstwhile permanent symbols such as jewel, rose, crown, moon, lion and the
rest that grow from them. Such poets begin and end with a
sensitivity to and love of the outer things which we all love.
By contrast we don't directly love other people's inner minds,
and so the act of expressing this inward search, already at the
boundaries of melancholy and unfulfilled desire, is an act of
courage too. The many curious mixtures of melancholy and
pleasure have to be present at this edge for the experience to
be bearable for the poet at all. The pleasure may be simply

pride that the pain is borne; it may risk the enjoyment of self-pity; or it may be that the desiring animal, the human being, has the imagination always to conceive desires which cannot be fulfilled. What one might call the cancellation of their own powerful sexuality in many of these poets itself seems to clear the way for the search into a universal void, or abyss, which they would mark or imprint (to use Derrida's insight) by an event of writing, an inscription of what it is to exist at all. Whatever the truth, this poetry's achievement, which is surely massive even if over, is that it poetically transformed a main aspect of the period of liberal individualism and its necessary search for self-consciousness and self-understanding, which they themselves were among the first to identify.

Today, there are some poets who, early in their careers, seemed to be likely to carry on the line this book has attempted to identify. Their strong response to the landscape of their countries of origin did not try to withhold the personal, subjective emotion motivating it. Such were R. S. Thomas, Ted Hughes and Seamus Heaney. But in all three cases these poets turned out, later at least, to be turning to different avenues and poetic modes of expression. The Heaney special edition of the magazine *Agenda*[3] referred impatiently in its editorial to Heaney's still 'ludicrously pastoral reputation', and R. S. Thomas had already moved from his early melancholic-bitter identification with the surviving Welsh peasantry to consciously aesthetic, scientific, theological and galactic concerns. Because Hughes already had something elemental in his psyche-nature identification, the evidently personal drive behind the poetry was not something he dwelt on in front of our eyes. It always picked on an element in nature, an animal, a rock, the power of the sea. The individual may do the experiencing of this, but in Hughes's poetry that aspect was marginal. One poet currently still writing in the English-line mode – though recently he too seems to have turned to other modes of writing – is Andrew Motion. He is one obvious possible successor to the English line on its earlier terms if one takes point-by-point detail. He is an orthodox bourgeois representative of that line, is seen as following in the tradition of Larkin and Edward Thomas and has said that Wordsworth is the poet he most admires[4]. His poems are gentle, approachable, subjective, limpid and somewhat indefinite. Yet there is a touch of reportage in the work which always prevents the characteristic inner-outer identification.

Another strand of poetry which for a while has perhaps replaced the older kind, also takes the natural physical world as theme, but in more energized, historical or scientific ways. The main poets here could well be Basil Bunting (now dead), Charles Tomlinson, Geoffrey Hill and Peter Redgrove. These poets differ from each other, but all have written about the land or natural matter (rather than simply landscape) as though the land itself is archaeologically layered and inhabited by creatures, organic life, history and spirit of its own. Thus their attention to the land is no longer wholly a matter of identification with the poet's inner troubled existence. Jeremy Hooker, a write of some commitment to the idea of relation between poetry and place, has put it that 'arguably, the most interesting poets now writing in English . . . are those, as in the case of Bunting and [David] Jones, with access to something larger than their own private minds'[5] (Hooker has also treated of Geoffrey Hill). The poet Thom Gunn has recently said that Bunting's *Briggflatts* (set in his native Northumberland) is one of the great poems of the century, because Bunting 'is able to combine the influence of Wordsworth and Pound – something that Pound never invisaged'[6]. That seems to be true, and a pointer to the future.

With Tomlinson habitation of the land is a matter of living an intellectual life of repeated absorption in the land's significance. He traces the interconnections of nature's parts as though disciplined human observation of those things unselfishly suppressed the self's problems and yielded up its true meaning. Donald Davie believed that the neglect of Tomlinson's poetry was a scandal[7], although this has been rectified somewhat since Davie wrote. Geoffrey Hill works to set the political events of England's history into a terrain where one can sense its successive continuities. Thus curiously Hill's poetry has a nearly tangible architectural quality; as Heaney puts it, 'Stone and rock figure prominently [in Hill's poetry, but] he is not the suppliant chanting to the megalith, but the mason dressing it'[8]. Since Hill is also a deployer of words with the full sense of their historical genealogies, he too goes clear to the outdoor of the mind, yet a territory is there. With Peter Redgrove, a mixture of anthropology, mythology and microscopic natural science energizes the work. It as at times subjective, but its materials are engaged with vigour. Many of his poems are first-person, some throughout, but their eye is permanently alert for the unexpected mysteries in pungent things, human bodies with their odour and sweat and sexuality, insects and birds, gardens and dirty buildings and hills, often futuristic in feeling, which with some relish he upturns. Whether Heathcote Williams' strongly environmental TV poems go along with this line remains to be seen. *Whale Nation* was immensely powerful and moving, but its aims and means were different.

By contrast, it seems as though it is women who have for some time taken up their 'I' voice, the first-person voice, which in their case stayed silent in times of male domination. Most leading male poets in contemporary Britain – for example Craig Raine, James Fenton and Tony Harrison – do not write after this fashion. But Anne Stevenson, Fleur Adcock and Carol Rumens all speak with at least some element of such a voice. Some impetus was given to this movement by the work of Sylvia Plath in the 1960s, although later women poets have been chary about taking her anguished confessional poetry as a model for women's poetry generally.

The question is of how women's poetry will develop in this situation. In Chapter 6 it was suggested that, when their role as creators was neither fully acknowledged nor (often) circumstantially feasible, women would take male models of poetry (in our case 'English line' poetry) and, in effect, make necessary adjustments to it from the woman's gender point of view. Today the woman poet is freer; if she wants to write her own poetry of mind and emotion – or indeed any other – she needs less and less to take man's poetry as model or inspiration for it. There has been a variety of results. A leading post-war poet has been Elizabeth Jennings, notably the one woman in the 'Movement' of the post-war period. Unlike them, however, her poetry has some intensity of commitment while still highly controlled. It is a continued meditation on her own devoutness. She detachedly assesses her mildly guilty experience of being human at all at the same moment as the guilt is reexperienced, re-felt. Ursula Fanthorpe writes small and terse observations of ordinary human weakness and humour in a provincial setting. Thus while entering the characteristic English tradition she stays away from her own emotional involvement beyond the level of ironic sympathy. Stevie Smith by contrast wrote a remarkable and apparently eccentric and whimsical poetry which, however, contained much personal pain and songful isolation. Rather more parallel to the Hughes-Redgrove pattern, the American poet Elizabeth Bishop wrote a powerful poetry of natural life and elements, charged with a feeling which, however, came out as a play of forces, colours and natural living plants and animals. The full entry of women, as of other cultures and races, continuing or not continuing this line, has open potential.

It is interesting then to wonder what if anything will fill the gap the English line is leaving. Maybe quite simply a robust, objective and international poetry is now needed and is coming. Wallace Stevens once wrote, 'The great poems of heaven and hell have been written. The great poem of earth has not been written'. The physical condition of the lump of real estate called Planet Earth would seem to be our chief problem. A more outward, corporate approach to global and cosmic awareness is growing, and for a long period may well have to dominate politics. The troubled, inward poetry may therefore have written itself out, and thus become a permanent possession from the past. Certainly poetically, the environment, 'the earth which is our home, or not at all', would appear to be a magnetic topic, an epic theme to outweigh all others. Meanwhile we can be grateful for the English line's beautiful articulation of at least some of our feelings, loves and anxieties, and for playing its part along with other lines, English and otherwise, in getting us to where we are now, as a whole new millennium, with a strange new psychological import entailed, confronts us.

Texts Used for Main Poets Discussed

GRAY & COLLINS, *Poetical Works*, ed. Austin Lane Poole (Oxford University Press, 1974)

WILLIAM WORDSWORTH, *The Poems, Vols I & II*, ed. John O. Hayden (Penguin English Poets, 1977)
The Prelude 1799, 1805, 1850, eds Jonathan Wordsworth, M. H. Abrams and Stephen Gill (W. W. Norton & Co, 1979)

S. T. COLERIDGE, *The Poems Of Samuel Taylor Coleridge*, ed. Ernest Hartley Coleridge (Oxford University Press, 1957)

JOHN CLARE, *Selected Poems*, eds J. W. and Anne Tibble (Dent, Everyman's Library, 1965)
The Shepherd's Calendar, eds Eric Robinson and Geoffrey Summerfield (Oxford University Press, 1964)

ALFRED LORD TENNYSON, *Poetical Works, Including The Plays* (Oxford University Press, 1953)
In Memoriam, eds Susan Shatto and Marion Shaw (Oxford, Clarendon Press, 1982)

MATTHEW ARNOLD, *The Poems Of Matthew Arnold*, ed. Kenneth Allott, second edition by Miriam Allott (Longman, 1979)

EMILY BRONTË, *The Brontës, Selected Poems*, ed. Juliet R. V. Barker (Dent, Everyman's Library, 1985)

CHRISTINA ROSSETTI, *The Complete Poems Of Christina Rossetti*, Vol. I, ed. R. W. Crump (Louisiana State University Presss, 1979)
Monna Innominata in Anthony H. Harrison, *Christina Rossetti In Context* (Harvester, 1988), pp. 191–200

ELIZABETH BARRETT BROWNING, *Selected Poems*, ed. Robert Browning (Smith, Elder & Co, 1902)
Aurora Leigh And Other Poems, Introduced by Cora Kaplan (The Women's Press, 1978)

G. M. HOPKINS, *Poems And Prose*, selected and edited by W. H. Gardner (Penguin, 1953)

THOMAS HARDY, *The Complete Poems*, ed. James Gibson (Macmillan, 1976)

A. E. HOUSMAN, *Collected Poems And Selected Prose*, ed. Christopher Ricks (Allen Lane, 1988)

WILFRED OWEN, *The Collected Poems of Wilfred Owen*, ed. C. Day Lewis (Chatto & Windus, 1967)

EDWARD THOMAS, *Poems And Last Poems*, ed. Edna Longley (Collins, 1973)

ROBERT FROST, *The Poetry Of Robert Frost*, ed. Edward Connery Lathem (Jonathan Cape, 1972)

LOUIS MACNEICE, *The Collected Poems Of Louis MacNeice* (Faber & Faber, 1966)

DYLAN THOMAS, *Collected Poems 1934–1952* (Dent, Aldine Paperbacks, 1971)

PHILIP LARKIN, *Collected Poems*, ed. Anthony Thwaite (Marvell Press and Faber & Faber, 1988)

Notes and References

1. Introduction

1. E.g. Bob Perelman, 'The First Person', *Hills*, Nos 6/7 Spring 1980; Anthony Easthope, 'Why Most Contemporary Poetry Is So Bad', *P. N. Review*, Vol. 12, No. 4, p. 36; Christopher Miller, 'Philip Larkin', *Agenda*, Vol. 20, No. 3, pp. 69–103.
2. Walter Pater, *Appreciations* (Macmillan, 1889), p. 57.
3. *Thomas Hardy*, ed. Samuel Hynes, (Oxford University Press, Oxford Authors, 1984), p. xxix; Andrew Motion, *Philip Larkin* (Methuen, 1982), p. 19. I regret that the present book was completed before John Lucas's book *England And Englishness* (Hogarth Press, 1989) appeared.
4. Maud Ellman, *The Poetics Of Impersonality* (Harvester Press, 1987).
5. E.g. 'It can hardly be denied that the canonical tradition, the poetry of the 'single voice', is now dying both from inward exhaustion and external erosion. . . . Bourgeois poetic discourse now has no real audience.' Anthony Easthope, *Poetry As Discourse* (Methuen, 1983), p. 161.
6. *The Prose Works of William Wordsworth*, eds. W. J. B. Owen and Jane Worthington Smyser, Vol. i (Oxford, Clarendon Press, 1974), pp. 123 and 130; ibid. Vol. ii, p. 85; Matthew Arnold, *Essays In Criticism* (Second Series) (Macmillan, 1888), p. 155; *Poems Of Thomas Hardy*, ed. T. R. M. Creighton (Macmillan, 1974), Appendix ii, p. 315; *Edward Thomas, Selected Prose*, ed. Edna Longley (Carcanet Press, 1981), pp. 150–61; Lawrance Thompson and R. H. Winnick, *Robert Frost* (Holt, Rinehart & Winston, 1986), p. 172; Philip Larkin, *Required Writing; Miscellaneous Pieces 1955–1982* (Faber & Faber, 1983), p. 80.
7. Michel Foucault, *The History Of Sexuality* (Allen Lane, 1979).

8. W. David Shaw, *The Lucid Veil* (The Athlone Press, 1987), pp. 131–4.

9. Harold Bloom, *Poetry And Repression* (Yale University Press, 1976), p. 146. For his wider theory, *The Anxiety Of Influence* (Oxford University Press, 1973), and *A Map Of Misreading* (Oxford University Press, 1975).

10. Jacques Derrida, *Of Grammatology*, trans. G. C. Spivak (Johns Hopkins University Press, 1974), esp. Part II, ch. ii; *Writing And Difference*, trans. Alan Bass (Routledge & Kegan Paul, 1978).

11. Roland Barthes, 'The Death of the Author' in *Image-Music-Text: Roland Barthes*, ed. Stephen Heath (London, Fontana, 1977); Michel Foucault, 'What is an Author?' in *Textual Strategies*, ed. J. V. Harari (Methuen, 1979).

12. Jacques Lacan, *Ecrits: A Selection*, trans. Alan Sheridan (Tavistock, 1977), p. 76.

13. Julia Kristeva, *Desire In Language: A Semiotic Approach To Literature And Art* (Basil Blackwell, 1981), ch. 5, esp. pp. 136–7.

14. Charles Altieri, 'An Idea and Ideal of a Literary Canon' in *Critical Enquiry* September 1983, pp. 37–60; Howard Felperin, *Beyond Deconstruction: The Uses And Abuses Of Critical Theory* (Oxford: Clarendon Press 1985), esp. ch. I, sect. vii.

PART I

2. Wordsworth's Precursors

1. See Jonathan Bate, *Shakespeare And The English Romantic Imagination* (Oxford, Clarendon Press, 1989), chs 4 and 5.

2. Matthew Arnold, 'Preface to the First Edition of *Poems*' in *Poetical Works*, eds Kenneth and Miriam Allott (Longman, 1979), p. 655.

3. Marilyn Butler, *Romantics, Rebels & Reactionaries: English Literature And Its Background 1760–1830* (Oxford University Press, 1981), esp. ch. 1, pp. 11–38.

4. Samuel Johnson, *Lives Of The Most Eminent English Poets* (Frederick Warne, 1911), p. 34.

5. Robert Langbaum, *The Poetry Of Experience: The Dramatic Monologue In Modern Literary Tradition* (University of Chicago Press, 1957, 1985).
6. Gerard Manley Hopkins, *Poems and Prose*, ed. W. H. Gardner (Penguin Books, 1985), p. 201.
7. Jerome J. McGann, 'George Crabbe: Poetry and Truth' in *London Review Of Books* 16 March 1989; Robert Gittings, *Young Thomas Hardy*, p. 121. However, another major biographer of Hardy, Michael Milgate, appears sceptical that Hardy actually learnt from Crabbe. (For details of biographies of Hardy cf. ch. 7, note 4.)
8. Samuel Johnson, op. cit., p. 502; F. R. Leavis, *Revaluation: Tradition And Development In English Poetry* (Chatto & Windus, 1959), p. 106.
9. Stephen Bygrave, 'Gray's "Elegy": Inscribing the Twilight', in *Post-Structuralist Readings Of English Poetry*, eds Richard Machin and Christopher Norris (Cambridge University Press, 1987), p. 164.
10. I take De Man's suggestion, that traditional criticism necessarily has a blindness at its moment of greatest insight, parallels this idea of the 'blind seer' in poetry. However, because (as De Man says) the poet uses language in the only way that acknowledges its fictional character, the poet's insight emerges as blindness's deliberate result: Paul De Man, *Blindness And Insight: Essays In The Rhetoric Of Contemporary Criticism* (Oxford University Press, 1971).
11. Milgate, op. cit. (see ch. 7, note 4), p. 400.

3. William Wordsworth

1. The standard biographies are Mary Moorman, *William Wordsworth: A Biography*, 2 vols (Oxford University Press, 1957 and 1965); and Stephen Gill, *William Wordsworth: A Life* (Oxford University Press, 1989).
2. Marilyn Butler, op. cit., p. 67; George Watson, 'The Revolutionary Years of Wordsworth and Coleridge' in *Critical Quarterly* Vol 18, No 3 1976, pp. 49–66; John Beer, 'The "Revolutionary Youth" of Wordsworth and Coleridge: Another View' in *Critical Quarterly*, Vol 19, No 2 1976,

pp. 79–87; E. P. Thompson, 'Wordsworth's Crisis' in *London Review Of Books* 8 December 1988 (Review of Nicholas Roe, *Wordsworth And Coleridge: The Radical Years* (Oxford University Press, 1988); answering letter by Nicholas Roe, same journal 6 February 1989.

3. Gayatri C. Spivak, 'Sex and History in *The Prelude (1805): Books IX to XIII*' in Machen & Norris, op. cit., pp. 193–226.

4. Paul Hamilton, *Wordsworth* (Harvester Press, 1987). George Watson, op. cit.; David Ellis, *Wordsworth, Freud And The Spots Of Time* (Cambridge University Press, 1985).

5. Bloom, *Poetry And Repression*, op. cit., ch. 3.

6. Cited in Appendix to William Wordsworth, *The Prelude: 1799, 1805, 1850*, eds Jonathan Wordsworth, M. H. Abrams and Stephen Gill (New York, W. W. Norton & Co., 1979), pp. 532, 534.

7. Jonathan Wordsworth, *William Wordsworth: The Borders Of Vision* (Oxford, Clarendon Press, 1982), p. 27; E. D. Hirsch, *Validity In Interpretation* (Yale University Press, 1967), pp. 227–9; Seamus Heaney, *Preoccupations* (Faber & Faber, 1980), p. 67; Jan Montefiore, *Feminism And Poetry* (Pandora Press, Routledge & Kegan Paul, 1987), p. 61; Jerome J. McGann, *The Romantic Ideology: A Critical Investigation* (Chicago University Press, 1983), pp. 68–9.

8. *Letters Of William Wordsworth: A Selection*, ed. Alan G. Hill (Oxford University Press, 19, 1984), p. 43.

4. *Samuel Taylor Coleridge and John Clare*

1. Coleridge's views on Wordsworth's poetry are found in S. T. Coleridge, *Biographia Literaria*, ed. George Watson (Dent, Everyman Books, 1956), esp. chs XVII-XXII. The remark to Godwin is found in *Letters of Samuel Taylor Coleridge* ed. E. L. Griggs (Oxford, 1956), Vol II, p. 714.

2. Harold Bloom, 'Coleridge: The Anxiety of Influence' in *New Perspectives On Wordsworth And Coleridge*, ed. Geoffrey H. Hartman (Columbia University Press, 1972), pp. 247–67; Thomas McFarland, *Coleridge And The Pantheist Tradition* (Oxford University Press, 1969), esp. pp. 111, 144.

3. K. M. Wheeler, *The Creative Mind In Coleridge's Poetry* (Heinemann, 1981), pp. 95, 99.
4. An account of the writing of the three poems is given in George Dekker, *Coleridge And The Literature Of Sensibility* (London, Vision Press, 1978).
5. Quoted in Mark Storey, *The Poetry Of John Clare* (Macmillan, 1974), p. 68.
6. *Letters Of John Clare 1818–1837*, eds. J. W. and Anne Tibble (Routledge & Kegan Paul, 1951), Introduction, p. 20.

PART II

5. *Alfred Lord Tennyson and Matthew Arnold*

1. The standard biography is R. B. Martin, *Tennyson: The Unquiet Heart* (Oxford, Clarendon Press, Faber & Faber, 1980). The incident of the coat is recounted on pp. 357–8.
2. Martin, op. cit., p. 291.
3. Langbaum op, cit., ch. 2; Carol T. Christ, *Victorian And Modern Poetics* (University of Chicago Press, 1984), chs 1 and 2.
4. *Tennyson: In Memoriam*, eds Susan Shatto and Marion Shaw (Oxford, Clarendon Press, 1982), Preface, esp. pp. 7–20.
5. *Princeton Encyclopedia Of Poetry And Poetics*, ed. Alex Preminger (Princeton University Press and Macmillan, 1975), p. 215.
6. W. David Shaw, op. cit., p. 277.
7. Hallam Lord Tennyson, *Alfred Lord Tennyson: A Memoir* (Macmillan, 1897), 2 vols, Vol II, p. 288.
8. Shatto & Shaw, op. cit., p. 15; Hallam Lord Tennyson, op. cit., Vol I, p. 294.
9. De Man, op,. cit., p. 11.
10. Marion Shaw, *Alfred Lord Tennyson* (Harvester Wheatsheaf, 1988), pp. 144–58.
11. Alan Sinfield for example notices the 'babe-faced lord' (Part II, section i, stanza 1, line 13) but sees him as epitomizing effeminacy. A. Sinfield, *Alfred Tennyson* (Basil Blackwell, 1986), p. 175. Cf. also Robert E. Longy, 'The

Sounds and Silence of Madness: Language as Theme in Tennyson's *Maud'* in *Victorian Poetry* (USA) Vol. 22 (1984), pp. 407–26.

12. Langbaum, op. cit.; Carol T. Christ, op. cit., p. 17.

13. Standard biography is Park Honan, *Matthew Arnold: A Life* (Weidenfeld & Nicholson, 1981); cf. also W. F. Connell, *The Educational Thought And Influence Of Matthew Arnold* (Greenwood Press, Connecticut, 1971).

14. J. Hillis Miller, *The Linguistic Moment* (Princeton University Press, 1985), p. 17.

15. In a letter to John Duke Coleridge, quoted in Lionel Trilling, *Matthew Arnold* (George Allen & Unwin, 1939), p. 142. 'Tennyson is another thing; but one has him so in one's head, one cannot help imitating him sometimes.'

16. Lacan, op. cit., p. xi; discussed by Elizabeth Wright, *Psychoanalysis And Criticism: Theory In Practice* (Methuen, 1984), p. 111.

17. Hillis Miller, op. cit., p. 35; Frank Kermode, *Romantic Image* (Routledge & Kegan Paul, 1957), p. 18. Honan states that it was the suicide that first drew Arnold's attention to the poetic potential of the Empedocles story; Honan, op. cit., p. 184.

6. *Emily Brontë, Christina Rossetti, Elizabeth Barrett Browning – Gerard Manley Hopkins*

1. Christina Battersby, *Gender And Genius* (The Women's Press, 1989), p. 23.

2. 'The rest of the world, which I define as the Other, has meaning only in relation to me, as man/father, possessor of the phallus'; Anne Rosalind Jones, 'Writing The Body' in *The New Feminist Criticism: Essays On Women, Literature And Theory*, ed. Elaine Showalter (Virago Press, 1986), p. 362.

3. Susan Gubar, ' "The Blank Page" and the Issues of Female Creativity' in ibid., pp. 292–313.

4. Montefiore, op. cit., p. 5.

5. Hallam Lord Tennyson, op. cit., I 262; Honan, op. cit., pp. 219–20.

6. Sandra M. Gilbert and Susan Gubar, *The Madwoman In*

The Attic: The Woman Writer And The Nineteenth Century Literary Imagination (Yale University Press, 1979), p. 552.

7. Lawrance Thompson, op. cit., p. 291.

8. A. C. Benson in *National Review* No. 24, February 1895; Ruskin relevant passage cited in Antony H. Harrison, *Christina Rossetti In Context* (Harvester Press, 1988), p. 40.

9. Jerome J. McGann, 'The Religious Poetry of Christina Rossetti', 'Critical Enquiry Vol. 10, September 1983, pp. 127–44.

10. Antony H. Harrison, op. cit., p. 47.

11. Quoted in ibid., p. 191.

12. Angela Leighton, *Elizabeth Barrett Browning* (Harvester Press, 1986), ch. 4, esp. pp. 82, 89.

13. Donald Thomas, *Robert Browning: A Life Within Life* (Weidenfeld & Nicholson, 1982), p. 177.

14. Kathleen Blake, 'Elizabeth Barrett Browning And Wordsworth: The Romantic Poet as a Woman' in *Victorian Poetry* (USA) Vol. 24 (1986).

15. Letter to Robert Bridges, 2 August 1871, in Hopkins, op. cit., pp. 172–3.

16. F. R. Leavis, *New Bearings In English Poetry* (Penguin Books, 1963), p. 134.

17. Letter to Robert Bridges, 30 December 1918, in *A. E. Housman: Collected Poems & Selected Prose*, ed. Christopher Ricks (Allen Lane, 1988), pp. 460–1.

18. *Correspondence of Gerard M. Hopkins and R. W. Dixon*, ed C. C. Abbott (Oxford University Press, 1935), pp. 147–8.

19. Ezra Pound, *Selected Prose 1909–1965*, ed. William Cookson (Faber & Faber, 1978), p. 431.

20. Hillis Miller, op. cit., p. 266.

21. *Letters To Robert Bridges*, ed. C. C. Abbott (Oxford University Press, 1935), 18 October 1882, p. 155.

PART III

7. *Thomas Hardy*

1. Donald Davie, *Thomas Hardy And British Poetry* (Routledge & Kegan Paul, 1973); Edna Longley, Preface to *Edward Thomas: Poems And Last Poems* (Collins, 1973).

2. Cf. Linda Dowling, *Language And Decadence In The Victorian Fin De Siècle* (Princeton University Press, 1986).

3. Quoted in Robert Graves, *Goodbye To All That* (Penguin Books, 1960), p. 251; Creighton, op. cit., p. 319.

4. The standard biographies are Robert Gittings *Young Thomas Hardy* (Penguin Books, 1975); Robert Gittings *The Older Hardy* (Penguin Books, 1980); Michael Milgate, *Thomas Hardy* (Oxford University Press, 1982), p. 439.

5. Florence Emily Hardy, *The Life Of Thomas Hardy 1840–1928* (London, 1962), p. 386. (This book was written largely by Thomas Hardy himself.)

6. J. Hillis Miller, *Thomas Hardy: Distance And Desire* (Oxford University Press, 1970), esp. ch. 2.

7. Florence Emily Hardy, op. cit., pp. 377–8.

8. Bloom, *A Map Of Misreading*, p. 20; Dennis Taylor, 'Hardy and Wordsworth' in *The Thomas Hardy Journal*, Vol. iv, No. 1 1988, p. 57.

9. Gittings, *Young Thomas Hardy*, pp. 57–61.

10. For example in *Tess Of The D'Urbervilles*, in ch. xxi Izz Huett kisses the shadow of Angel Clare's mouth on the wall, and in ch. xxxvii Angel kisses Tess while he is sleepwalking.

11. Florence Emily Hardy, op. cit., pp. 209–10.

12. Larkin, op. cit., p. 175.

13. *Letters Of Ezra Pound*, ed. D. D. Paige (New York, 1950), p. 294.

14. John Carey, *John Donne: Life, Mind And Art* (Faber & Faber, 1981). p. 261.

15. Tom Paulin, 'Hardy and the Human Voice' in *The Thomas Hardy Journal*, Vol. III, No. 1 1987, p. 30; Ralph W. V. Elliott, *Thomas Hardy's English* (Basil Blackwell with André Deutsch, 1984).

16. Florence Emily Hardy, op. cit., pp. 105, 128.

17. These remarks are taken from longer passages, all cited at the start of Ralph Elliott, op. cit., pp. 13–17.

18. John Stuart Mill, *Collected Works*, ed. J. M. Robson (University of Toronto Press, 1963–84), Vol. I, pp. 152–3; Harriet Martineau, *Autobiography* (Virago Press, 1983), Vol. II, p. 239.

19. Davie, op. cit., p. 62.

8. *A. E. Housman, Wilfred Owen and Edward Thomas*

1. The standard biography is Richard Perceval Graves, *A. E. Housman: The Scholar-Poet* (Oxford University Press, 1981).
2. Edmund Wilson in *A. E. Housman: A Collection Of Critical Essays* ed. Christopher Ricks (Prentice-Hall, 1968), pp. 14–25.
3. Larkin, op. cit., p. 265.
4. Graves gives only one attested reference to a visit, although there may have been unrecorded day trips in childhood. Graves, op. cit., p. 108.
5. Christopher Ricks, 'A. E. Housman: The Nature of his Poetry' in *The Force Of Poetry* (Oxford University Press,1987), pp. 163–78; also his Introduction to *Collected Poems* (op. cit.), pp. 7–18.
6. Dominic Hibberd, *Owen The Poet* (Macmillan, 1986), p. 110.
7. Ibid. p. 105.
8. Ibid. p. 166.
9. Ibid. and Jon Stallworthy, *Wilfred Owen* (Oxford University Press, 1974).
10. Edna Longley 'Editor's Preface' in *Edward Thomas* (op. cit.), p. 9. I am grateful to William Cooke for sending me his list of 27 poets who have written poems to Edward Thomas or about him.
11. R. George Thomas, *Edward Thomas: A Portrait* (Oxford, Clarendon Press, 1985), esp. chs 10–12.
12. Cf. for example Walter Pater, op. cit., and *The Renaissance* (Macmillan, 1873).
13. Edward Thomas, *Selected Prose* (op. cit.), pp. 25, 27.
14. Sigmund Freud, *The Interpretation Of Dreams* (Penguin Books, Pelican Freud Library, 1976), p. 422.
15. Ralph Waldo Emerson, 'Nature' in *Essays: First And Second Series* (Oxford University Press, World's Classics, 1927), pp. 377–98, esp. near the end; Elizabeth Wright, op. cit., p. 143.

9. *Robert Frost*

1. For example the 'huge peak' (*The Prelude* 1805 Book I), the Winander Boy episode (Book V) and the underground

river (Book XIII) find counterparts in 'The Mountain', 'The Most Of It' and 'Hyla Brook' respectively.

2. Standard biography is the three-volume work by Lawrance Thompson (Vol. III with R. H. Winnick), abridged to Lawrance Thompson and R. H. Winnick, *Robert Frost* (Holt, Rinehart & Winston, 1986). Cf. also William H. Pritchard, *Frost: A Literary Life Reconsidered* (Oxford University Press, 1984).

3. On 26 March 1914, having already met Thomas a few times, Frost wrote to a friend Sidney Cox, 'I have no friend here like Wilfred Gibson'. R. George Thomas, op. cit., p. 228.

4. L. Thompson, op. cit., p. 179; *Selected Letters Of Robert Frost*, ed. Lawrance Thompson (Holt, Rinehart & Winston, 1964), pp. 217–20; *Poetry Wales*, Vol. 13, No. 4 Spring 1978, pp. 22–3.

5. See ch. 8 note 10.

6. Edward Thomas, *Selected Prose* (op. cit.), pp. 125, 130, 128, 127 respectively.

7. Sylvia Plath, *Letters Home: Correspondence 1950–1963*, ed. Aurelia Schober Plath (Faber & Faber, 1975), pp. 313–4; Karl Miller, 'Robert Frost Crosses the Missouri' in *Doubles: Studies In Literary History* (Oxford University Press, 1985), p. 285; Wallace Martin, 'Frost's Thanatography' in Machen & Norris, op. cit., p. 395; Yvor Winters, 'Robert Frost, or the Spiritual Drifter as Poet' in *The Function Of Criticism* (Routledge & Kegan Paul, 1962).

8. In *Selected Literary Criticism Of Louis MacNeice* (Oxford, Clarendon Press, 1987), pp. 246; W. H. Auden, 'Robert Frost' in *The Dyer's Hand* (Faber & Faber, 1975), p. 343.

9. Lacan, op. cit., p. 46.

10. Cf. for example 'Adam's Curse', 'The Fascination of What's Difficult', 'The People', 'The Choice'. *Collected Poems Of W. B. Yeats* (Macmillan, 1958), pp. 88, 104, 169, 278 respectively.

11. Richard Poirier, *Robert Frost: The Work Of Knowing* (Oxford University Press, 1977), p. 198.

12. L. Thompson, op. cit., p. 172 (a summary of many of Frost's remarks on the subject).

13. Wright, op. cit., p. 44.

14. Norman Holland, 'The "Unconscious" Of Literature: The Psychoanalytical Approach' in *Contemporary Criticism*, eds M. Bradbury and D. Palmer, *Stratford-upon-Avon Studies*, No. 12 (Edward Arnold, 1970), pp. 131–54.

PART IV

10. *Louis MacNeice and Dylan Thomas*

1. Edna Longley, 'MacNeice and After' in *Poetry Review*, Vol. 78, No. 2 Summer 1988, p. 6.
2. MacNeice, *Selected Literary Criticism*, op. cit., pp. 32–3, 43.
3. Edna Longley, *Louis MacNeice* (Faber & Faber, 1988), p. 66; Samuel Hynes, *The Auden Generation* (Bodley Head, 1976), p. 369.
4. MacNeice, op. cit., and *The Strings Are False: An Unfinished Autobiography* (Faber & Faber, 1965).
5. R. George Thomas (op. cit., p. 236) gives November, but silent action no doubt preceded. That month Edward Thomas also began thinking of enlisting, and may well have been to Wales that summer.
6. Dylan Thomas, 'Notes on the Art of Poetry' in *Modern Poets On Modern Poetry*, ed. James Scully (Collins/Fontana, 1966), pp. 195–202.
7. Blake Morrison, *The Movement* (Methuen, 1980), pp. 147, 149.
8. Ferdinand de Saussure, *Course In General Linguistics*, trans. Wade Baskin (Fontana/Collins, 1974), esp. ch. I, sections i-iii; Lacan op. cit., p. 154, quoted and discussed in Easthope, *Poetry As Discourse*, op. cit., ch. 3.
9. Walford Davies, *Dylan Thomas* (Open University Press, 1986), p. 115.
10. Scully, op. cit., p. 197.
11. Gwen Watkins, *Portrait Of A Friend* (Gomer Press, 1983), p. 4.
12. John Bayley, *The Romantic Survival* (Chatto & Windus, 1957), p. 198.
13. Scully, op. cit., p. 199.
14. Walford Davies, op. cit., p. 122.

210 *The English Line*

15. Paul Ferris, *Dylan Thomas* (Penguin Books, 1985), ch. 2, esp. pp. 25, 27.
16. Walford Davies, op. cit., pp. 94–101.
17. MacNeice, 'Autumn Sequel' in *Collected Poems*, pp. 327–439, esp. canto XX.
18. Al Alvarez, *The New Poetry* (Penguin Books, 1962), p. 19; Davie op. cit., p. 64.

11. *Philip Larkin*

1. Larkin, op. cit., p. 86.
2. Ibid., p. 174.
3. Barbara Everett, 'Philip Larkin: After Symbolism' in *Essays In Criticism*, Vol. XXX July 1980, pp. 227–42.
4. For example Peter Porter (*The Independent* 8 October 1988) believes it adds considerably to Larkin's stature; Ian Hamilton (*London Review of Books* 13 October 1988) does not.
5. Davie, op. cit., p. 72.
6. Harold Bloom, 'The Breaking of Form' in *Deconstruction & Criticism* (Bloom, De Man, Derrida, Hartman, Hillis Miller) (Routledge & Kegan Paul, 1979), pp. 1–38.
7. Anthony Thwaite, in Philip Larkin, *Collected Poems* (Marvell Press and Faber & Faber, 1988), p. xviii.
8. As yet there is no biography of Larkin. Andrew Motion is currently working on the authorized one.
9. Andrew Motion, *Philip Larkin* (Methuen, 1982), p. 80.
10. Ibid. p. 76.
11. Michael Ignatieff, 'Paradigm Lost' in *Times Literary Supplement* 4 September 1987, pp. 939–40.

12. *Conclusion*

1. W. B. Yeats, 'A General Introduction for my Work' in *Yeats: Selected Criticism And Prose* (Pan Books, 1980), pp. 255–69.
2. Foucault, op. cit., 1979.
3. *Agenda*, Vol. 27, No. 1 1989.
4. Andrew Motion, 'Who's Reading Whom' in *The Sunday Times* (Books) 26 March 1989.

5. Jeremy Hooker, *The Poetry Of Place: Essays And Reviews 1970–1981* (Carcanet Press, 1982), p. 151.
6. In Jim Powell, 'An Interview With Thom Gunn' in *P. N. Review* Vol. 16, No. 2, p. 54. (In rating Larkin an 'exquisite but unimportant' poet Gunn is I believe wide of the point about Larkin; namely, that Larkin is at the end of the line.)
7. Davie, op. cit., p. 2.
8. Seamus Heaney, op. cit., p. 159.

Index of Names

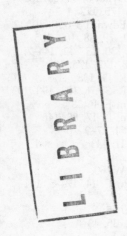

Index of Main Characteristics Discussed